Withdrawn
AVIATION INSIGNIA

DEVILBIRDS

The Story of United States Marine Corps Aviation in World War II

DEVILBIRDS

THE STORY OF UNITED STATES

MARINE CORPS AVIATION

IN WORLD WAR II

☆ ☆ ☆

John A. De Chant

CAPTAIN, USMCR

Foreword by
GENERAL A. A. VANDEGRIFT

COMMANDANT
UNITED STATES MARINE CORPS

NEW YORK AND LONDON

HARPER & BROTHERS PUBLISHERS

DEVILBIRDS: THE STORY OF MARINE CORPS AVIATION IN WORLD WAR II

☆

This book has been compiled from official sources; yet it is not an official publication. The Marine Corps is in no way responsible for any points of view expressed, nor for the factual accuracy of statements made herein.

CONTENTS

☆ ☆ ☆

v

ILLUSTRATIONS

☆ ☆ ☆

ACKNOWLEDGMENTS

☆   ☆   ☆

The author is initially indebted to Major Generals Field Harris and James T. Moore of the Marine Corps Division of Aviation and Brigadier Generals Robert L. Denig, Franklin A. Hart, and William E. Riley of the Division of Public Information for their aid in getting the book under way. No one has contributed more, or more graciously, than Captain Edna Loftus Smith, USMCWR, Division of Aviation, through her innumerable hours of painstaking historical research and helpful advice. Editorially, the labors of Lieutenant Hal Goodwin and Major Frank O. Hough have been invaluable. A complete and colorful account of Marine ground operations, only briefly covered herein, will be found in the recently published book by Major Hough called *The Island War*. The author is very thankful for the conscientious, accurate, and colorful reporting of the Marine Public Information Officers and the Combat Correspondents, many of whose stories are used herein with and without by-lines, and for the many others who have given time and advice in preparing this book. Lastly, he is most grateful for the patience, encouragement, and constant assistance of his wife.

FOREWORD

☆ ☆ ☆

The vast scale and diverse nature of the war in the Pacific created a kaleidoscopic pattern which is far beyond the scope of any one historical study. This book, then, brings but one facet of the war under the microscope of history and the author has thus been enabled to give a dramatic and coherent account of the men and the organizations who made Marine Aviation a synonym for terror to our enemies.

To the general public, Marine Aviation is best known for the tiny but venomous air force that helped to make Wake Island a saga of heroism and for the gallant fliers and ground crews who at Guadalcanal matched their blood, nerve, and skill in an unequal battle for air supremacy in the skies over the Solomons. Like their fellow Marines in the jungle foxholes, the flying Leathernecks of Guadalcanal held and won against almost overwhelming odds.

The author has thrown new light on these last-ditch battles and on the men whose cunning and courage won them. At the same time, he has gone behind the scenes and analyzed the toil and planning which went into the forging of the Marine spearhead which was equally effective on land, sea, and in the air. He has likewise traced the path of havoc wrought by Marine aircraft and pilots from the South Pacific to Tokyo itself.

Here for the first time is a balanced account of the planned versatility of the more than 150,000 officers and men who were the aviation component of the Marines' Pacific team. Spectacular aerial combat was but a part of Marine aviation's mission. Time after time Marine pilots blasted a path of destruction close ahead of advancing infantry, both Marine and Army. Again Marines flew mission after mission against Japanese forward bases and by-passed islands. They swept the skies and systematically wiped out ground installations. These strikes rendered such bastions as Rabaul, Wotje, and Mille impotent and in turn released Marine ground forces for their rapid march across the Pacific.

In accordance with their mission, Marine Aviation personnel took a vital share in naval operations, flying from land bases to attack and sink troop-carrying transports and barge flotillas as well as combatant ships. They even joined in the carrier defense against the Kamikazes and in the fleet's rampaging sweeps against the Japanese home islands.

These were only a few of the aspects of the task our Marine fliers did so well in the Pacific. All of the phases are dramatically related in the pages of this book and each phase is an exciting story in itself. Taken altogether they provide the first real picture of the over-all concept of Marine aviation—an organization planned, designed, and battle tested to fit into the demanding science of amphibious warfare. The story of how the airplane was developed as a weapon for the landing force is a part of the story of how the Marine Corps conceived and developed the tactics that made the seizure of defended beachheads possible. It is a story of "banana wars" and rebellions in the jungles of Haiti and Nicaragua and of savage, all-out fighting on Iwo Jima and Okinawa.

The full story of Marine Aviation is a story that needed telling. Through this one aspect of the war the reader can catch many a revealing glimpse of the efforts of all arms in the Pacific. To anyone who wants to know, as we all should, the details of modern war and the national defense measures needed to prevent it, I recommend this book.

The author, Captain John A. De Chant, USMCR, is eminently qualified to interpret this story. He was one of the first officers to join the Marine Corps organization of combat correspondents and was instrumental in setting the pattern for a new kind of service journalism. His unit was the first to send back combat recordings from the Pacific, taking the sounds and voices of the war off the printed page and bringing them to the American people via their

radios. Captain De Chant lived, flew, and fought beside the men of
whom he writes from Guadalcanal to Okinawa. This book presents
a moving and analytical account of the great job that they did.

A. A. VANDEGRIFT
General, USMC

INTRODUCTION

☆ ☆ ☆

Devilbirds, the title of this book, acquired its Marine Aviation historical significance much in the same manner as the legendary Marine term "Devildogs" which the retreating Germans of 1918 applied to the Marines fighting them in France.

When Marine planes winged over the jungles of Haiti during the 1920's, the native Cacos likened the planes to the mythical flying bats which West Indian natives held in awesome fear. The Haitian bandits named the winged men and their planes the "Devilbirds." So common did this usage become in Haiti that the Marine squadron there (VMS 3) adopted as its official insignia a winged devil and the heraldic inscription "Osieux Diable."

Later, in World War II, the natives of the Pacific jungle islands often referred to the planes of the Air Arm as "Devilbirds" as did the sometimes poetic war diaries of dead Japanese infantrymen.

Devilbirds is the story of United States Marine Corps Aviation in World War II. It is not an official history in the precise definition of the term. It is, instead, a well-documented, reportorial, and necessarily unilateral account of what the Air Arm of the Marine Corps did in the recent war. It is not a critique or judgment in the armchair sense. Nor does it offer the sadly misused theme that this branch or that branch of the Allied air services won the war in the Pacific. None of them did; nor could they have, as the war actually occurred.

Marine Aviation has been, since its inception in 1912, an integrated part of an air-ground team which is unique in military annals—the U. S. Marine Corps. As a part of Naval Aviation, the Marine Air Arm is organized and trained primarily as a highly mobile and versatile force to support Marine infantry in amphibious operations.

Secondarily, it furnishes replacement squadrons for fleet air groups. In the recent war, it performed both of these tasks, along with a variety of others, in a manner which the records show was extremely creditable.

The prologue chapter is included to record the activities of Marine airmen in nearly thirty years of action prior to the recent war and to show the continuity of personnel and action which made this story possible. It was this combination of veterans and experience which was ready to meet the immediate challenge of combat aviation when America entered abruptly into war.

It is difficult for this book or for any written record to recount in perfect focus and in adequate tribute the complete story of the Marine Air Arm in World War II, or of any unit in any war. The most earnest searcher after the skein of truth in war eventually stumbles over the two dominant factors of combat—the unknown and the uncertain. Add to these the undeniable "fog of war" and the weakness of the human memory in recalling exact detail, particularly in combat. All of these factors must be taken into consideration in evaluating any story of war. Insofar as any general account is affected by them, so is this one.

Although many of its statistics are incomplete because of conditions early in the war, Marine Aviation's accomplishments show that its airmen shot down nearly 2,400 Japanese planes; that they sank some 900 enemy ships and small craft, including more than 20 warships, while damaging some 800 other enemy surface vessels; that they supported 55 amphibious landing operations. The scoreboard shows that 120 Marine fighter pilots shot down 5 or more enemy planes to become aces, and that 10 won the nation's highest award, the Medal of Honor.

When one adds these precise figures to the intangible but equally significant record of courage, skill, determination, and sacrifice which made those statistics and all the other accomplishments possible, then the sum total of Marine Aviation's efforts in the Pacific war can neither be denied nor be mutely praised. That is true even in contrast with its larger compatriots with whom it worked so closely and so well. For the criterion of military excellence and efficiency

is not how much was accomplished by the many, but how well **it**
was done by the few.

It is to all those of the Air Arm, who made this story possible, that
this book is dedicated. It is the end result of nearly four years of
close study and intimate association with the members and campaigns
of Marine Aviation. The book is motivated by a sincere respect for
all that the Marine Air Arm has accomplished and an understanding
of the odds of all kinds that it overcame to do it.

This story is as fair and accurate as it was humanly possible to
put down at this time. Some of its facets will never be known. They
are locked in the hearts and minds of the airmen themselves, many
of whom are dead. To those who probed deeply enough, those airmen,
men who flew anywhere in combat, were somehow a different breed
of men. Regardless of who or what they were on the ground, when
they flew they had it within themselves to reach out and "brush
the face of God."

JOHN A. DE CHANT

Washington, D.C.
December 30, 1946

DEVILBIRDS

The Story of United States
Marine Corps Aviation
in World War II

☆ 1 ☆

THE BROOD OF NOISY NAN

NOISY NAN was the beginning. Quite feminine by name and by nature, she cavorted around the Philadelphia Navy Yard in the year 1911. She received far more notoriety than was proper for a woman in those days. Moreover, Nan was the object of enough blasphemy to skin the hide clean off a mule. Obviously, Noisy Nan wasn't a lady. She was a man-made dodo bird—an airplane that wouldn't fly. Her constant companion, one Alfred Austell Cunningham, a first lieutenant of the U. S. Marines, so recorded her antics:

"I called her everything in God's name to go up. I pleaded with her. I caressed her. I prayed to her, and I cursed that flighty Old Maid to lift up her skirts and hike, but she never would."

This happened in the days when *The Literary Digest*, weighing the future of aviation in the light of a plane crash, stroked its beard and wrote: ". . . it raises the question whether the aeroplane is not to be classed with the tightrope and the 'loop-the-loop' rather than be considered seriously as a practical means of locomotion."

Were Noisy Nan his only criterion, Cunningham would certainly have agreed with that pompous judgment. He was, however, as persistent as Noisy Nan was perverse, and out of their experiences grew the Brood of Noisy Nan—the Air Arm of the U. S. Marines.

Cunningham's aviation story began in 1903. In a field near his Georgia home, he watched a balloon ascend into the afternoon sky. The next time it went up, Cunningham was in its basket beneath the great bag filled with illuminating gas. It rose until the country below was a mottled miniature, then bumped to earth again. Cunningham stayed aboard for a second ride. He landed a "confirmed aeronautical enthusiast."

1

While on duty at the Marine Barracks in Philadelphia, Cunningham, a second lieutenant, haunted the local airfields, such as they
were, and buttonholed everyone connected with the flying game.
His biggest find was an inventor named Brown who had built a
contraption with wings and a motor but had gone broke trying to
get it to fly. The Marine rented the machine for twenty-five dollars
a month.

After considerable persuasion, Cunningham received permission
from the local commandant to use a half-mile-long field inside the
Navy Yard. He was warned, however, that no one would tolerate his
noisy infernal machine for very long, and that even if he did get it
off the ground the net result would be calamity.

Cunningham dubbed his contraption Noisy Nan. Her two-cycle,
four-cylinder motorboat-type engine made more noise than a thresh-
ing machine run amuck. The remainder of his pusher-type craft was
a concoction of bamboo poles, wires, and warping wings. He perched
up forward in front of its wings with nothing between him and
eternity but a heavy wheel on a stick.

His test runs were more trouble than pitching hay in the broiling
sun. It often took an hour of cranking before the engine took hold.
Then the Marine would go "grass-cutting" down the field at what
should have been flying speed. Noisy Nan thought otherwise, and
would not take off. The homemade plane was too heavy for its
stuttering motor. Cunningham stripped her of all nonessentials but
she remained a grass skimmer. So he built a bump on the end of the
runway to jolt the plane into the air. On one trial after another,
Noisy Nan traipsed down the field, hit the bump, fluttered 20 and
even 50 feet into the air, and promptly settled right back down
again.

Noisy Nan never did fly but, in her fashion, she taught Cunningham much about airplanes and managed to fire his enthusiasm about
the military prospects of flying. He joined the Aero Club of Pennsyl-
vania and sold its members on the need of a Marine flying field at
Philadelphia. They in turn put pressure on Congress. In the contro-
versy that followed, Cunningham wound up in the middle. The
lieutenant finally had to admit to the Major General Commandant

of the Corps that he was behind the pressure campaign. In return for calling it off, Cunningham was ordered to aviation duty.

The Air Arm of the Marine Corps was born on May 22, 1912, when the gleeful Cunningham reported for flight training at the Navy's embryonic aviation camp at Annapolis, Maryland. As one of its class of five students, the Marine found that the naval airmen were having their troubles too.

For several years prior, a few civilians and naval officers had been experimenting with the airplane for use with the Navy. Their pioneering had little official approval or encouragement. America had invented the airplane and the seaplane but relegated them to the stunt-and-toy department of its thinking. The European nations were much more foresighted. In 1912, France was spending $7,500,000 for military aviation. Russia had an air budget of $5,000,000. Germany, Italy, and Great Britain invested $2,000,000 apiece to test this new weapon of war. Even Japan spent $600,000. That same year, the American Congress and this country's military commanders felt that $140,000 was more than ample to spend on aeronautics.

Fortunately, some of the American experiments were successful. The first flight from the deck of a warship was made in 1910, and the first landing on one a year later. In 1911, the first hydro- or seaplane made a successful water landing near a ship. That year the Navy purchased its first three planes—a Wright B-1 and two amphibians made by Glenn Curtiss.

Cunningham received his actual flight training at the Burgess-Curtiss air factory at Marblehead, Massachusetts. After two hours and forty minutes of instruction from a high-priced civilian instructor, the Marine volunteered to solo. He took off in the seaplane, circled the bay several times, and managed a fair landing in a spray of foam. Then and there, Cunningham became the first Marine airman and the fifth naval aviator.

First Lieutenant Bernard L. Smith, who was to play a vital role in Marine Aviation, reported at Annapolis while Cunningham was still there and shortly became the second Marine flight officer.

In 1912, the Marine Corps officially reported that it had two officers and one enlisted man on aviation duty "in view of the great benefit to an advanced base force that might result from trained aviators." Because of the usual budget pinch, this number had been increased to only five officers and eight men in 1916, when it was recorded that "Aviation has made great strides in the present war and has become of great importance to the military and naval services."

The original handful of naval aviation pioneers were regarded as harebrained zealots by their fellow officers afloat and ashore, for there were very few of the latter who believed that the flying machine was here to stay. The airmen felt otherwise but had to prove their point the hard way by sweating out hazardous experiments in inadequate planes.

Cunningham made the first catapult take-off attempt from a warship under way. His Curtiss flying boat was hurled into the air from an improvised flight deck on the stern of the battleship *Carolina*. But the catapult failed to function properly and the plane crashed into the ocean off Florida, breaking Cunningham's back.

Recovering from that accident, Cunningham asked permission to attend the Army aviation school at San Diego, California. He became the first Navy or Marine officer ordered to "purely land flying," and his two-way versatility became the hallmark of Marine Aviation.

Though the European nations were far ahead in matters of expenditure, design, and improvement, they had no edge on the Americans' zest for painstaking tests and the courage it took to make them.

Typical was Captain Francis T. Evans, who was curious about the flight characteristics of the seaplane. The experts said it was impossible to loop a seaplane. Evans was not convinced of this when he took off one day in February, 1917, at Pensacola. He climbed his heavy, cumbersome N-9 to 3,000 feet and looped it twice before a crowd of frightened onlookers. Evans also had been told that it was impossible to bring a seaplane out of a spin. He whip-stalled the N-9, forcing it into a tight, corkscrew spin and pulled out of it safely a few hundred feet over the water. His double gamble was made even more dangerous by the fact that he wore no parachute. Aviators did not use them in those days.

The early flying Marines saw one of their dreams become a paper reality when a Marine Aviation Company was authorized in 1916 for duty with the Advance Base Force or expeditionary troops. With that step, the Marine Corps formally took to the air after nearly a century and a half of fighting on land and sea. Whether this new unit was the result of foresight or concession, it was evidence that the general military skepticism about air power was abating. In any case, it was fortunate. Less than a year later America entered World War I.

Air War with the Germans

The day war was declared against Germany in 1917, the Marine Aeronautic Detachment at Pensacola was prepared to meet the crisis with a total of 5 officers and 30 enlisted men. [The three new officers who had completed their flight training by 1917 were William M. McIlvain, Francis T. Evans, and Roy S. Geiger.] Proportionately, the air services of the Army and Navy were not much stronger, although the nations fighting in Europe were making extensive use of aviation in combat. This rapid development in European plane types and tactics had been under the scrutiny of several American officers, including Marine Lieutenant Bernard L. Smith. He had been sent to Paris in 1914 as assistant to the Naval Attaché at the American Embassy and spent three years touring the fighting fronts, observing the progress of aerial warfare.

Cunningham, now a major, supervised the hectic expansion program of the Air Arm in the early months of World War I. The unit in Florida was ordered to the Marine Barracks at Philadelphia in the spring of 1917 and reorganized as the Marine Aeronautic Company. Its early training facilities consisted of one hangar and an assigned quota of "two land aeroplanes, two sea aeroplanes, one school land aeroplane, and two kite balloons." The hangar was built on the river bank with openings at either end—one for seaplanes and one for landplanes.

Within six months, the Company had expanded to 34 officers and 330 enlisted men. Combat flight training was very meager in comparison to what Europeans were getting. American equipment was sadly outdated and unavailable in any quantity because of the neglected state of the country's aviation industry. Rudimentary flying was about all the early pilot learned, due to a lack of instructors and of planes that were built to fight.

In October, 1917, the detachment at Philadelphia was divided into the First Marine Aviation Squadron and the First Aeronautic Company. The First Squadron of 18 officers and 180 men moved to Hazelhurst Field at Mineola, Long Island. It trained there for several months in Army landplanes during one of the severest winters in the history of New York. With a pneumonia epidemic raging at a near-by camp, the squadron flight surgeon pronounced the air camp unfit to live in. On New Year's Day, with the temperature at 16 degrees below zero, the First Squadron entrained for Washington.

The unit reported to Headquarters, Marine Corps, hoping for orders to an airfield that was at least habitable. The duty officer had no new orders for them; in fact, he had never heard of the squadron. He advised going anywhere that suited the pilots. Days later, Captain McIlvain's unit ended up at Gerstner Field, Lake Charles, Louisiana. After some confusion, the camp commander made room for the Marines and they trained under the Army's air program.

The First Squadron trained at Lake Charles until March, 1918, when it joined Geiger's Second Squadron and Pressley's Third Squadron, which were operating at the new Marine flying field at Miami.

Cunningham, meanwhile, had gone to Europe to study operating conditions and the prospects for Marine Aviation's utilization. Returning January, 1918, he recommended that the Marine squadrons operate as the Day Wing of the U. S. Navy's proposed Northern Bombing Group. This unit was assigned to the Calais-Dunkirk sector for missions against the growing German submarine menace.

Sailing from Weehawken, New Jersey, aboard the U.S.S. De Kalb, the Marine overseas air contingent of 109 officers and 657 men arrived at Calais on July 31, 1918. This new First Marine Aviation Force consisted of a headquarters company and three squadrons. After several days, Squadrons A and B moved to the town of Oye, France and Squadron C to La Fresne. This latter unit was joined at the end of September by D Squadron, commanded by Captain Douglas Roben. Wing Commander Cunningham's headquarters were established at Bois-en-Ardres with rear-area supply bases at Pauillac, France and Eastleigh, England.

Aerial combat was at its height when the Marine squadrons arrived at their new bases, but because of a plane shortage it was many weeks before they flew as squadron units. They had been assigned the first 72 De Haviland-4 bombers (DH-4) off American production lines, but when these finally arrived in France they had been so hurriedly constructed that every one of them required a major overhaul before it could be flown.

During this lull, Marine day-bomber crews received operational training at Moutchic and Clermont-Ferrand in France and at Stonehenge, England. They were then assigned to RAF squadrons for further training. However, the additional training and lack of planes of their own did not keep the Marines out of combat. The pilots spent their time at near-by bases of British and French squadrons on active duty. After wangling several successful volunteer missions in Allied pursuit ships and bombers, senior Marine pilots were assigned to a British replacement pool. For weeks, the Marines flew the fast single-seater pursuits—Nieuports, Camels, and Spads—and the Handley-Paige bombers on successful sorties over France, Germany, and Belgium.

The Marines drew their first blood on September 9, when Sergeant Thomas L. McCullough flew a mission over Coremarch, Belgium. His plane was attacked by eight German Fokker pursuits. McCullough shot down one and fought off the others until a jammed gun forced him out of action.

During a raid over Courtemareke, Belgium, on September 28, Lieutenant Everett Brewer and his rear-gunner, Sergeant Harry Wershiner, were jumped by 15 German scout planes. They shot down three of the Germans before Sergeant Wershiner got a bullet hole in his lungs and Brewer was seriously wounded in the hips. On the same day, the Aviation Force suffered its first battle loss when Lieutenant Chapin Barr fought off a number of German planes until he was seriously wounded in the leg by cannon fire. After bringing his plane back safely, Barr died the next day in a Dunkirk hospital.

The Marines flew their only spectacular air support mission of

World War I when they aided a French regiment which had been surrounded by Germans near Stadenburg. After the French had been without food for several days, it was decided to supply them by air. Captains Francis P. Mulcahy (who was to become a major general) and Robert S. Lytle, Lieutenant Frank Nelms, and Gunnery Sergeant Amil Wiman loaded their bombers with canned food and bread. The Marines flew over the besieged unit at 100 feet to make their supply drops. Despite heavy machine-gun, rifle, and artillery fire from the Germans, the Marines made four supply drops to the Frenchmen, and were later awarded Distinguished Service Medals for the action.

On a mission near Cunel in the Verdun sector on October 7, Lieutenant William O. Lowe tangled with eight Fokker pursuit planes. He shot down one and disabled a second Fokker before breaking off the fight. Later on the same mission, Lowe fought a running battle with five more German planes and drove them off.

The only Marine airmen to be awarded the Congressional Medal of Honor for action in France were the pilot-gunner team of Second Lieutenant Ralph Talbot and Gunnery Sergeant Robert Guy Robinson. The awards were received for air actions on the 8th and 14th of October.

While on a raid over enemy territory with planes of the RAF's 218th Squadron, the Marines' bomber was attacked by nine German scout planes. In the dogfight that followed, Talbot shot down one German. In the October 14 engagement, their plane was forced out of formation by motor trouble during a raid at Pittham, Belgium. Twelve German fighters dove on the bomber. Robinson shot one of them down in flames just as a machine-gun burst ripped away most of his elbow. His gun jammed, and Talbot pulled away from the fight to give him time to clear it. They rejoined the battle, with Robinson using his gun with one hand. They continued the dogfight until Robinson collapsed from wounds in his stomach and thigh. He recovered, but Talbot was killed several weeks later when his plane crashed into a bomb dump.

By early October, the Marine squadrons had received sufficient two-place DH bombers to begin combat operations as units. Their first raid in force was carried out on October 14 when seven planes of Squadron C hit the railroad yards at Thielt and destroyed a troop train.

For several weeks, the four squadrons of the Day Wing flew missions against German installations at Thielt, Steenbrugge, Eecloo, Ghent, Deynze, and Lorken. Only one mission was flown against the submarine bases on the Channel coast before the Germans abandoned them. Operations were temporarily suspended October 27 to establish a new airdrome at Knesselaere, Belgium. The Marines continued their bombing runs against the retreating German armies until the Armistice on November 11, 1918.

The First Aviation Force, with a loss of 4 dead, reported that during its brief period of operation it had shot down a dozen German planes, made 5 supply drops, and dumped 52,000 pounds of bombs on 57 missions.

Sub Searches Off Azores

United States and British naval airmen carried on an increasingly successful warfare against the strong German submarine fleets and their bases in the last year of the war. Earlier, however, when the U-boats appeared far out in the mid-Atlantic, it was feared that the Germans would expand the scope of their convoy raids in the Atlantic from secret bases in the Azores. With the permission of the Portuguese government, Marine Aviation took over the Azores guard detail when the British withdrew in September, 1917.

In mid-October, the First Marine Aeronautic Company moved from Philadelphia to the airbase at Cape May, New Jersey, where it trained extensively in seaplane operations. During the first weeks of 1918, the unit, commanded by Major Francis T. Evans, disembarked in the Azores. Within a month, its 18 seaplanes were on antisubmarine patrol over the convoy lanes from a base at Ponta Delgada.

The Aeronautic Company maintained a heavy schedule of sunrise to sunset flights throughout its tour of duty, but made no contacts with either enemy surface raiders or U-boats. The unit's only casualty was the death of a Lieutenant Pogue in a crash shortly after the Armistice. Duty in the Azores ended in January, 1919, when the Company was ordered to Miami, Florida, and demobilized.

One segment of the Marine air program which did not see action in the war was the Balloon Company. A small lighter-than-air unit began training at Philadelphia in the spring of 1917, using several types of kite balloons. The Company was organized at the new Marine flying field at Quantico, Virginia, in June, 1918. It operated extensively there in observation and spotter work for heavy artillery units until the end of the war. A balloon unit continued as part of the Air Arm until 1930.

The Years of Nominal Peace

The size, hopes, and gusto of the Marine Air Arm dropped sharply after the Armistice. During the 20 war months it had expanded from 35 personnel to 280 officers, 2,200 men, and 340 planes. In 1918, there were provisions to raise these totals to 1,500 officers and 6,000 men, but rapid demobilization put an end to these plans.

At the high tide of war, after a decade of fumbling, America had grasped its aviation opportunities—and now almost as promptly released them. Marine airmen were plagued for twenty years by a shortage of new planes, personnel, and funds to make the most of their combat assignments, let alone the training programs. All of the nation's military and naval services suffered severely from this traditional shortsightedness and pacifism which held the country in its grasp until the eve of World War II.

Unlike the Army and Navy fliers, the Marines were fortunate in having a number of actual combat assignments during the years of peace at home. On these expeditionary missions, the Air Arm was able to improve its knowledge of combat tactics and operations. These missions, though small in scale, provided the only opportunities the nation had for actual combat experiment and experience.

Dive-Bombing the Cacos in Haiti

A series of revolutions on the island of Haiti was climaxed in October, 1918, when companies of the Marine Brigade on duty there set out again to restore peace and order as they had in 1915. They campaigned against the Cacos, or native hill-country bandits, led by Charlemagne Peralte, who were terrorizing the civilian population.

The Fourth Marine Air Squadron of 12 planes was sent to duty with the Brigade in February, 1919. Operating from its main base at Port au Prince, the six landplanes and six seaplanes flew regular missions in support of patrol actions by the Marines and the Haitian Gendarmerie, which was largely officered by Marines. During the prolonged campaign against the elusive Cacos, the pilots flew attack missions and scouting patrols, did aerial photography, and kept isolated units in contact with headquarters by flying messages, official papers, and staff officers. It also maintained a regular airmail service between the infantry units.

During the jungle and mountain operations against the forces of Peralte in 1919 and, after his death, against those of the bandit, Benoit, the Air Arm began its first combat experiments with the type of air attack which was to be called dive-bombing.

Since the infantry units were operating in close quarters against the Cacos in rugged terrain, the airmen were wary of the questionable accuracy of their horizontal bombing. There was an evident need for a new type of ground support which would result in better bombing without harming friendly troops.

Using a makeshift bomb rack fashioned from a sack, and a rifle barrel for a sight, Lieutenant Lawson H. M. Sanderson made several "glide" attacks on practice targets at Mirabelais in September, 1919. He dove his plane at an angle of 45 degrees and released its bomb low over the target. "The accuracy was astounding," according to Sanderson's report made some years later. Most of the squadron fliers were trained in this new tactic and in October, 1919, glide-bombing was used against the Haitan rebels "with excellent results," Sanderson reported.

The Marine Brigade hunted down the last of the Cacos revolutionaries in early 1921, and peace and order were maintained in Haiti until a brief outbreak in 1929 which was quickly quelled. During this period, the Marine air unit, redesignated several times, became Squadron VO-9M and continued training and operational flights, flew aerial survey and mapping missions, and maintained regular air-mail runs until Marines were withdrawn from the island in August, 1934.

Banditry in the Dominican Republic

Concurrent with the action in Haiti, Marine expeditionary forces were operating against guerillas and bandit gangs in the Dominican Republic. Marine troops maintained order in the Carribean Republic from 1914 until a new outbreak in 1919. This flare-up called for in-tensified campaigning, and the First Division, Squadron D (later called the First Air Squadron), was ordered to Santo Domingo where it was attached to the 15th Regiment.

The six-plane squadron, flying DH-4's, operated with regimental troops based at San Pedro de Marcoris from February, 1919, until March of the following year when it was moved to Santo Domingo City and attached to the Second Marine Brigade.

Throughout its combat tour, the squadron served the ground forces much in the same manner as aviation had in Haiti. It bombed and strafed bandit positions and flew routine tactical missions including reconnaissance, the evacuation of wounded, and ferrying doctors and medical supplies to patrols and forward outposts. Although order was restored in the Republic by June, 1922, the squadron remained on garrison duty until it was recalled to the United States in July, 1924.

Outpost Duty in the Pacific

The first harbinger of the Air Arm's future role in the Pacific was the ordering in 1920 of Flight L, Fourth Squadron, to duty at Guam in the Marianas where its small detachment operated on a shoestring basis for more than a decade. Its four planes were used in training flights and gathering meteorological data. Although nearly 100 offi-cers and men from its lone unit—Scouting Squadron One—(VS-IM) —left Guam in April, 1927, for duty in China, Marine airmen con-tinued to fly from the base at Sumay on Guam until 1931, when they were withdrawn.

World War I saw the first test of U.S. Marine tactical aviation. Here one of its two-place light bombers of 1917 is being readied for a mission over the German lines in France

China patrol flights occupied several Marine squadrons in 1927 during a civil war period there when Allied forces were on the alert. Camp MacMurray (below) served as a Marine air base in China.

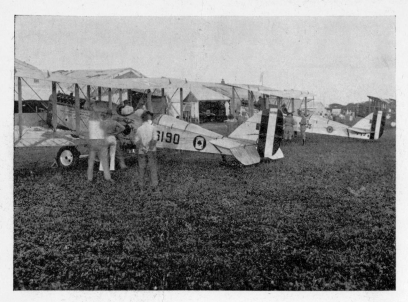

Port au Prince was a regular duty station for Marine airmen in Haiti during the peacetime years. (Above) Planes of the Ace of Spades squadron prepare for a mission over the island.

Air evacuation of wounded was an early Marine innovation in tactical support for the infantry. Here casualties arrive by plane from a Nicaraguan battle area for hospital care.

Aerial message drops to front-line patrols was a regular service by Marine fliers in Nicaragua. Waiting infantrymen get out from under just in case the weighted sack misses a ground panel bulls-eye.

Lieutenant General Roy S. Geiger

Major General Ross E. Rowell

Major General Ralph J. Mitchell

Major General James T. Moore

Major General Field Harris

Major General Louis E. Woods

Major General Claude Larkin

Major General Francis P. Mulcahy

Marine carrier airmen shown aboard the carrier *Lexington* in 1936 trained extensively in peacetime on both land and sea for their role in a vanguard air arm.

Wake Island lies below the laden bomb rack of an SBD during one of a series of carrier raids which pounded the atoll after it was wrested from its Marine garrison in December, 1941.

The Battle of Midway was in its crucial hours when these two Marine SB2U Vindicators took off to find and batter onrushing Japanese fleet units.

Midway buries its dead after the June, 1942 victory in which Marine airmen suffered severe casualties while playing a major role in turning back the enemy invasion armada.

The Pagoda at Guadalcanal overlooking Henderson Field served as headquarters for the Marine generals commanding the Allied air forces during the early stages of the battle for the Solomons.

Grumman Wildcats which played the dominant fighter role in the bitter air war over Guadalcanal are gassed and armed for another mission on a taxiway at Henderson Field.

With the Third Brigade in China

Perennial civil war in China kept the Marine forces there on the alert throughout the 1920's and early 1930's. A serious threat to American lives and property in 1927 occasioned the landing in China of the Third Marine Brigade. Joining U. S. Army and British units, the Marines were rushed to the Tientsin–Peking area in Northern China, where the Brigade remained on security duty until the end of 1928.

Although the Marines were never drawn into the civil war, they were continually on the alert for developments which might threaten American lives and property. Planes of the Marine squadrons, attached to the Brigade and based near Tientsin at the mouth of the Hai Ho River, maintained a daily reconnaissance patrol over an 8,000-square-mile area to keep the American forces informed of the activities of the opposing Chinese armies. During 18 months of operation in China, pilots of Patrol Three, Fighting Three, and Observation Squadron Five amassed a total of 3,800 flights which included photo missions, reconnaissance, and a regular airmail and passenger service between ground force units.

Air Infantry Support in Nicaragua

A period of anarchy, banditry, and revolution in Nicaragua provided Marine Aviation with its major combat role in the years of "peace." Marine guard detachments and expeditionary forces were in action sporadically in Nicaragua from 1910 until 1927 when, after a civil war ended, the bandit leader, Sandino, began a five-year guerilla war against the country's government and the Marine forces supporting it.

Several Marine air units were sent from Quantico to duty with the Second Brigade in Nicaragua in early 1927. They flew reconnaissance and maintained contact between some forty garrison units scattered throughout the country. Order was temporarily restored, but Sandino secretly gathered several hundred armed followers in northern Nicaragua and attacked the Marine and native constabulary garrisons at Ocotal on July 15, 1927.

Sandino's night attack was driven off and at daylight the battle was resumed. Two Marine patrol planes operating out of Managua arrived over Ocotal in midmorning. On instructions from the besieged garrison, the two planes strafed the bandit forces until out of ammunition. During the strafing, one plane was sent back for reinforcements. Five bombers, led by Major Ross E. Rowell, commander of the air units in Nicaragua, returned to Ocotal after flying through a tropical storm. Rowell's planes dive-bombed and machine-gunned the Sandino positions until the bandit forces scattered. This air attack was so successful that bandit casualties from it were estimated at up to three hundred dead.

Rowell's planes operated aggressively against the bandit groups throughout the final months of 1927 and made several attacks against the Sandinistas. During one of these, in October, a Marine plane crashed near Quilali. Patrols attempting to rescue its crew fought several decisive actions with the bandits but failed to locate the grounded airmen. The pilot was later found hanged from a tree by Sandino's orders.

Considerably understrength because of the personnel which had been withdrawn for service in China, the Marines took the offensive against Sandino's forces roving the wild jungle terrain of Neuva Segovia province. Two Marine columns operating in the vicinity of Quilali were ambushed by six to eight hundred bandits in early January. While planes covered the relief expedition, the wounded from the clash, including the two Marine commanders, were evacuated to Quilali. There an emergency airstrip was prepared by burning and leveling a part of the town.

Lieutenant Christian F. Schilt volunteered to fly out the wounded. Using a Corsair two-seater biplane, Schilt made ten trips into Quilali, landed on the small rutted road, loaded his patients, and took off again in the face of considerable hostile fire. Schilt, who was later to serve in a command position at Guadalcanal, was awarded the Medal of Honor for his "extraordinary heroism" in performing the Quilali rescue mission.

Less than a week after the Quilali incident, the Marines attacked Sandino's camp at El Chipote. While infantry patrols assaulted a main outpost, planes bombed and strafed the bandit camp "inflicting heavy damage on material and apparently heavy losses to personnel."

During the spring and summer of 1928, the air squadrons of the Brigade harassed the bandit groups in both eastern and western Nicaragua, either in support of patrols or on independent attack missions. Flying from crude forward fields, the Marine planes on numerous occasions bombed and strafed outlaw forces on the jungle trails and in their mountain hide-outs. When guerilla operations were localized in early 1929, and Sandino fled the country, planes of the Air Arm heckled the small bandit forces then operating under new leaders. [During one twelve-month period at this time, the Marines completed 1,275 combat sorties in their total of 5,000 flights.]

Sandino returned to Nicaragua in the summer of 1930 to make new forays from his headquarters in the mountains of Jinotega. The new uprisings were met by Guardia forces led by Marine officers and supported by the air squadrons. These native-constabulary units maintained constant though minor contact with the bandit forces until late 1932. Marine squadrons supported the Guardia actions until they were withdrawn to the United States in January, 1933.

As a result of their six years of combat and expeditionary service in Nicaragua, the squadrons of the Marine Air Arm made a major contribution to America's meager knowledge of aviation in combat. Though severely hampered by the number of planes available, Marine Aviation's extensive service in support of the ground forces was warmly praised by the infantry. With the exception of air opposition, the Marines flew the gamut of tactical operations under conditions not unlike those which the Air Arm would face years later in the Pacific war. A decade later, many of the same airmen who saw active service in Nicaragua, and were decorated for valor there, played key roles in the campaigns of Marine Aviation in World War II.

The variety of air missions which they performed in Nicaragua included the actual coverage of a boat-to-shore landing at Saclin on the Coco River by Guardia troops, rations drops to isolated units, aerial message pick-ups, evacuation of the sick and wounded, airmail and airfreight service for personnel and supplies, photo missions, scouting and reconnaissance flights over partially unexplored mountain and jungle terrain, mosquito dusting of camp areas which eliminated malaria, and rescue flights during the earthquake at Managua in March, 1931.

Those tactical missions, plus the improvement of its vital dive-bombing techniques, resulted in recognition of the Air Arm as a major component of the Marine Corps' tactical striking force.

When Things Were Bad All Over

In the decades between the world wars, Marine Aviation and its service counterparts grew up the hard way. They were weaned on pot-luck and "drug up by their own bootstraps." The nation's aviation industry, which had boomed spasmodically during the war years, collapsed like a pricked balloon immediately after the Armistice. It had been badly in need of the practical subsidy of military orders for experiments and new types of planes. It did not get them, and both the industry and the air services suffered accordingly.

Military budgets were gutted regularly each year, and the softest spots for cuts were the new air services. It was thought wiser to pay for new battleships and pack howitzers than for better air forces. Besides, there were scores of old warplanes and engines around the country, and in the interests of economy the fliers were told to use those and forget about progress.

During the 1920's, the "Aeronautic Organization of the Marine Corps" struggled along with its four partially active squadrons, which were scattered from the main airbase at Quantico to the field at Parris Island, South Carolina, and overseas in five different countries. Though many of its expeditionary missions were concurrent, few planes, new or old, were available and the squadrons spread themselves thinner and thinner.

During the peace years, the Air Arm nurtured its painful progress and expansion side by side with its supplier and senior partner, Naval Aviation, which had serious troubles of its own with battleships and budgets. There was a like situation within the Marine Corps itself. Some officers realized the impact of air warfare and many did not. Of those who did, some had a firm grasp on the shape of things to come.

Joel D. Thacker, an historian, notes that, "as early as July, 1919, the Major General Commandant submitted . . . specifications for a Marine Corps 'expeditionary plane.' They called for a two-seater plane with one or two fixed guns firing forward and one machine gun on a scarf mount in the rear cockpit; a flying speed of 90 to 100 mph, a landing speed of 45 mph, and a climb of 5,000 feet in seven minutes; a cruise radius of 300 miles; able to land and take off from small fields; to carry 200 pounds of bombs with bombsights and racks; a radio-telephone and telegraph set; guns, ammunition, and camera; interchangeable landing gear . . . these specifications also called for pack-type parachutes and *self-sealing fuel tanks*."

It was almost a full twenty years before all of those visionary specifications of 1919 were met and exceeded. In that time, the Marines graduated slowly from their Curtiss Jennies and De Havilands. Searching for suitable combat types, the Marine and Navy pilots experimented with foreign makes. They flew Austrian, British, French, Italian, and German military aircraft until a few American models appeared. It was not until 1928 that the Marines replaced their 1918 workhorses. Then, Curtiss Falcon fighter-observation planes were sent to duty in China and the new Loening amphibian proved ideal for Nicaraguan operations, as did Chance-Vought's two-seater biplane, the O2U.

Marine and Navy airmen were assigned the Curtiss biplane Helldiver and a series of two-place fighters produced by Curtiss in the late 1920's and early 1930's. The O2C-1 Helldiver, considered the first dive-bomber in the naval service, was replaced in 1935 by the Great Lakes BG-1. During the 1930's, Vought turned from fighters to observation planes while Boeing produced new pursuit models. Standard Air Arm fighter planes from 1936 to 1940 were the F2F and F3F Wildcats made by the Grumman Company. These biplane pursuits were replaced by the F4F-3 monoplane fighter which fought at Wake Island. Vought's SBU scout-bomber series of 1936 evolved the SB2U Vindicator used at Midway. The outmoded Great Lakes and Curtiss biplane bombers were finally replaced by the Northrop BT-1, the prototype of the Douglas SBD scout-bomber which became the workhorse of attack aviation in the Pacific war.

This tedious evolution of plane types produced the Air Arm's starting line-up for World War II—Wildcat and Brewster fighters, SBD's, SB2U's, and the DC-3 Douglas transports used by the civilian airlines. This array was hardly a frightening one to America's potential enemies, who knew too well that this country was only a fifth-rate world air power. Only because of several years of undeserved grace before and after 1941 was the United States able to catch up with and surpass Axis air power in quantity and quality.

Pathfinders and Progress

When the Brood of Noisy Nan returned from France in 1919, it was still a fledgling in search of a destiny. Public and military apathy to the contrary, its fliers believed in aviation's war potential. Fortunately, they were pioneers in the manner of Cunningham, Smith, and Evans, and anxious to test their wings against any challenge.

The airmen had two excellent reasons for their eagerness. Their whole new world of aerial flight was clouded with questions, and the strange Lorelei that is flying demanded the answers. Moreover, they wanted desperately to sell the public and the older branches of the services on military aviation.

It was not enough that they were the pathfinders in the small wars overseas. The airmen at home etched paths of their own to the far horizons along with the pioneers of the Army and Navy. Some of these Marine exploits made headlines. Others added to the lore and laurels of the Air Arm in the growing world of aviation itself.

The longest unguarded flight ever made over both land and water won the Distinguished Flying Cross in 1921 for Lieutenant Colonel Thomas C. Turner when he led two De Havilands from Washington, D.C. to Santo Domingo City and return, with an elapsed flying time of 46 hours and 17 minutes.

Two Marine De Haviland bombers broke another landplane record in 1923 by completing a 10,953-mile flight from Haiti to San Francisco and return. In addition to being an American distance record, the flight was credited with being the second longest of its kind in the world.

Pilots of the Air Arm stationed in the United States participated regularly in battle maneuvers with their own infantry and in joint exercises with the Army and Navy from the Civil War battlefields of Virginia to the beaches of Hawaii. [*Pilots received their flight training at Pensacola and were assigned to Army or Navy air schools for special training or to the Marine fields at Quantico, Parris Island, and San Diego.*]

No call for their appearance in the name of aviation was unanswered. At the christening of each new civilian airfield or the opening of an air meet, Marine planes were there. More than likely, it was the crack Helldiver unit doing acrobatics with its wings tied together or giving an exhibition of dive-bombing. Rescue and emergency flights, whether for Mississippi flood victims or forest-fire patrol, became part of the Marine stock in trade.

In the Army Air Service bombing competition of 1926, Marine pilots placed second, third, and fourth. Captain Harold D. Campbell, later a brigadier general, was awarded the Herbert Schiff trophy by the President for safety in flying during 1925-1926.

Captain Arthur H. Page received the DFC for a record "blind" flight from Omaha to Washington in 1930. He negotiated a distance of almost a thousand miles, through storms and heavy cloud cover, flying only on instruments. Two months earlier, Page had won the Curtiss Marine Trophy race at Anacostia. His average speed for the course in an F6C equipped with pontoons was 164 mph. Page died several months later when his plane crashed during the Thompson Trophy race at Chicago.

When polar explorer Richard E. Byrd discovered a new mountain range in the Antarctic in 1929, the pilot of his plane was Marine Captain Alton N. Parker. Two Marine enlisted men were awarded Navy Crosses on this expedition for their technical exploits. One of the men, Czegka, (later a warrant officer) won the Navy Cross again as general manager of the second Byrd expedition to the South Pole.

The Air Arm moved into new fields of operation when two of its squadrons were assigned to regular carrier duty with the fleet in 1931. They served aboard the *Lexington, Saratoga,* and *Langley* for three years. In 1934, the old Haitian observation squadron became the garrison air force for the Virgin Islands in the Carribean. It operated from the town of Charlotte Amalie on St. Thomas Island until it was decommissioned as VO-9M in 1944.

By the eve of World War II, the Marine Air Arm dropped out of the headlines to concentrate its wealth of tactical experience on training and maneuvers with the infantry and the fleet. During the decades of "peace," it had grown measurably in stature and experience, but not in size. From 1,000 on duty in 1921, the Air Arm had grown to 192 pilots and a grand total of less than 2,000 in its ranks by June, 1940. Comparatively, the Army and Navy air services were no larger and they lacked the twenty years of combat experience Marine aviation had earned.

By any measure, American air power was not quite ready when, less than eighteen months later, the Japanese Zeros roared over Pearl Harbor.

2

THE HOLDING PHASE—PEARL HARBOR–WAKE–
MIDWAY

THREE hundred miles east out of Midway, the carrier *Lexington* plowed through the rich, improbable blue of the Pacific. Combers broke from its bow and curled back along the sides. Now and then schools of flying fish spurted from the waves like iridescent sun showers.

On deck, the pilots and gunners of VMSB 231 lolled in the warming sun and the Sunday morning quiet. From the bridge came the order to clear the decks for their SB2U's to take off. Reluctantly, the airmen eased out of their reveries and into the planes.

Suddenly, the bullhorn blared everything else into silence:

"Now hear this! Hostilities commenced this morning with a Japanese attack on Pearl Harbor. This is not a drill! I repeat, this is not a drill!"

Back in a cottage at the abrupt little Ewa Beach on the western shore of Oahu, Captain Dick Mangrum, a Marine dive-bomber pilot, thumbed through the comic strips of the Honolulu paper. He shrugged off the muted sounds of machine-gun firing. The Fleet was always holding some kind of light-weapons exercise. Strange, though, that this one was so early on a Sunday morning. Then bomb explosions mingled with the soft, distant snapping of the gunfire. Thinking how damned odd that was, Mangrum looked out and saw a tight formation of planes flying low along the beach, right past his front door, in the direction of Pearl Harbor. They had bright-red meatballs on their wings.

Three miles inland from where Mangrum stood, the Officer of the Day at the Ewa Marine airbase had just finished his breakfast when he heard a large number of planes approaching. Stepping outside the mess hall, he saw two formations winging in. One was to the left; it had about 18 torpedo planes and was close to the beach, moving toward Pearl Harbor at one thousand feet. To the northwest, and coming almost directly at him, was another pack of gnats. They were sweeping in from the direction of Nanakuli over the long, gentle slope that passes through a spectrum of mottled greens and browns from the mountains down to the sea. These were single-seat fighters— Mitsubishi Zekes. The sun spilled off their fuselages and focused sickeningly on the red-blobbed insignia on their wings and sides. Passing over the squat shacks of Ewa town about a mile north of the field, the Japanese formation wheeled right and peeled off in string runs for the airbase.

It was 0755. The surprise was perfect. Some of the Marines looked up and scattered for their duty stations. A few were puzzled—then got the word and ducked for cover.

The Zekes whipped in, expertly and disdainfully, their wing guns stuttering red with incendiary, explosive, and armor-piercing fire. First targets were the tactical planes, neatly lined up in the parking areas, and concentrated at the paddle-bat end of one of the two intersecting runways.

Barely twenty feet off the deck, the Jap pilots squeezed off short bursts of machine-gun and cannon fire into one plane after another. The sitting ducks smoked, flamed, or sat there briefly and were holed like collanders as streams of gas spurted out of their tanks and burned or puddled on the runway waiting for a bullet.

Out of their runs, the Japs kicked the Zekes over the treetops, stood them on one wing, and came in again. A dozen minutes of this squirrel-cage attack and Ewa's planes were out of commission. For ten minutes more the Zeros kept at it, beating up the utility planes, personnel, and planes under repair.

The Marines, recovering from their original surprise, fought back as best they could. Some of them broke out rifles and set up a firing line in the operating area near the burning planes. Little three-year-old Hank Anglin took a stroll from the photo tent where he and his father had been taking cover. All this excitement was rare fun for a Sunday at Ewa and little Hank had to see more of it. The youngster was well out on the landing mat watching the Zekes zip by before his father missed him. Sergeant Anglin dived after him and, with the boy underneath, crawled back some thirty yards while puffs of tracer dust patterned around them. The Anglins had just got inside a radio trailer when a slug carved a hole above its door.

Pfc James Mann was refueling the ambulance when the attack began. He rounded up Pharmicist Mate O. D. Smith and started for the burning planes. The strafing fighters bored in on their ambulance. Mann stopped short and they crawled underneath it. Minutes later, the corpsman had copped a bullet in his left leg. Their ambulance had 52 holes in it. Mann drove his patient through Jap fire to the sick bay.

Halfway to the same area, a Marine named Shaw, wheeling the bright-red fire truck, got the strafing treatment. When the Zeros shot the tires off its wheels, Shaw abandoned his loud target, grabbed a rifle, and went on the firing line.

Thirty or forty Marines found shelter in the excavation for the swimming pool. Captain Milo Haines ducked behind a tractor with its driver. The shield worked well until one Zeke came in from the wrong side. Its first burst clipped Haines' necktie off just below the chin and nicked the back of his head. When their trailer hideout got too warm, Sergeant Anglin and his son darted back to the photo tent. While the sergeant was breaking out his photo gear to get pictures of the fracas, little Hank obediently stayed under a wooden bench. As the Sergeant stepped into an adjacent tent, a machine-gun bullet went through his upper right arm. Staunching the flow of blood, he went back to the photo tent where his little boy, still under the bench, pointed to a spent bullet on the floor and warned, "Don't touch that, Daddy, it's hot!"

The first wave of attackers pulled off and Lieutenant Colonel Claude A. Larkin, with shrapnel wounds in both legs and one hand, marshalled his meager defenses and checked his planes. None of the fighters nor dive-bombers could be flown. All available weapons were passed out—rifles, pistols, a few .30-caliber machine guns assigned to the squadrons, and several others cannibalized from the rear seats of wrecked dive-bombers. They were mounted on anything handy. One of the less damaged SBD's was hauled into a tent area off the field. Two Marines manned its guns. Others were posted as extra guards in the fields and roadways leading to the airbase. Trucks and cars, those that were left, were driven out on the runways to prevent a landing of airborne troops. Though the sick bay had been set on fire by the first passes, doctors and corpsmen saved some medical supplies and gave first aid to the wounded. Serious cases were evacuated to the Ewa Plantation Hospital.

Meanwhile, the Jap carrier planes were lambasting other targets in their coordinated attack. Kaneohe Naval Air Station, on the far side of the island, was hit a few minutes before Ewa, and 17 were killed. Army fields at Hickam, Bellows, and Wheeler were carefully neutralized. The heaviest impact of the morning was directed against fleet units in Battleship Row off Ford Island where the final havoc was disastrous.

Ten or fifteen minutes after the Zekes left, Ewa got its second and heaviest attack of the morning, beginning at 0835. A straggling column of about thirty low-wing dive-bombers, Aichi (99) Vals, skimmed in over the trees from the direction of Pearl Harbor. After the first planes made their runs, it was evident to them that the tactical planes on the ground had been knocked out in the first raid. Then the dive-bombers concentrated their strafing and bombing on camp areas, buildings, and personnel. Light bombs erupted on target after target as the Aichis weaved in and out looking for bait.

This attack was met by heavy ground fire from rifles, Tommy guns, and .30-caliber machine guns. Master Technical Sergeant Emil Peters and Private William Turner, who had manned the free gun in the parked SBD, gave the Vals a going over throughout the second and third raids. Peters put bursts into every plane that came within range, while Turner fed belted ammunition into the machine gun.

Firing from a completely exposed position, the Marines drilled a burst into the underbelly of a bomber which smoked and crashed beyond the end of the runway. Then the Vals turned on them.

Two planes strafed repeatedly and one bomb exploded ten feet away, but neither Marine was hit. Bullets finally made a sieve of the SBD. Peters still crouched and fired, but Turner fell from the wing, mortally wounded. He died a few days later.

The Vals weaved in low, strafed from their forward guns, then pulled up in a steep wingover to let their rear-gunners answer the ground fire. From their firing position inside the swimming-hole pit, Marines had planes come in so low they could see the Jap pilots and gunners grinning at them. A technical sergeant by the name of Turnage sawed a heavy gunburst into another Val that staggered out of sight and probably crashed.

After thirty minutes, the enemy dive-bombers joined up and headed out to sea. In the lull, the Marines reorganized their defenses, put out fires, and treated the wounded.

Fifteen Nakajima I-97 fighters roared in for the final raid on Ewa. Flying in a treetop column, they duplicated the tactics of the Zeros. After a few quick strafing runs, they got tired of the sport, or found the heavy ground fire uncomfortable. A large part of the formation broke off and flew seaward over Barbers Point. Five or six fighters stayed behind, making sporadic runs on personnel. They killed Sergeant Carlo Micheletto as he sniped away at them from an exposed position. As the sergeant died, the last I-97 made its run and headed out to sea.

This was the finale of the December 7 raid for the Marines at Ewa. Colonel Larkin reported his command condition to CINCPAC at Pearl Harbor: 3 men dead, another dying, 11 enlisted men and 2 officers wounded. Only one Marine plane was flyable and that was down in the repair shops at Ford Island. All other fighter, bomber, and transport planes of MAG 21 were destroyed or damaged. [VMJ 252 had 2 planes left out of 8; VFM 221 lost 7 of its 9 fighters; VMSB 231 all of its 7 planes; and VMSB 232, 10 dive-bombers out of 22. Those planes not destroyed were all in need of repair.]

Throughout the rest of the day and night, radio channels on Oahu were alive with rumored sightings of Japanese planes and ships in the area, but none materialized. At dawn five Army fighters landed for operations. On the 10th, the 18 Marine SB2U's off the Lexington

26 DEVILBIRDS

landed. For weeks after the attack, the Marines at Ewa serviced planes from five Navy carriers and those of the 47th Army Pursuit squadron whose base at Wheeler Field couldn't handle them. As the days passed and the alert lessened, Larkin's command cleaned up its debris, repaired its planes, and rebuilt the airbase in preparation for things to come.

[Ewa (pronounced Eh-Vah) Field is on the coral flatlands on the leeward side of Oahu, 17 miles from Pearl Harbor. In 1925 it had been developed as the Ewa Mooring Mast for the airship Shenandoah. Marine Air Group 2 landed at Pearl Harbor for temporary duty on January 21, 1941. Commanded by Lieutenant Colonel Lewie G. Merritt, the group moved to Ewa. Its squadrons—VMF Two, VMB Two and VMJ Two—landed at Ewa on February 3 for training and patrol operations. Merritt was detached November 18 and replaced by Colonel Larkin. Ewa served as the main staging and training area for Marine squadrons going into combat at Wake, Midway, and the Solomons, and as headquarters for the operational command, Marine Air, Hawaiian Area (MAHA).]

Sixteen Days at Wake Island

Far out on the mid-Pacific horizon a tight knot of 12 planes flew dead-on for the lonely outpost. Minutes later, they swept over the coral, brush-topped wishbone of an island, startling a flock of pirate birds, and broke out into a landing circle. They were the stubby, blue, clipt-winged F4F-3's of VMF 211. In the cockpits were Putnam, Elrod, Tharin, Freuler, Kinney, Graves, Kliewer, Holden, Webb, Davidson, Hamilton, and Arthur. The latter two were flying sergeants, the others captains and lieutenants, except for Putnam, the major, who commanded that forward echelon. It was Thursday, December 4, 1941.

The Wildcats had taken off from a carrier at sea several hours earlier and were landing now on the new runway. They were the first land-based planes of the garrison air force for this most isolated island possession of the United States. Wake was the only link between Guam and Midway, and a stopover for the Pan American Clippers.

15358

As the last plane pancaked and taxied into the parking area, Marine Aviation's strength on Wake Island numbered 12 officers and 49 enlisted men. Major Walter L. J. Bayler and Lieutenant C. R. Conderman had come ashore with a detail of 47 enlisted men from the *U.S.S. Wright* on November 29 to establish the airbase.

Putnam and his pilots, in the midst of raucous noises from the bosun birds, received a royal welcome from the 1,200 civilian construction workers, nearly 400 enlisted Marines of the Wake Detachment, First Marine Defense Battalion, a small group of Army radio men, and the island's military commanders. Putnam reported in first to Commander Winfield S. Cunningham, skipper of the Wake Naval Air Station. He was introduced to Commander Campbell Keene, in charge of the patrol-plane facilities; Dan Teeters, head of the construction detail; and the lean, sharp, bemoustached little commander of the Marines ashore, Major James Patrick S. Devereux.

On the day that VFM 211 landed, Wake was not much of a citadel. There are three islands in this coral atoll group, which is 2,000 miles southwest of Honolulu and directly north of the enemy-mandated Marshall Islands. The crooked wishbone of Wake is the largest atoll —two and a quarter square miles. On its western finger was Camp No. 2, home of the construction workers. Across the green lagoon, on the first knuckle of the other finger, was Marine camp No. 1. At the fat point of their joining was the airbase. Across Peale Channel, below Camp No. 2, was Peale Island. Its one-half square mile contained the Pan American facilities. On the eastern side of the atoll was Wilkes Island, one third of a square mile in area and rectangular in shape. The three islets were fully ringed by a jagged coral reef which, if nothing else, offered a natural barrier to enemy landing parties.

Defense-wise, Wake was still in a primitive state, but through no fault of those ashore, who were sent out at the last minute to develop its military potential. Devereux had worked out a clever defense, making good use of what little he had. [*His heavy armament of 18 guns was paired off in batteries and emplaced at the extremities of the island. Three 2-gun batteries of 5-inch coast artillery and three 4-gun batteries of 3-inch anti-aircraft guns were concealed and strung*

*out from Toki Point on Peale, to Heel Point on the bulge above the
construction camp, down island to Peacock Point off the airfield, and
back down to Kuku Point on Wilkes. For light armament, the Marines
had twenty-four .50-caliber machine guns, and thirty .30-calibers.]*
The Marine forces finally totaled 15 officers and 373 men. These,
plus 11 naval officers and 58 men, the unarmed Army radio unit of
5 men under Captain Stanley Wilson, and Teeter's civilians, brought
Wake's population to 522 military and 1,200 civilians.

Major Putnam, in his last letter aboard the carrier wrote, "He [the
task force Admiral] made it plain to me that nothing should be over-
looked nor any trouble spared in order that I will get ashore with 12
airplanes in as near perfect condition as possible . . . all hands have
vied with each other to see who could do the most for us. I feel a bit
like a fatted calf being groomed for whatever it is that happens to
fatted calves. . . ."

Once ashore Putnam had ample worries. None of his pilots had
more than thirty hours' flying time in the new F4F's, nor had they
dropped a bomb or fired a gun from them. There had not been time.
His Wildcats were to double as bombers, but the bombs ashore did
not fit their racks and had to be hitched on precariously with bands
from light practice bombs. The new planes had no armor, no self-
sealing tanks, no IFF homing devices. Wake itself had no radar for
warning purposes. The air camp and repair shops on the south side
of the runway were still in the rugged stages.

There was a fretful tension in the air at Wake, and, as there had
been for weeks, talk of war. The Marines worked hard under the prod
of a shapeless urgency. Four Wildcats took off at dawn Friday to begin
routine patrols. At dusk another four took over the chore. Saturday
morning, the planes made dummy runs on the AA batteries to warm
up their crews and get a little strafing practice themselves. That afternoon and Sunday, the Marines on Wake had a breathing spell,
except for the duty stations and the air patrols. Bayler broke out a
bottle of beer in the tented Officers' Club, tore a page out of his note-
book, and finished a letter to his wife. He wrote, "It's a beautiful
spot . . . and so utterly peaceful!" That night all hands slept well

under a blanket of sound—the dull, booming roar of the surf pounding on the reefs.

At 0630 on the Monday morning of December 8, Captain Wilson telephoned from his quarters to the radio trailer at the airfield. His sergeant on duty kept saying, "I don't believe what I'm hearing . . . it's . . ." and then put the earphones to the mouth of the telephone. The Morse code was obviously from their Hawaiian transmitter— "SOS SOS Japs attacking Oahu. This is the real thing . . . Hickam Field and Pearl Harbor under attack . . . this is no drill!" [*It was December 7 in Hawaii. Wake is on East Longtitude Time, being beyond the International Date Line.*]

Wilson headed for the Marine camp on the double and found Devereux in his tent, shaving. The Major read the message, wiped off the lather, and went to his near-by office. Shortly the bugler called Wake to arms. Laughing and joking, the Marines grabbed rifles and gear and headed for their battle stations. At 0800 sharp, colors sounded and men all over the island snapped to, smartly. The flag went up for keeps, its halyards lashed to the pole.

Putnam had sent up four of his planes under Captain Hank Elrod to patrol the southern sector until they ran low on gas. Four more would take over when they came back. Pan Am's Clipper had taken off at dawn for Guam, but was recalled by radio. It landed at 0930 and Hamilton, its Captain, agreed to make a search around the island for 100 miles. Two pilots would escort when it took off at 1330. After the first flight was off, Putnam's men continued to gas and arm the remaining eight fighters which were dispersed at widely separated points in the parking area. Over the noise of their revving motors and the roar of the surf, every man on the island cocked an ear to the sky, listening for whatever it might hold. Near noon, Putnam and his pilots waited under the squadron tent, on the parking apron, for chow.

At 1158, the deep-throated roar of many motors rose above the local turmoil. As the pilots watched, 24 bombers flew out of a rain squall in the south and headed directly for Wake at about 3,000 feet. Someone said, "They're B-17's!", and got a sharp answer, "Hell NO, they're Japs!"

Slick and gleaming, the Mitsubishis held their tight V-of-V-formation as they passed the reef. Down came the tumbling salvo of bombs in a neat checkerboard pattern which blanketed the airfield. Once beyond the island, the Jap formation split. One section returned to strafe the airbase. The other veered over Peale to bomb and strafe the Pan American camp.

It was all over in ten minutes. Wake's own bombs still exploded erratically while out of the crackling flames, a wild hail of machine-gun bullets and tracers from the burning planes swept over the low atoll. Putnam's camp was a shambles. Beyond it, heat belched from two 25,000-gallon gas tanks and 600 oil drums.

VMF 211's pilots had sprinted across the open areas for their planes at the first alarm. As Graves reached his cockpit, a bomb exploded directly behind him, throwing his body under the wing. Conderman was riddled with shrapnel fragments and died that night. Frank Holden was cut to pieces in the strafing attack. Lieutenant Harry "Spider" Webb was knocked flat by the concussion and crippled for the rest of the siege. Nine of the ground crewmen were killed outright. A dozen others were wounded, including three of the eight remaining pilots. Seven of the eight F4F's on the ground were gutted and destroyed either by direct hits or from their own exploding bombs. The last plane had a wing tank ripped beyond repair.

Elrod's air patrol, which had been searching a sector away from the path of the bombers, landed. One plane failed to clear the debris on the runway. Its wrecked propellor was replaced from a damaged plane. Three-quarters of Wake's tiny air force had been wiped out in ten minutes. There were four planes left.

Putnam and Bayler worked out the timing on future raids. The bombers were obviously based somewhere in the Marshalls (actually on Kwajalein). To make the round trip by daylight, they would arrive roughly between 1100 and 1300.

Four fighters were up on Tuesday when, at 1145, 27 Mitsubishis came in from the East. The Japs hit the construction camp and ignored the airfield. Their accuracy was off, but one bomb hit the well-marked hospital and killed 21. Ten were wounded civilians, the

others were Marines of VMF 211. Technical Sergeant Hamilton cut
one bomber out of the pack and sent it down in flames, with
the help of Kliewer and Davidson, for Wake's only blood of the
day.

As rescue squads picked up the remains of the civilian dead, they
found that the shell fragments were easily identifiable American
scrap—nuts, bolts, scissors, farm machinery pieces, and two radiator
caps with the well-advertised trademarks still on them.

The next day, three javelins of nine bombers came in again, one
hour earlier than usual, but on the same course and altitude. Stray
bombs killed one line Marine and three from VMF 211. Their bodies
were not found for ten days. Wilkes Island took the brunt of the raid.
Its dynamite dump blew up, flattening everything in the area. In return, Captain "Baron" Elrod shot down two of the bombers. That
afternoon Freuler mined the airstrip and ringed the flats around it
with bulldozers to prevent any landings by Jap planes.

At midnight, lights flared at sea to the south. In the dawn, two
patrol planes spotted the invasion fleet bearing down on the southwest side of Wake. The F4F's went low enough to identify the 14
ships—light cruisers, destroyers, small gunboats and transports.

Devereux's batteries held fire to conceal position until the lead
ships were 4,500 yards from shore, then opened up. In the front-yard
duel, one battery scored four hits on a cruiser which retreated out of
range. Another sank the lead destroyer with three salvos, then holed
a transport and the second cruiser. A battery on Toki Point sank another destroyer and the invasion fleet withdrew.

After the shore batteries had opened up, the Grummans tackled the
fleet. Elrod and Tharin wove a pattern over the ships and picked out
their target . . . "See that big fat —— straight ahead? . . . I'll go
down on this side . . . you sashay off to the right . . . we'll divide
his fire." They reported back to Wake by radio, debating whether
two medals or two cups of "Joe" (coffee) should be held for them.
Then they pushed over. Three of their bombs were plate-rattling
near-misses. One started a fire forward on the target ship, while
their gunfire rattled over its deckplates and superstructure.

Elrod and Tharin came back to Wake for more "nourishment."

They taxied into the rearming pits and were off again in minutes. This time they were ordered to observe results when the shore guns fired. One full salvo hit a gunboat and the F4F's laid in a bomb apiece to finish her off, while their earlier target disappeared over the southern horizon, trailing smoke. Back for another load, they reported in to Putnam and asked permission to get a destroyer which looked like the enemy flagship. They got it, but with instructions to bring back the planes.

Over the destroyer, the Marines dived again. Tharin's guns failed to work so he feinted a frontal attack while Elrod came in from the side. One bomb scored a hit. The two pilots swore all the way back to the field about jammed guns and erratic light bombs that would not go where they were sent. Back on the field, they stayed in their cockpits while the armorers rebelted the guns and hung on bombs. Back south they flew. Again they dove, and again and again. The Baron and the Duke made four round trips against the *Kisaragi*. When they left her finally, she was ablaze from stem to stern from eight direct bomb hits and well serrated by their strafing. Its crew was abandoning the warship with considerable alacrity.

After turning the invasion attempt, the men in the dugouts had no time to relax. At 0945, some 20 two-engine bombers were overheard. The formation stayed at 20,000 feet and its bombs were all wide. These fish-butchers were jumped by four pilots—Kinney, Davidson, Freuler, and Elrod—who were patroling on oxygen above the enemy formation. The F4F's poured down through a hail of fire from the enemy rear-gunners. Bullets punched through Elrod's engine and the motor sputtered weakly as he staggered back to the field. Seconds too soon, his motor stopped and the F4F crashed among the boulders on the beach. Elrod walked away, heartbroken that he was responsible for the loss of a plane. Freuler, too, was forced out of the fight with bullets in his engine, but he managed a neat deadstick landing.

Carl Davidson worked the tail of the bomber formation and sent its two rear planes splashing into the ocean. Kinney got a probable, the AA downed one and smoked three. That afternoon over Radio Tokyo a singsong voice that was to become infamous as that of

Tokyo Rose lilted the news that the Japanese had made a landing on Wake and captured it. As in the months to come, the Rose was always good for a lie and a laugh.

On the afternoon of December 12, Lieutenant Dave Kliewer was patroling high when he spotted a black object on the surface about 12 miles south of the island. Corkscrewing down, he found it was a Jap sub, charging its batteries on the surface. Kliewer closed, strafing. Low over the black cigar on the water, he released his two bombs. Both seemed direct hits. Seconds later, he was back for another attack but found only an oil slick.

After five days of bombing, bad weather kept the Japanese away from Wake on the 13th. It was a breather in the monotony of destruction, but no rest. Those ashore worked furiously repairing what was left of Wake's military potential. Both the Navy and Marine radio communication units had long since been knocked out. Wilson's Army crew maintained the only contact the island had with its own planes and the outside world. At the airfield, VMF 211 kept performing minor miracles of salvage, invention, and repair—anything to keep the planes in the air. Hank Freuler rigged a system for transferring oxygen from the contractors' big tanks into the small bottles used in the planes. He was too weak from diarrhea to explain how he did it. It was said that Kinney and Hamilton never slept. If they were not up on patrol, they were in the repair shops, building and rebuilding engines and swapping plane parts back and forth until none of the original F4F's was identifiable. Their ingenuity added a third plane to the available list. It was rebuilt from the wrecks.

A few hours later, Wake again had but two planes to fly. During a take-off, the rebuilt F4F veered wildly toward a group of workmen. Freuler couldn't kick it back on course so he tried horsing the plane into the air. It was too ramshackle to respond and crashed in the brush. Freuler escaped serious injury and they propped his plane up as a dummy along with Elrod's.

For six more days, with one exception, the raiders came in and the patrols went up. The bomb barrage slowly ground down the remnants of Wake, its defenses and defenders, and days and events became a vague blur. One of the Wildcats was set on fire and, while it was still smoking, its undamaged engine was transferred into Freuler's plane.

After 41 bombers struck on the 16th, Tharin was on dusk patrol when a lone four-engine flying boat came over, dropped its bombs, and returned for a low, insolent strafing run. Tharin patiently chopped away until the Mavis flamed and settled to a water landing, burning. Tharin went back for a load of bombs to give it a final gutting, but when he returned minutes later, the charred hulk settled beneath the surface.

By the morning of the 20th, half of Putnam's air command were casualties—28 dead and 6 wounded. Out of a morning rain squall, slid a PBY patrol plane with mail and dispatches and the word that all but 250 key civilians would be evacuated on the 24th, and that reinforcements were enroute. [*The promised rescue task group, including the carrier Saratoga, was within 24 hours of Wake when it was diverted to Midway.*] When the PBY splashed off next morning, Major Bayler was aboard on orders to duty at Midway. With him went the last dispatches and final eye-witness account of what happened in the siege at Wake until the end of the war freed the survivors from Japanese prison camps. These told the story of the last desperate hours.

On the 22nd, Freuler and Davidson were at 12,000 feet when the bombers came in. Freuler shot down one on his first pass. On his second run, he got a bullet through his shoulder as the second bomber exploded in front of him, scorching the F4F. Its engine stopped turning over as he brought the plane in for a landing. Davidson never returned. The planes they tangled with were carrier-based Zero fighters and bombers. Davidson was last seen diving on a Zeke with one on his tail. Freuler's plane was marked off when it landed.

With the carrier raid, the air defense of Wake was at an end and the final invasion was imminent. What was left of Putnam's squadron joined the defense forces as infantrymen.

One hundred minutes past midnight on the 23rd, vague activities at sea suddenly materialized when the first Jap landing barge ground ashore on Wilkes Island. There was a flurry of machine-gun fire and silence. The cable link with the main island was severed. By 0300, it was evident that the main enemy landing effort would be concentrated on the southern side of Wake.

By 0430, there were 1,000 Japanese troops ashore on the south of Wake. They were faced by about 85 Marines, including the airmen. Other knots of defenders were in zones along Wake and on Peale. At 0730, with the fight on the beaches still raging and the defenders under attack from carrier planes, Devereux contacted Cunningham who advised that there were no friendly ships within 24 hours of Wake. Slowly, Cunningham said, "I guess we'd better give it to them."

Shocked and equally broken-hearted, Devereux passed the word to the batteries to destroy their weapons. Tieing a white rag to a mop handle, Devereux went out to contact the Japanese. Sporadic firing continued. Some of the Marines had not got the word. Others just would not believe it. He met the Jap advance and, turning the surrender details over to Cunningham, went on to pass the word to those still in action.

At Peacock Point, Devereux found 12 Marines holding some 200 Japs at bay. He shouted to stop firing. After a silence, Paul Putnam came out. He had been shot in the jaw and his face was smeared with blood. "I'm sorry," he said, "but poor Hank is dead." Captain Elrod, the fighter pilot, had been killed throwing a hand grenade. [A year after the war was over, Elrod received the Medal of Honor, posthumously. He was the tenth Marine pilot in World War II to receive the nation's highest military honor.]

They found Kliewer in a revetment trying desperately to work the detonator, that would set off the charges under the airstrip. By sundown on the 24th of December, the American flag had been struck and the last of the Marines rounded up. That night the Marines buried their dead. It was not until five years later that the survivors of Wake heard the First Presidential Unit Citation of the war. Awarded to them, it read, in part:

"The courageous conduct of the officers and men of these units [First Defense Battalion and Marfitron 211] who defended Wake Island against an overwhelming superiority of enemy air, sea and land attacks from December 8 to 22, 1941, has been noted by their fellow countrymen and the civilized world, and will not be forgotten so long as gallantry and heroism are respected and honored."

These words of high praise, others from the Japanese, and the welcome home they received, were a bit bewildering to the emaciated survivors of Wake Island. They were just Marines, one said, who had been in a hell of a fight . . . and lost it.

The Battle of Midway—David vs. Goliath

Captain Toshikazu Ohmae, former chief of operations for the Imperial Japanese Navy, declared in a postwar interview that the American pilots who turned back the powerful Japanese naval armada at Midway in June, 1942, wrecked Japan's plans for a compromise peace based on a stranglehold of the Pacific from outlying bases.

In his statement to Allied newsmen in Tokyo, December 5, 1945, Ohmae named the battle of Midway as one of the two engagements regarded by Japan as the most decisive battles of the war. His country sent 11 battleships and 75 other combat ships against Midway, but when "dive-bombers and fighters smashed the Midway thrust on the first fiery day, June 4, sinking four carriers and destroying the Japanese air strength," the Japanese abandoned the campaign without sending their "overwhelmingly superior surface forces against the defenders."

The fighter planes of Marine Air Group 22 were the first to blunt the attack on Midway in the early morning of June 4, 1942, and while they were breaking up the enemy air assault on the island, MAG 22's dive-bombers were blasting the Japanese carriers and their support units.

Midway Atoll and its two small islands are a part of the Territory of Hawaii, yet the City of Honolulu is 1,300 miles south by east of their position. Where Wake Island served as the barrier outpost of American mainland defense in the south central Pacific, Midway, 1,000 miles northeast of it, was the key U. S. base in the central Pacific. It was the outer shield for Hawaii, a major trans-Pacific air terminal and cable station, and the only American base standing between Pearl Harbor and the mainland of Japan.

From the air, Midway looks like two muddled egg yokes in a green frying pan, nestling against the side of the coral reef. Sand, the larger island, was the site of the Naval Air Station and headquarters for the Sixth Marine Defense Battalion. Eastern Island is two miles east of the big island, and site of the Marine airbase. Midway had no land-based air protection on December 7, 1941. The planes of VMSB 231, intended as part of its original garrison, were within flight distance of Midway aboard the *Lexington* when hostilities began. But they turned back to search for the enemy fleet. It wasn't until December 17 that seventeen SB2U's took off from Hickam Field and, navigating behind a PBY, made the nine and one-half hour flight to Midway without incident. The hop was the longest overwater flight on record at the time for single-engine planes. [*On the night of December 7, Midway was shelled by a Jap cruiser and destroyer. The Marines ashore under Colonel Harold Shannon held fire until the enemy ships were 4,500 yards out. Firing by searchlight, the Marine guns hit both ships several times and sprayed them with machine-gun fire. The Japanese Navy kept away from Midway after this attack until June, except for sporadic night appearances of the submarine "Oscar" which surfaced and shelled the atoll on several occasions.*]

The Marines found their new airbase at Eastern not vastly different from what had confronted VMF 211 at Wake. Aviation radio facilities hadn't been installed and other vital improvements had been delayed because the initial aviation personnel had been pressed into service as beach defenders. There were compensations, however. The Navy airbase at Sand was the source of a few supplies and assistance. The island was within air transport flight of the supply base at Ewa, and the airmen were quartered underground—no simple feat, since Eastern was only five or six feet above sea level.

Lieutenant Colonel William Wallace arrived in early January to command the Midway Detachment of MAG 21 which then comprised two squadrons, VMSB 231 and VMF 221, which had landed on Christmas Day from carriers. In March this composite became

MAG 22, forward echelon of the Second Marine Air Wing. With Wallace's arrival, the civilian contractors erected individual bunkers or revetments for the land-based planes. Previously they had been merely dispersed and protected by a series of "Rube Goldberg" machine-gun mounts—a free gun mounted on a gas drum inside a sandbagged position near each plane. Fighter, bomber, and radar training programs began in earnest along with the regular daylight patrols. As a precaution against sneak attacks, all planes were manned and ready for take-off a half hour before dawn. The alert procedure was repeated at dusk, while during the daylight hours four fighters and four bombers were on patrol.

The tension at Midway eased a bit as February passed. The prospect of imminent invasion became more remote, but Oscar, the submarine, kept the garrison on the prod. Not until March 10 did the air Marines have their first contact with the enemy. It was brief and to the point. Radar picked up a four-engined enemy plane approaching the island. Four VMF pilots intercepted the khaki-colored flying boat and shot it down, 45 miles out. The only Marine casualty was Bob Dickey, a flying sergeant. He was shot up making an underside run on the well-gunned snooper, but continued his attack. Dickey radioed for an ambulance in his welcoming committee and came in with one arm useless, weak from loss of blood, and his instrument panel full of holes. His landing was smooth but he quietly fainted when the plane taxied to a stop.

Throughout April and the early days of May, the Marines began looking over their shoulders again, with the feeling they were in the middle of a predetermined bull's-eye. Midway was an obvious target and, while the Japanese marshalled their invading armada, the U. S. Navy, by "planned premonition," was doing what it could to meet it.

As the springs of crisis wound tightly around them, the Marine squadrons increased their training and patrol work, praying and pushing their antiquated planes to the limit. VMF 221 had only the creaking, side-winding Brewster Buffaloes (F2A-3's) which the pilots felt were not even good training planes. The dive-bomber pilots had a like regard for the decrepit, fabric-covered SB2U Vindicators which required more tinkering than a Model-T.

Midway's garrison air strength was drastically increased in the last weeks of May. Lieutenant Colonel Ira L. Kimes, who replaced Wallace, had his field facilities taxed far beyond capacity with the arrival of a Catalina patrol squadron, an Army B-17 Flying Fortress squadron, 4 twin-engine B-26 Marauders, and 6 Navy TBF torpedo planes. Barely a week before the battle, MAG 22 received 19 SBD-2's the new-type dive-bomber, 19 pilots fresh from flight school, and 7 new F4F's. Kimes had barely time to get his new pilots squared away when the first reports of the oncoming enemy fleet filtered in.

A few minutes past nine on the morning of June 3, a high-flying PBY uncovered a convoy of ships steaming toward Midway. Successive reports that morning confirmed the situation and the size of the enemy armada. Kimes sent out his calling cards; a strike of nine Army B-17's took off past noon to hit the nearest column—cruisers covering a convoy. They bombed through spotty clouds from medium altitude in the Army's pattern fashion. Results were unobserved. Three PBY's made an historic night torpedo attack and reported possible damage to several ships.

These feeler attacks were little better than pebbles against a giant, but the desperate situation called for anything in the book, and then a little. That night, in the camouflaged dugouts at Midway, few if any slept. There were too many urgent questions on their minds: Just how big was the entire Jap task force? Where were its carriers hiding, and how many were there? How many planes would they send and from what directions? Was this to be a raid or a full-scale invasion?

While he sweated over these intangibles, Colonel Kimes tallied his defensive strength on Eastern: two full squadrons and a small headquarters unit, some 350 to 375 aviation Marines plus a company of infantry Raiders to help the ground crews; 27 fighter planes, most of them the ancient Buffaloes; some 30 flyable dive-bombers, and some 80 pilots and gunners. These Marines, plus the Army and Navy units ashore and a small Navy task force with three carriers somewhere in the area, made up the defenders of Midway. It was not much better than David against Goliath.

Reveille sounded at 0300 in the troubled darkness of June 4. The airmen tumbled out of their dugouts, wolfed a few bites of breakfast or sloshed down hot coffee, and headed for the revetments where the mechs were standing by the planes. By 0350, the pilots and gunners were in their cockpits with the motors turning over. In the next half hour, 11 PBY's and 14 B-17's took off with 12 planes of VMF 221 furnishing air cover. With the patrol airborne, engines were cut on the field until about 0525, when the naval station received word from a patrol plane that the enemy carriers had been sighted.

At 0545, a plain-voice message from a PBY crackled over the earphones at Midway: "Many planes heading Midway—bearing 320—distance 150." The radar screen on Sand Island confirmed this, moments later. On Eastern, the air-raid siren wailed. An officer messenger carried the word to all bomber commanders: "Attack enemy carriers—distance 180 miles—bearing 320—course 135—speed 25."

Snarling down the eerie runway, the fighters were first away. Three divisions, under Parks, Curtin, and Carey, were vectored out by the fighter director toward the incoming raid. Two more divisions, ten planes in all, under Hennessey and Armistead, were told to orbit ten miles out as a reserve should the Jap planes strike from several directions.

Thirty miles out of Midway, Captain Carey's division made a wide, diving turn. Carey radioed the "Tallyho!" reporting at 0614 "large formation of bombers," then a slight pause, "accompanied by fighters." Below the Marines were more than 100 enemy carrier planes in tight V-formations. Oddly, the bombers had no top cover. The 40 or 50 Zeros were underneath—expecting to strafe and then pick off Midway's interceptors as they took off.

As the Marine planes whipped down on the bombers, the Zeros broke formation and rose sharply to intercept. Even before some of VMF 221 had time to complete their first runs, the Zeros, in quantity, were closing on them from the sides, from the rear, and head on. The actual fighter odds against the Marines were better than 2-1 when the dogfight started. When the Zeros began their dancing acrobatics, running rings around both the F2A's and the new F4F's, those odds rose another 25 to 50 percent.

Lieutenant Canfield got a Val flamer to start. Joining up on Carey for a second run, they were hit from the left by a pack of Zeros.

Seconds later, Carey was badly wounded in the legs and barely able to fly his plane. Canfield's stitched-up fighter had its undercarriage collapse in landing while the field was under a strafing attack.

Fifteen more Zeros filtered up through the bombers to meet the Marines. Captain Marion Carl made a high side run on one below him and, as he clawed back up, the Zeros followed easily on his tail. He nosed over with everything to the firewall [an aviation slang expression meaning the plane is moving at utmost speed] and lost them. Climbing again, Carl made a run on three Zeros. One fell off smoking and went straight down out of control.

Kirk Armistead's division left its reserve sector at the "Tallyho" and climbed to 17,000 feet, where they pushed over. Tracers from Armistead's Brewster sewed through the leader and one whole side of a bomber V. As he looked back, two of the bombers fell out in flames. Three Zeros took him over as he returned for another run. He kicked over in a violent split-S and escaped through a screen of fire that perforated his plane.

Humberd, a captain and leader of Armistead's second section, destroyed one bomber on his first attack. While riddling a second Val, two Zeros climbed his tail. One followed him down to the water in a shrieking dive, then Humberd turned into the Jap. One burst at 300 yards and the Zero caught fire and tumbled into the water.

Captain McCarthy and Lieutenant Corry, who had been up on dawn patrol, refueled and joined the fracas. At 8,000 feet, eight Zeros cut off their run on the bombers. McCarthy got one and Corry shoot another off his wingman's tail. With three Zeros riddling him, Corry pounced on a Val returning from its attack on Midway. One burst dumped the bomber into the sea. Corry lost the Jap planes low on the water. On landing, he reported seeing two Buffaloes shot down and one of their pilots strafed by Zeros after bailing out.

The water highway to Midway was littered with flaming wreckage, both Marine and enemy, but the VMF 221 attack had fended off the major portion of the huge carrier raid. Only a dozen Jap dive-bombers and escorts broke through and hit the islands.

Lieutenant Brooks came back after a full half hour of nothing but woe. Pulling up from his first attack on the bombers, his wheels jammed one-third down as two Zeros riddled his tabs, cockpit, and instrument board. Unable to outdive them, he weaved violently and got in several bursts as the Zeros went by. Brooks then took out after two planes dogfighting in the sun. Instead of a wingman in trouble, it turned out to be two Zeros. Both turned on him. He outran one and put a burst into the second in a head-on run. The Zero wobbled down out of sight. As he circled to land, Brooks chased two Japs on the tail of an F2A, with only one of his wing guns firing. He was a little too late.

Kunz, in another F2A, flamed two bombers, got the Zero treatment, and came in dizzily with a bullet crease on his forehead. He made no bones about the relative merits of the Zero and the F2A in his report: "The 00 [Zero] fighter has been far underestimated. As for the F2A-3 [or Brewster trainer] it should be in Miami as a training plane, rather than be used as a first-line fighter."

Of those who came back, none had a kind word to say for the Buffalo fighter. One captain added, "It is not a combat aeroplane. It is inferior to the planes we are fighting in every respect. The F2A-3 has about the same speed as an Aichi 99 Val Dive-Bomber." Another pilot, grounded by engine trouble, watched two Brewsters dogging Zeros strafing the field. "One was shot down and the other saved by the ground fire covering his tail. Both looked like they were tied on a string while the Zeros made passes at them."

By 0715, the last of the carrier raiders left Midway. They had been only a small portion of the enemy force and they had done no devastating damage. Fourteen bombs fell on Eastern, putting out the power plant and cutting off the main fuel supply. Forty more hit Sand Island. Four Marine Ordnance men were killed by a direct hit. Another died near the engineering tent. If it had been the Japanese purpose to pulverize the air and ground defenses at Midway, their airmen were not quite up to it.

When the all-clear sounded, the carcass of a Zero was scraped off the runway. It was one of a half dozen shot down by ground fire. Kimes at the CP called repeatedly to his fighter force to return and refuel. For a long time, his only answer was loud silence. Then a handful of stragglers limped in to deposit their wrecks on the runway.

When the time limit passed, Kimes gave up hope and tallied what was left. If there were another air attack that day, Midway had two fighter planes to send up. Fifteen of his 27 fighter pilots were dead or missing, including Major Floyd Parks, commander of VMF 221. Six of the surviving pilots were wounded. Six of his ground crew were dead. Kimes could only hope that his dive-bombers were a little luckier.

The bombers had gotten away immediately after the fighters. Navy's six TBF's and the four B-26's went off on a torpedo run. The Zeros were waiting at three levels. Only one Navy plane got back, and two of the Marauders. The three were badly shot up.

By prearranged plan, the Marine dive-bombers joined up 20 miles east of Midway in two groups—16 SBD's under Major Lofton R. Henderson and 11 SB2U's under Major Benjamin W. Norris. They were to get the carriers.

At 0755, Henderson's flight sighted the enemy fleet and he passed the word for runs on two carriers. It was to be a glide attack because his pilots had more experience in that tactic. They had barely an hour's training in the new SBD's. At 9,000 feet they started their approach in wide let-down circles, to reach the attack level of 4,000 feet for final runs. All the way down, the formation was under heavy attack from Jap fighters and violent AA fire.

The bombers held tightly to their box formation for protection, as the rear-gunners laced back at the diving Zeros. After several runs on it, Henderson's plane burned along the left wing. In spite of the flames, Henderson continued his glide, holding course until several hundred feet from a carrier. His bomb was a near-miss.

Captain Elmer Glidden took the lead when Henderson's plane caught fire. The fighter attacks were so heavy that he led the formation into a cloud layer. Coming out at 2,000 feet they found two large Jap carriers immediately below sporting big red meatballs on their yellow flight decks. The flat-tops were protected on all sides by task-force elements. Glidden signaled for the attack and his bombers glided down at five-second intervals with Zeros and Nakajima fighters tailing them.

The carriers took violent evasive action while the battleships, cruisers, and destroyers belched up an umbrella of flak. Glidden made his drop at 400 feet and went right down to water level to avoid the AA and fighters. Looking back, he saw two direct hits and one near-miss alongside the bow of the carrier, which was pluming smoke. He reported the air filled with "flaming planes heading for a watery grave." The Zeros rode Glidden's plane until it was 40 miles away.

Lieutenant Daniel Iverson came down behind Glidden. He picked out one of the three carriers in sight and peeled off with three fighters chasing. His bomb was a close-miss, astern of the flight deck. As he leveled out, four fighters started overhead runs on his SBD. One pass severed the mike cord around his neck. Another shot out his hydraulic system. Iverson made a one-wheel landing at Midway.

Zeros were drilling holes in the wings and fuselage of Captain Richard Blain's SBD as it weaved away, after hitting one carrier with its 500-pounder. Blain ducked into a cloud as his fuel pump went out of commission. Forty minutes later, Blain and his gunner were in the water pumping up their life raft. It had a hole at the waterline and they bailed all night. They were rescued by a PBY on the morning of their third day at sea.

When the last of the SBD stragglers reached Midway, the rear-gunners were credited with shooting down several fighters. Three direct bomb hits and two near-misses were chalked up by the pilots on either one or two of the Japanese carriers.

Norris' SB2U formation rendezvoused and arrived at another position over the enemy fleet 10 or 15 minutes after the SBD's were through. At 13,000 feet, the bombers were heavily attacked by Zero and 1-97 fighters on all sides. Unable to search further for the carriers, Norris put the finger on a battleship below the spotty clouds and radioed, "Attack target below!"

His 11 Vindicators spiraled through the flak, fighting off the Jap planes all the way. The gunners flamed one Zero. At 2,000 feet, their glide runs started on the battleship. Its return fire was so heavy the pilots found it impossible to hold the bucking planes on course. One by one the turgid bombers went in, and their eggs ringed or hit the battleship, which was now smoking amidships. One bomb failed to release and the pilot pulled out and made a run on a destroyer. No results reported. He was too busy with the Zeros. When the last SB2U jinked away, the battleship had turned off course. It was "listing heavily and smoking badly."

Two planes failed to return from the raid and Lieutenant Dan Cummings crash-landed five miles out of Midway. His plane sank quickly, but he had time to verify that Starks, his rear-gunner, was dead. Starks had been killed in the fighter attack. Cummings was picked up by a PT boat.

Throughout the rest of the morning and afternoon, planes from the carriers *Hornet, Enterprise* and *Yorktown* worked on the Japanese invasion fleet. At a cost of 35 torpedo planes and 18 dive-bombers, they hit three carriers, a battleship, and a cruiser. Two enemy carriers sank and a submarine finished off a third, the *Soryu*, later in the day. The *Hiryu* escaped in flames and its planes hit the *Yorktown* twice on the 4th.

Back at Midway, Kimes and his two-plane fighter force and beaten-up dive-bombers waited for a second raid from the carriers. It never came. At 1700, an enemy carrier was reported on fire, 180 miles out. Norris favored a night attack on two counts: the target would be self-illuminated and there would be no Zeros to intercept. Past 1500, 12 dive-bombers took off, with Norris leading 6 SB2U's and Captain Marshall Tyler the 6 SBD's. They searched the pitch-black night and found no trace of the carrier. The SBD's homed in safely, but Norris' flight ran into squalls. After a long delay, they wandered in singly, guided by an oil fire and a searchlight. Norris failed to return.

Again Midway had a sleepless night. At 0545, Kimes received orders to attack two Jap battleships 140 miles out. Anything that could fly went on the line and, at 0730, 12 dive-bombers got off. Tyler had his half-dozen SBD's. Captain Richard Fleming, who was wounded twice on the 4th, led the SB2U's. Forty-five minutes out they picked up the spoor—wide oil slicks left by the damaged BB. They followed it for 30 miles and found the two ships. Tyler ordered a two-type attack. His SBD's would dive-bomb from 10,000 feet and Fleming's planes would glide-run from 4,000.

Tyler's bombers ringed the damaged battleship. Captain Fleming started down, but as he pushed over, his SB2U was set afire by the flak. According to Lieutenant George Koutelas, who was last man down, "Fleming stayed in his dive even though he was in flames and dropped his bomb at 500 feet, scoring a near-miss on the stern of the ship." His plane crashed into the sea. Months later, Fleming was posthumously awarded the Medal of Honor, the first Marine airman to receive it in World War II.

That was the last of the flaming glory for the Marines at Midway. Again Kimes penciled out his sad statistics: 15 fighter pilots, 11 dive-bomber pilots, and 12 rear-gunners dead or missing in action. Thirty-eight of his 84 airmen. Seventeen more were wounded. There were not a dozen planes in combat condition. In return, his VMF 221 pilots had shot down 37 and a possible 43 enemy planes. The rear-gunners were certain of perhaps 10 more over the enemy fleet, while their pilots had scored direct hits on 2 carriers and 2 battleships. The invasion had been turned back. Theirs had been a major contribution, but at a terrible price.

The survivors read the letter directed by Admiral Nimitz to the Marine airmen at Midway:

"The sacrifices of your heroic men have not been in vain. I am deeply grieved over the losses and they shall help us remember Midway instead of Pearl Harbor. When the crisis came, they were ready. They met courageously and unflinchingly the onslaught of greatly superior numbers and made the attack ineffective. They dealt the enemy carriers the first blow and they spearheaded our great victory. It is a new and shining page they have written in the history of the Marine Corps."

3

EAGLE HATCHERIES AND GROWING PAINS

B RIGADIER GENERAL LEWIE G. MERRITT was the first
  and last Marine flier shot down by the Nazis in World War II,
but he was not the only Marine who might have been. The Air Arm
had its observers roaming the globe in search of new tactics and new
ideas long before the country was concerned with "someone else's
war." These Marines operated on a thesis as old as war itself, that one
stands a better chance of combat success if he knows beforehand the
timbre, tricks, and techniques of his opponents and his allies.

Merritt's episode occurred on January 7, 1942, while he was serving
out of Cairo with the British Royal Air Force. Their Eighth Army
was probing Rommel's positions when Merritt took off in a Wellington bomber making a reconnaissance mission near Halfaya Pass.
Several miles south of Bardia, the Wellington was hit by Nazi 88mm
flak and machine-gun fire. An exploding shell ruptured its hydraulic
lines and control wires, forcing the plane to land within sight of the
battery that winged it. After the crash, the German artillery laid
down a heavy barrage which pinned Merritt and the crew to the
desert until two British armored cars broke through and rescued
them. Though his right side was injured, General Merritt was released from the dressing station to continue his study of Fighter
Command operations of the RAF.

Brigadier General Harold D. Campbell, USMC, received the
Legion of Merit for services with the British Staff of Combined
Operations. He was the Navy and Marine Corps aviation advisor for
Lord Louis Mountbatten in the planning and execution of the famed
Dieppe raid.

While Marine airmen served in many foreign countries as naval attachés during the years of peace, their travels to Europe and Africa increased in early 1941. Brigadier General Ross E. Rowell, senior Marine aviator, was ordered to London as Air Attache for duty in Cairo, Egypt. Based on his observations in the desert war and on the Western Front, Rowell made many recommendations to improve the Marine Air Arm. Perhaps the most far-reaching of these, made in November, 1941, was for a medium-sized, long-range, high-speed bomber to be used in night harassing missions against distant enemy targets. Out of such advice, and the rigorous combat experiments of Major Jack Cram in the Pacific, grew the Marine PBJ night bomber program which operated against Japanese shore bases and shipping in the last years of the war.

Through the medium of attachment to British Empire Forces, Marine pilots gained a firsthand knowledge of the Axis forces wherever the Allies engaged them.

Brigadier General Walter G. Farrell and Colonel Perry O. Parmalee watched the costly impotence of land and sea forces in the face of superior enemy air power while serving with the British Eastern Mediterranean Fleet in the spring of 1941. They saw the Allies' almost futile effort to stem the flow of supplies which poured into North Africa across the Sicilian straits under an umbrella of shore-based Italian and German planes. Then came the Luftwaffe field day at Crete where its air superiority easily knocked out three-quarters of the supporting British ships, and permitted a shuttle relay of Nazi air transports to spill parachutists on the Meleme airdrome and then reinforce them at will with airborne infantry.

These graphic examples of air superiority convinced Farrell and Parmalee, among others, of the vital need in any air organization of a fighter plane force strong enough to immobilize the enemy's air efforts. Such recommendations contributed to the 4-1 ratio of fighters to bombers which our forces attempted to maintain ashore and afloat in Pacific campaigns.

Singapore was the first step for Major General Claude A. Larkin and Colonel Frank N. Dailey when they left the U. S. in the summer of 1941. From the British fleet base, they traveled via Malaya, Thailand, Burma, India, and Arabia to Iraq, where they arrived at Basra near the end of the Iraqui revolt. Larkin and Dailey later saw duty with the RAF and Australian ground forces in action in the Middle East.

After duty as an observer in Europe and Africa, Lieutenant Colonel Michael Sampas urged that a photo-reconnaissance squadron, equipped with the best available fighter planes, be attached to each air wing.

Many other Marine airmen traveled to Europe and Africa before and after America went to war, and their observations contributed greatly to the rapid, effective expansion of the Air Arm during the war years. Among them there was a unanimity of conviction on a number of vital subjects: that a high ratio of fighters to bombers was essential for successful bombing missions; that aerial reconnaissance and photographic work be intensified; that nonflying personnel be assigned in quantity to all air units for staff duty; and that immediate provisions be made for adequate airdrome defense.

Probably their most important single contribution to the later success of the Air Arm in combat was in the field of night fighting. The first night unit in naval aviation to enter Pacific combat [VMF (N) 531] was commanded by Colonel Frank Schwable, who had studied British methods in intercept control and radar at their fighter Director school at Stanmore, England. Working with Schwable after their round-the-world tour was Colonel Edward C. Dyer, who recommended that Marine air wings and defense groups have a complement of night fighters as the only adequate answer to the enemy's night bombing. Subsequent Pacific actions bore out Dyer's contention, and a contingent of officers and enlisted men was sent to England in early 1943 for training in night air operations. Some of the Marines flew the British Beaufighter on numerous night patrols against the Luftwaffe. Though there is no record of their shooting down Nazi planes, these airmen returned to enhance the Marine training program and to engage in Pacific operations.

Growing Pains of the Air Arm

The Marine Corps air organization, which for twenty years had pioneered in the use of planes in support of the ground forces, was pitifully small when it entered the period of prewar expansion. In the summer of 1939, it totaled only nine squadrons and two air groups. Fortunately, its veteran personnel had a wealth of training and combat experience to bulwark the rapid development ahead.

A naval air fleet of 15,000 planes was included in the "Two-Ocean Navy" bill which Congress, almost on the eve of war, authorized in late 1940. Marine Aviation was allotted some of these planes to be formed into two air wings, with 32 operating squadrons. Significantly, the two wings were assigned to duty with two Marine infantry divisions soon to be activated. This expansion program had hardly begun when a joint board of Navy and Marine observers returned from the European theaters and, upon their advice, the Navy and Congress approved a plan which almost doubled the strength of Marine Aviation.

Under the expansion program, the First Marine Aircraft Wing was commissioned at Quantico, Virginia, on July 7, 1941, under Lieutenant Colonel Louis E. Woods, who served until Brigadier General Roy S. Geiger took command in late August. The First Marine Aircraft Group, which had been the highest air echelon on the East Coast, became the Wing's first component. The First Wing's early months of existence, like that of other major units of the armed forces at the time, was replete with growing pains. Its allowance of four air groups with 16 operating squadrons was a dream on paper, because Geiger couldn't get planes enough to fit out even a single group.

His appeal barrage to the Navy Department and the Marine Corps for planes, men and materiel to prepare the Wing for combat was denied. The scanty supplies available went to higher-priority units. After the attack on Pearl Harbor, the First Wing was ordered to the West Coast. When General Geiger reported at San Diego on December 10, he advised that his Wing had only 67 planes capable of making the trip and that only 15 of these were ready for combat— and they were dive-bombers, while the crying need was for fighter planes. The balance of the Wing's planes were unfit for combat because of a lack of self-sealing gas tanks, armor plate, guns, and radio equipment. By June, 1942, after its first group, MAG 13, had been sent to Samoa, the First Wing still had only four air groups, with ten operating squadrons flying a grand total of 95 planes, less than half its allowance.

Colonel Francis P. Mulcahy took command of the Second Marine Aircraft Wing on its activation at San Diego July 10, 1942. The old Second Aircraft Group, which had been on duty at Ewa in Hawaii since January, 1941, was assigned to the Wing, bringing it some of the oldest squadrons in Marine Aviation—Fighting Two, Bombing Two, Scouting Two, and Utility Two. [VMF 2 was renamed VMF (Marine Fighter) 211 under the Marine unit system of designation which assigned Wings numbers of one digit; Air Groups numbers of two digits, the first to correspond to that of its Wing; and three-digit numbers to squadrons, the first two of which corresponded to its Air Group. The forward echelon of the new VMF 211 fought at Wake Island. VMS Two and VMB Two became VMSB 231 and 232, the first two dive-bomber squadrons to operate off Guadalcanal. VMJ Two became VMJ 252, the nucleus of SCAT transport in the South Pacific.]

Brigadier General Ross E. Rowell took over the Second Wing and its lone air group September 15, 1941, and encountered the same headaches as Geiger had in attempting to build up the command to a semblance of combat strength and efficiency.

In the summer of 1942, as units of the two Wings shoved off for combat in the Pacific, the Division of Aviation, Marine Corps, in Washington, was struggling to meet the current deficiencies and future requirements from its training and expansion program. Its authorized strength was one-fifth that of naval aviation, in keeping with a similar ratio between the Navy itself and the Marine Corps. Some 5,000 planes were allotted to the Marine Air Arm to operate in two wings, six base defense groups, two fighter groups, two bomber groups, and one replacement and training wing, in addition to the glider program. Marine pilot strength in June, 1942, was 1,273 with slightly more than a thousand additional fliers expected by the end of 1943.

With an anticipated pilot attrition of four percent a year, the requirements of Marine Aviation by December, 1943, would be some

6,800 pilots—a shortage of 5,500 under the then current program. Although immediate steps were taken to remedy this serious situation, it was not until late in 1943 that the pilot shortage was considerably lessened. [On July 1, 1943 there were 4,989 Marine pilots. One year later the number was 10,483 with the final figure slightly under that when demobilization began in August, 1945.]

Marine Aviation had its own aviation-cadet procurement program until July, 1942, when it was taken over by the Navy. Under this Navy program, the Air Arm had three sources of pilots—regular Marine infantry officers assigned to flight training, naval aviation cadets who were commissioned second lieutenants in the Marine Corps after flight training, and Naval Aviation pilots—the NAP's or Marine enlisted men who earned their wings.

Training of the Marine pilots paralleled that of the Navy's own airmen through completion of intermediate training. Three months before getting their wings, the cadets asked for duty either with the Navy or Marine Aviation. After 14 to 18 months in advanced flight training at the Naval Air Stations at Pensacola, Florida or Corpus Christi, Texas, the aviators were designated pilots in either the Naval or Marine Reserve.

During operational training at East or West coast Marine airbases, the major emphasis was placed on mastery of the offensive plane type to which the pilot was assigned. After joining a squadron, the flier concentrated on formation flying, night operations, all phases of gunnery, air tactics, instrument training, and carrier landings, where required. This aerial work was thoroughly implemented by weeks of previous, rigorous classroom schooling in allied subjects.

East Coast Air Bases

The pilot factories of the Air Arm, by tradition and expediency, were divided between the two coasts, with the largest Marine Air Station located at Cherry Point, North Carolina. Pilots of land-based planes reported there upon completion of their naval training. Literally carved out of swamplands and forests, Cherry Point was primarily a training station. Work on its runways did not begin until two weeks before war was declared.

On November 10, 1942, the Third Marine Aircraft Wing was commissioned at Cherry Point "to prepare for and carry out combat operations." Until it moved to Ewa, Oahu, T. H. in May, 1944, the Third Wing trained dozens of squadrons, groups, and ground units and shipped them to the combat areas. [The Third Wing was successively commanded at Cherry Point by Lieutenant Colonel Calvin R. Freeman and Colonel C. A. Larkin, and overseas by Brigadier Generals Walter G. Farrell, Byron Johnson, and Lewie G. Merritt. Its training mission at Cherry Point was taken over in April, 1944, when the Ninth Marine Air Wing was commissioned. Intervening Wing numbers between Four and Nine were assigned to special groups—night-fighters, medium bombers, etc. The Ninth Wing, which remained in North Carolina until the end of the war, was commanded by Colonel Christian Schilt, General Merritt, Colonel Burke, and Brigadier General Campbell.]

At Cherry Point, tactical air training in maneuvers with infantry units, dive-bombing, high- and low-level bombing, strafing, intruder tactics, air combat with gun cameras, and antisubmarine patrols was carried on extensively. Night fighting and the training of air warning squadrons in group control interception and ground-to-air fighter direction occupied the nocturnal phases. As the program expanded, 11 airfields were established. [The training command became Marine Corps Air Bases, Cherry Point, with the addition of bases at Atlantic, Bogue, Oak Grove, Kinston, Camp Lejeune (at the infantry base), and Congaree and outlying fields at Beauford, Greenville, New Bern, Washington, and Wilson—all in North Carolina.]

The Air Arm established its first operational training squadron at Cherry Point in February, 1943. This school for PBJ (B-25) training was one of the few solely under Marine direction. It became Marine Operational Training Group 81 in January, 1944, when it was transferred to Edenton. During the two-month course, pilots, aircrewmen, and ground crews received intensive ground and flight instruction before being sent to the combat zones.

From the establishment of the first night fighter squadron at

Cherry Point in November, 1942, until March, 1943, when its 12 pilots were attempting to practice airborne interceptions in the squadron's lone, radar-equipped plane, Pacific commanders pressed for an increase in the program. Seven more Marine VMF (N) squadrons were organized by May, 1943, to fly Corsairs, Hellcats, and, toward the end of the war, the new, twin-engine Grumman F7F Tigercats. Marine Night Fighter Group 53 was commissioned at MCAS, Eagle Mountain Lake, Texas, in April, 1944, and the airmen received final polishing there after initial training at Vero Beach, Florida. The ground portion of the night operation began with the organization of AWG 1, the first Air Warning Group, in July, 1942. Air Warning Squadron One, the first of 19 such units, was activated two months later to handle the radar-interception and fighter direction for the night pilots.

Balloons, Gliders, and Paratroopers

Early in 1941, Marine observers studied the barrage-balloon program activities of the Army at Fort Sill, Oklahoma. They reported that the Army planned to use the bomb-shaped gas bags in its air defense sectors. Since it was anticipated that the Marine Corps might be charged with putting up balloon barrages at naval bases not defended by Army units, a school was organized at the Marine Base, Parris Island, South Carolina in June, 1941, under Major Bernard L. Smith, the veteran aviator who learned to fly in 1912 and had been recalled to active duty. It trained personnel in the handling of the balloons as an adjunct of Marine defense battalions guarding vital bases. ZM One and Two, the first Marine balloon squadrons in World War II were commissioned in October, 1941, and four more were later added. Four ZM squadrons remained in the United States to guard Navy yards and bases while two went overseas. One of these served as infantry with a defense unit at Tulagi in the Solomons, but raised no balloons. The other was stationed in New Caledonia where it had further training. It was soon discovered that this static type of air defense created just as great a hazard to friendly planes as it would to those of the enemy, and the balloon program was disbanded in December, 1943.

Because of the tactical and terrain situation in the Pacific areas where the Fleet Marine Force was operating, the Marine paratrooper program suffered a fate similar to that of the balloon squadrons. Although Marines pioneered the art of dropping troops by parachute as early as 1927, it wasn't until late 1941 that they were assigned a paratrooper program by the Navy. [In 1927, Marines established a record when 12 infantrymen were dropped from transports in 14 seconds during a demonstration at Anacostia, D.C.]

After attending an Army demonstration in August, 1940, Marine observers recommended that the Corps should train a nucleus of such jump-troops "as soon as practicable, to include combat elements, engineers for demolition, and saboteurs. There are many foreseeable situations in which such elements would prove invaluable."

Paratroop training began at Quantico and the naval base at Hightown, New Jersey. The jump-troops gave their first demonstration late in December, 1940, and by the end of 1941, more than two hundred men had been trained. The jungles, swamps, mountains, and tiny atolls of the Pacific islands were found to be unsuitable for paratroop combat jumps and the program was disbanded in December, 1943. Troops of the Parachute Regiment, however, fought up the Solomons from Tulagi to Bougainville, and their survivors later formed a part of the Fifth Marine Division.

In the summer of 1941, the Air Arm was studying another program which never saw combat—troop-carrying gliders. Finally activated in July, 1943, it called for 150 pilots to man 75 twelve-place gliders. Glider pilot proficiency required a large number of flight hours which were obtainable then only in power planes. Rather than use the badly needed power pilots to fill the glider quota, the Air Arm sent 240 volunteer officers and men to Civil Aeronautics Authority stations to get power flight time, prior to their lighter-than-air training. A glider detachment was organized at Parris Island in January, 1942, for primary and advanced work, but was disbanded on the formation of Marine Glider Group 71, which was later stationed at Eagle Mountain Lake, Texas, under the command of Lieutenant Colonel Vernon M. Guymon.

Three factors finally ended the glider program in June, 1943: the required 200 gliders failed to arrive from the factories; Pacific island terrain was found unsuitable for their use; and the program proved too great a drain on the limited number of pilots available for the powered-plane squadrons.

Marine Air Infantry Training

Early in 1944, Marine Aviation undertook the first step in resuming its long-standing practice of infantry training for its airmen. Prior to the war, its fliers were invariably pilots who had months and even years of line training before assignment to flight school, on the premise that they were Marines first and pilots afterward. This was in keeping with the Marine air-ground team policy.

After a temporary lull due to wartime pressure, Camp Larkin was established at Cherry Point, where pilots reporting from naval flight schools were given a two-week infantry indoctrination course. Living as enlisted men, the fliers were given a curriculum which included night patrol actions, 35-mile hikes, judo, demolition, and the use of basic infantry weapons. At its finale, the airmen participated in an amphibious landing under simulated combat conditions.

Half the trainees set up beach defenses, complete with TNT charges, bangalore torpedoes, machine-gun emplacements, and foxholes. The invading pilots landed in the surf from small boats and waded ashore behind a smoke screen laid down by other fliers who had completed the course. At Camp Larkin, the aviators learned the value of precision in close air support and, basically, how the other half of the Marine team lived and fought. Originally an interim measure due to a scarcity of training planes, the school was continued at the request of the pilots themselves.

A permanent step toward greater teamwork between aviation and the infantry was the Marine Air-Infantry School at Quantico, Virginia. Originally called the Aviation Ground Officers School, it was redesignated MA-IS in February, 1945. Its mission was to indoctrinate Marine aviators and ground officers in the conduct of air-amphibious operations and the functions of amphibious infantry. Stress was placed on the integrated operation of the battalion landing team and the air squadron.

Many of the first airmen ordered to the school in October, 1944, were combat veterans from the Solomons, and succeeding classes in the 16-week course had a high ratio of experienced combat officers. Making like "Mud Marines" was not a well-loved chore for the birdmen at first, but they found it much less objectionable as they worked to overcome the failings common to precision air-infantry support in the field. Scores of Marine fliers and ground officers completed the course before the end of the war, with early graduates going directly to combat units and air-support operations in the Pacific.

Blind Tigers of the AVS

To relieve pilots from nonessential ground duties and implement its squadrons with civilian specialists, the Air Arm began its Aviation Volunteer Specialist program. Early in 1942, it was recommended that 1,100 nonpilot officers be assigned to air units. Because of the high age bracket of the first AVS class at Quantico—many of them retreads from World War I—the officers dubbed themselves the Blind Tigers.

Sixty-four Reserves completed the two-month training period in July, 1942, and, as did succeeding classes, went directly to tactical units or to specialist schools throughout the country for Intelligence, Photography, Photo-Interpretation, Fighter-Direction, Gunnery, Engineering, or Radar training. Some were assigned to universities for more intensive schooling as aeronautical engineers, aerologists, and radar specialists.

By September, 1945, there were 1,441 AVS officers on duty in the United States or in the Pacific in every conceivable ground capacity from camp commanders to mess officers. [From a total of 39 aviation ground officers in January, 1939, there were 5,000, including the AVS, in aviation at the end of the war.]

Bulwark of the Air Arm

The old military truism that an outfit is only as good as its corporals was very much to the point in the Air Arm, where the captains and the colonels admitted readily that it was the enlisted men who contributed that rare mixture of brains and brawn, guts and ingenuity which made Marine aviation possible. After their tough recruit or "boot camp" training with the infantry Marines, enlisted men were transferred to air units, where their duties varied from the "bull gang" or police detail through several dozen categories to aircrewmen and pilots.

From a roster of 2,500 men in January, 1941, the peak was reached four years later when 94,500 enlisted white and Negro Marines were on duty. One-third of them were trained as aviation specialists in Navy or Marine schools. Another third were given apprenticeship schooling. The balance made their stripes the hard way on routine Marine duties.

Overseas, the enlisted men were invariably the first ashore and the last out of the combat areas, sweating out one island-hopping campaign after another to keep up with the flight echelons from atoll to island or aboard carriers. Their combat performance was nothing short of magnificent whether under fire, garrisoning the atolls, or gouging some semblance of civilization into an island that did not deserve it.

Infantry Marines often griped that air duty was a "soft touch" until they had some of it. Then they knew all too well why the rear-gunners and the ground crewmen were an undeniable part of the blood brotherhood of the Marine Corps.

"Ye Gods, Mac, Women!"

One wartime measure that temporarily broke the salt-encrusted hearts of the "Old Corps" was the enlistment of women Marines. A Women's Reserve of 18,000 to relieve men for combat duty was begun in February, 1943. That part of the idea was acceptable to the old hands in Aviation, but the thought of doing military duty side by side with "them glammer girls" was beyond belief—until they saw the dungareed WR's tear down a Corsair engine, or slide out, greased and grimed, from under a six-by-six truck, or handle a fouled-up air traffic pattern from a control tower with the same ease as they did a typewriter. Then the male Marines dropped their well-chewed pencils, wrenches, and doubts, and put in for another tour overseas.

After basic training, the enlisted WR's received the same specialist schooling as the men and they performed and were rated accordingly. Aside from the administrative staff work, the WR's were on duty as aerographers; parachute riggers; control tower operators; gunnery, recognition, and Link-trainer instructors; radio operators; and mechanics, from Cherry Point to Ewa, Oahu. Three hundred and fifty officers and 7,000 enlisted WR's were on duty at aviation commands and bases across the country and at Pearl Harbor in August, 1945.

Marine Fleet Air, West Coast

As a part of the Fleet Marine Force, battle arm of the Corps, and as a junior partner in Naval Aviation, Marine Air was jointly responsible to both the Navy's Bureau of Aeronautics (BuAer) and the Marine Corps. In supply and aviation technical matters, it received its directives from BuAer, while personnel, policy, and administrative matters were decided by Headquarters, Marine Corps, and its Division of Aviation. Tactically, the Air Arm was controlled by the Commander, Fleet Marine Force, Pacific; the Navy's Commander, Aircraft, Pacific Fleet; or the commander of the foreign shore base to which it was attached. The Assistant Commandant of the Marine Corps (for Air) was Director of the Division of Aviation and in that capacity had control of the East Coast air commands and stations and supervision of all Marine Aviation units. The system of Marine air commands and stations on the Pacific coast was under the jurisdiction of the Fleet Marine Force and its air component.

Traditional center of Marine operations on the West Coast in 1941 was the Naval Air Station at North Island, San Diego. The need for a command higher in echelon than a Wing was filled by the establishment of Marine Air Wings, Pacific, in August, 1942, under Major General Rowell. MAWP assumed command of all Marine air organizations in the Pacific, except those attached to specific task organizations. Tactically, it was under COMAIRPAC and administratively under FMF, Pacific, at Pearl Harbor.

In September, 1942, Rowell took down his flag at San Diego and ran it up several weeks later at the Marine Corps Air Station, Ewa, Oahu, where the senior Marine air command in the Pacific remained for the balance of the war. From its base at Ewa, MAWP controlled the air units operating in the Pacific areas and its own network of supply and training bases on the West Coast.

Marine Fleet Air, West Coast (MARFAIRWEST), the senior air command on the West Coast, was activated under Colonel Lewie G. Merritt in January, 1943, and given control over the Marine airbases, stations, and auxiliary air facilities being built in southern California and up the Pacific coast. The huge Marine Corps Air Depot and field at Miramar—15 miles northeast of San Diego—became the clearinghouse for a widening river of men and supplies fed into Pacific combat units.

Four new major Marine air stations were opened in rapid succession. El Toro, near Santa Ana, in the San Joaquin Valley, opened in January, 1943, and was soon handling the largest tactical airdrome traffic on the Pacific coast. MCAS, Santa Barbara, formerly a municipal airport, had fliers operating off its runways months before it was officially opened in December, 1942.

The station at El Centro was some one hundred miles due east of San Diego in the Imperial Valley. Two hundred miles north of it was the base at Mojave, where the airmen simmered in the desert heat. A further outlying field for training transport squadrons was opened later in the war at Corvallis, Oregon.

At these tactical stations, often called the "eagle hatcheries," many thousands of Marine pilots, aircrewmen, and ground units received their finishing touches in combat tactics and close support operations with near-by Marine infantry units before sailing for duty overseas with combat echelons of Aircraft, Fleet Marine Force, Pacific. [MAWP was redesignated AIRFMFPAC in September,

1944, when Major General Mulcahy relieved General Rowell. Mulcahy continued in command until he took over the Okinawa operations and was succeeded by Major General James T. Moore, who remained in command until the end of the war. On January 1, 1945, Mulcahy's AIRFMFPAC consisted of the First, Second, Third, and Fourth Marine Air Wings—all on duty in the Pacific; MARFAIRWEST and its Stateside echelons, including the Marine Carriers Groups organized at Santa Barbara in October, 1944; and the Provisional Air Support Command at Ewa, which was activated at the same time under Colonel Vernon E. Megee to train air-support liaison teams and supervise the complexities of the expanding FMF close air-support program.]

☆ 4 ☆

THE CACTUS SHIVAREE

GUADALCANAL is peaceful now . . . the once-embattled island is kept only by the bat and the lizard, plus a handful of Navy and a few bored and home-weary New Zealanders who care for the health and well-being of the glowering, fuzzy-haired natives who lived there before the white or yellow man came.

"It is only a little more than three years since first we went ashore there to give the Jap his first bloody nose and turn back the tide of his attack. Already the vine and creeper have retaken Bloody Knoll, choking the old entrenchments with their tangle. The Lunga still rolls, gray-green as motor-oil, and nothing disturbs its steaming peace except the splash of a fish, the quick dart of a bird. Grass pokes green and rank through the metal mat that formed the airstrip of Henderson Field.

"All up the waters they called The Slot, the track between the islands that once were the most dangerous seas in all the world, there now is peace.

"All is tranquil below and aloft. Through the skies where Zeros once swarmed thick as mosquitos . . . battered Douglas transports of a Marine freight-hauling air group now trudge peacefully, as if in Stateside flight, past islands whose names were once in every headline, on every tongue, but which are remembered now only by the men who fought there and the families of the men who died there.

"Savo, Tulagi, Munda, Rendova . . . are just check points now on a pilot's map . . ."

In part, so wrote hulking Harold Martin, Georgia columnist turned

Marine correspondent, when, in the late summer of 1945, he passed through what had been for four terrible months in 1942 the hellhole of the South Pacific.

It was a long nostalgic piece, skillful in its portrait of the aftermath of jungle war, yet, except for the lingering legends and the frightening fecundity of the jungle, it is not how Guadalcanal will be remembered by the Marines who fought there.

This island, which was made the bursting place for the high-tide of Japanese aggression in the southern latitudes, they had many names for—"The Rock," "The Canal," "Guadal," "The Island," and many others far more pertinent which were Marine in origin and unprintable.

Cactus was its code name and it fitted well into their clipt, tired jargon, yet it had no unusual significance when it was assigned.

Once the Marines were joined to the place called Cactus, to have and to hold it at all costs, they committed themselves to an unholy, Martian shivaree unlike any other in the long history of their Corps.

The Target Group

The Solomon Islands, which lie in the Coral Sea across the western approaches to northern Australia, were called by prewar explorers "The Land That God Forgot." It was not a misnomer.

Volcanic in origin, they fester on the southern seas beneath the equator like an inverted, rough-hewn necklace of green mold. Bougainville is the pendant and the Solomons stretch south from its tip in a double line for 700 miles to the southeast below New Britain. The upper or northern row begins at Choiseul, then Santa Isabel, and lastly Malatia, called Maluou by the natives. The inner row and path of the counteroffensive against Nippon begins with Vella Lavella, then Kolombangara, New Georgia, Rendova, the Russells, then Guadalcanal (meaning "dry river bed"), and lastly San Cristobal.

Somewhat picturesque in a garish tropical fashion to those who flew high enough above them, the Solomons steam and stew in their own tropical juices. Hot sun, high humidity, constant rains, disease, and brier-thick jungles perform together like a primitive incubator

which works double-time to the advantage of everything in nature
except the mores of the white man. Stark and weird in contrasts,
like the red blood which so often spattered their lush orchids, the
Solomons were reputed by Marines to be the only place on earth
where you could stand hip-high in mud and get dust in your eyes.

Four-hundred-odd miles south of Guadalcanal were the New
Hebrides, part of this same family of islands. South by west from the
New Hebrides and 1,000 miles northeast of Sydney, Australia, is the
large French-mandated island of New Caledonia. [*Pushing warily
up from their original defense line in the Samoan group, Marine
planes landed on their new advance field at Tontouta, New Caledonia, on May 10, 1942. It was at this mountain airbase that MAG 25,
a transport air group and nucleus of SCAT (South Pacific Combat
Air Transport) later began operations as the flying lifeline to the
Solomons. On June 8, 1942, Marine planes pancaked at Efate in
the southern New Hebrides, and on July 29 probed even closer to the
enemy when they landed at Espiritu Santo. This main island of
the Hebrides, occupied by May 29, was the advance staging base in the
air battle for Guadalcanal.*]

Guadalcanal from the air looks like the twisted carcass of an
iguana lizard sans legs and tail. About 90 miles long and less than
half of that in width, it is serrated by three mountain ranges rising at
one place to 8,000 feet. Its most accessible, populated, and livable
area is the northern coastal plain. This begins along the razor coral
shore with its sandy interludes at Sealark Channel and moves inland
several miles through head-high kunai grass which is broken on the
coastline by ordered coconut groves and clutters of native huts. Ideal
for airbases, the inland plain is broken at times by a number of
ridges, rivers, and streams. Further inland it abruptly joins the high,
matted green wall of jungle which stretches back to the mountains.

On this northern plain, between the Lunga and the Tenaru rivers,
was the tip of the Japanese spearhead. They had driven it in there to
stay in the advance down the Solomons. The enemy installations,
begun in the early summer of 1942 and developed rapidly, were
centered around the small airstrip, heart and trophy of the Guadalcanal battle, which was to be named Henderson Field (after Major

Lofton Henderson, the Marine dive-bomber commander in the Battle of Midway).

After their quick successes in the Philippines, the Indies, and Malaya, the Japanese swung south and invaded New Guinea and New Britain. Rabaul, on northern New Britain, was taken in late January of 1942 and became their key base and staging point in the drive to encircle the Coral Sea. The Jap Southeastern Fleet operating out of Rabaul had three main missions—to develop Rabaul, and to extend its hold on the Solomons and on New Guinea. Aided by ships of the Jap Eighth Fleet and planes of the 11th Air Fleet, they moved across to Buka at Bougainville's northern tip and leapfrogged south as far as Guadalcanal.

Concentrating on the drive of their 17th Army in New Guinea, the enemy had been slow to develop the holdings in the Solomons, their second line of offense. Their airfield at Guadalcanal was almost completed on August 5, 1942. And on the very day (August 7) that the Japanese planned to send elements of the 11th Air Fleet to garrison Guadalcanal, U. S. Marines made their well-timed landing on that and several islands across Sealark Channel.

The Invasion Forces

Vice Admiral Robert L. Ghormley, USN, head of all United Nations forces in the South Pacific Area, divulged plans for the operation on June 26, 1942, in a hurried conference with Major General A. A. Vandegrift, USMC, commander of the First Marine Division (Reinforced), who had arrived in New Zealand with its forward echelon only two weeks before.

The operation at Guadalcanal was to be the first major Allied offensive in the Pacific. This first taking of the initiative was a far more dangerous affair than the American people knew.

There was too little of everything—time, planning, reconnaissance, material, personnel, and support. But the offensive had to be launched then or the enemy would have had time to recover from the blows at Midway and the Coral Sea and to entrench himself deeply in the Solomons. Then the South Pacific situation would have had a second tombstone. Its inscription would have been old and apt for the Allies: "Too LATE."

They gambled on the first one. The dice were Marines. Rear Admiral John S. McCain, the doughty air sailor, headed up a new command: the small, motley air force which he scraped together of Army, Navy, Marine, and New Zealand components. His title was ComAirSoPac (Commander, Aircraft, South Pacific). His land-based task force had a total of 291 planes of all types. His entire force was divided in seven groups of which Six and Seven were commanded by Marine airmen, Major Harold "Joe" Bauer and Lieutenant Colonel John N. Hart.

At 0650 in the steaming dawn of August 7, 1942, the bullhorns on the transports in Sealark Channel howled "Land the Landing Force!" and Vandegrift's Marines went over the side to make separate landings on Tulagi, Gavutu, Tanambogo, and Guadalcanal.

The main attack force met no opposition on Guadal's Red Beach and the landing came off with "the precision of a peacetime drill" according to the official report.

The well-constructed Japanese air installations were overrun on the second day. Thus the first objective in the first major offensive in the Pacific war for airfields was accomplished. The hell came in holding it.

Early Jap air and sea opposition mounted quickly. The situation finally forced the carriers and the small naval support force to withdraw. By sunset on August 10, the sea forces hove out of Sealark, bound for the safety of Noumea. That left the Marines on their own with only part of their supplies and no air support.

That same day, with the help of captured enemy rollers and equipment, the Seabees began expansion and improvement of the enemy airfield. In almost coolie fashion and under constant fire, they extended the runway to 4,000 feet in six days.

It was formally named Henderson Field by General Vandegrift on August 17. The nerve center of the airbase was a hilltop shack with the turned-up eaves, Nippon style. This Pagoda on a hill overlooking the field became the symbol, rallying point, and target of the Guadalcanal operation.

A primitive air-raid system was installed at the Pagoda to give at least a token warning of the Japanese shuttle-bombing service that pounded the congested perimeter and field at will.

The first effort was a captured siren, though its banshee wail too often mingled with the sound of falling bombs. Fortunately, the Coastwatchers gave enough warning so that at least the Marines knew the bombers were coming down the groove.

Two weeks later a radar system was installed. Then the puny mast over the Pagoda carried flags as air-raid signals to those out of earshot of the siren. As part of the typical order within madness, a black flag was the final warning and meant "Condition Red"—that enemy planes were within two minutes of the field—or overhead. The alert pennant was a white flag which, happily, meant "Condition Yellow" —bombers en route. No flag on the Pagoda mast—no planes.

Like an occupational disease, Condition Red became the byword for Cactus. Day after day the flag was run up and at night the black skies served the same warning.

The First Division was without air cover until late in the afternoon of August 20, when two Marine squadrons landed at Henderson. They were the forward echelon of MAG 23, led by greying Lieutenant Colonel Charles L. Fike, Group executive officer. The 19 Grumman Wildcat F4F fighters of VMF 223 were commanded by Major John Lucian Smith and the 12 SBD-3's of VMSB 232 by Lieutenant Colonel Richard C. Mangrum.

Next day, five P-40's of the AAF's 67th Fighter squadron landed, bringing the defense force to 36 fighters and bombers. It was not much, but it was something to pit against the 40 to 50 bombers and fighters which the Japanese 11th Air Fleet sent down the Slot each day from Bougainville and Rabaul.

The Cactus Air Command

Bull-like, genial Colonel William Wallace, the Midway veteran and commander of MAG 23, succeeded Fike on August 30. The first SCAT transport into Henderson brought with it stocky, white-haired Roy S. Geiger, who had been twice Director of Marine Aviation and a flying captain in World War I. After his arrival at Cactus, Geiger received word of his appointment as major general.

The energetic Geiger had the joint status of Commanding General, First Marine Air Wing, and Commander of all Allied aircraft based at Henderson. On the day of his arrival, Allied aircraft totaled 42 planes, less than the operational strength of an air group.

MAG 23 and its component squadrons VMF 223 and 224 and VMSB 231 and 232 were the Marine tactical nucleus in the early stages of the air battle.

By October, the skeleton air force got some meat on its bones with the arrival of additional Army, Navy, and Marine squadrons which necessitated setting up a separate Fighter Command under Colonel Bauer, and a Search and Attack Command for bomber activities directed by Lieutenant Colonel Al Cooley. This latter unit became known as the Strike Command.

Geiger was relieved on November 7 as Commander, Aircraft, Guadalcanal by his First Wing chief of staff, Brigadier General Louis E. Woods. Geiger returned to Espiritu Santo, where the First Wing had set up headquarters on September 14.

The brilliant, fast-moving Woods, a 21-year veteran in aviation, commanded the Henderson Field force at what was probably its lowest ebb and the most critical period in the entire campaign. He also had the joint title of Commander, Forward Echelon, First Wing, until he was relieved the day after Christmas, 1942, by robust, ruddy-faced Francis Patrick Mulcahy, the brigadier general commanding the Second Marine Air Wing. [Rear Admiral C. P. Mason, USN, relieved Mulcahy in mid-February, 1943, as senior naval aviator at Guadalcanal, and assumed duties as head of the new combined command, ComAirSols (Commander, Aircraft, Solomons), which fused again the widely diverse Allied air units into a single operating unit. Marine airmen of the First and Second Wings comprised a major portion of the new command, as they had ComAirGuadal.]

The arrival of the staff of the Second Wing at Guadalcanal meant no relief to the operating units of the First Wing. They stayed on. The First Wing never left the Solomons as a command until the war ended.

The early phases of the air battle for Guadalcanal so knotted and interwove the personnel, units, and planes of the two Marine Wings that a precise definition of their workings together reads like a treatise by Einstein.

In addition to MAG 23 and 1/ the major groups involved in the First Wing's early activity at Henderson Field were MAG 25, kingpin of the SCAT transport operation [although SCAT planes flew in and out of Henderson, headquarters for MAG 25 was at New Caledonia] and MAG 11, which, like 23 and 14, was a fighter and bomber unit.

The Cactus Bumblebees

The Grumman Wildcats, sea blue on top and sky grey on their underbellies, snarled through the tropical skies like stiff-winged bumblebees. Until the arrival of the Corsair fighter in February, 1943, the Wildcat was the mainstay of the air defense of Guadalcanal. It took an almost mechanically impossible punishment in the air and on the ground and kept on flying. It has been rightly said that if any single weapon saved Guadalcanal, it was this Grumman fighter. It became such a symbol to those on the ground that they resented for a while the arrival of the Corsair.

As for the brand of men, both Marine and Navy, who flew the F4F's and the bombers in those first months, random notes on their chaotic lives were put down by an operations officer, Lieutenant Wayne Kelly, himself a pilot:

"They lived right next to the field . . . in the middle of the bull's-eye . . . in anything that offered camouflage or concealment . . . early flight pilots were up an hour before dawn . . . ate a slim breakfast or gulped coffee . . . bumped down to the field . . . warmed up their engines . . . and were ready to go at dawn . . . planes often had to be horsed out of revetments and on to the runway by tractors . . . tried to give the pilots three meals a day . . . sometimes though there wasn't enough food or time to eat it . . . only thing good about the chow was the hot coffee . . . rest was cold hash, spam, or sausage and those damn dehydrated spuds . . . often ate standing up . . . no mess hall . . . only a tent . . . had to borrow their mess gear from ground troops . . . no liquor except what the Doc had . . . they were always tired . . . and weak . . . flew at high altitudes all day . . . sucking that oxygen increased pilot fatigue and made them groggy . . . the Doc kept stuffing them with vitamin pills to keep up their resistance. Sometimes the pilots got so hungry they would corral a mess sergeant and knock off one of the stray cattle out in No Man's Land . . . wasn't healthy but it meant rare beef.

"No PX's . . . no candy . . . no gum . . . smoked Jap cigarettes . . . not even any soap . . . mail came infrequently . . . no extra clothes . . . in a few weeks they looked like a ragged rebel army . . . they lived right on the ground . . . no flooring in tents . . . bunks just sank into the stinking, black mud . . . any gear or equipment they had was so moldy in a few weeks it wasn't fit to use . . . but it had to be . . .

"There was no entertainment . . . no radio . . . news came through Communications . . . they used to lie in foxholes at night and laugh at the broadcasts from San Francisco about how secure the place was . . . when they never knew if tomorrow would be their last day. They used to call themselves the Nameless Wonders or the Bastard Air Force . . . the communiques and news broadcasts always babbled about the Army this . . . or the Navy that . . . but when the Marines did it, they were seldom mentioned by name, but called 'our planes' or 'our fighters.' It made them a little bitter when they didn't get the credit . . . but 'what the hell' . . . they said, 'at least the Japs know we're here.'

"Pilots had never heard enemy shelling or bombing before . . . didn't know what to fear . . . they soon learned . . . too much strain and no sleep made their hands shake while smoking cigarettes . . . crouched in the foxholes . . . couldn't see what was coming over . . . couldn't fight back . . . a feeling of nervousness and bewilderment got them . . . pilots in the air knew only the sound of their own motors and chatter of their own guns . . . the whispering whistle of those bombs at night got under their skins . . . everyone strained his ear for the off-beat motors of Washing Machine Charlie or Louie the Louse when they came over at night . . . no lights to pick them out . . . no protection except foxholes . . . you feel yourself shrinking into the smallest possible space . . . and edging close to the other guy because he seemed to give you some protection . . . you could hear Charlie settle down on his bombing run . . . no one ever said a word . . . just shrank and waited . . . a very faint swish . . . as the bombs started down . . . just before they hit, everybody would holler 'here it comes' or some damn thing . . . then open their mouths to reduce the concussion in case it landed too close . . . then you'd think . . . 'God, you better do me some good—right now!'

"Praying you did upstairs or down . . . and it was private . . . something quick . . . to make the other guy think you weren't afraid . . . but he knew better because he was . . . the pilots feared the shelling most . . . no warning . . . express train whine . . . harder to hide from . . . the more you took and the more you heard and the longer you were alive . . . gave you a smoky dread inside . . . like your luck was running out . . . and your number was getting close to the top . . . like the Irish sweepstakes drawing . . . you wonder if you won't win tonight . . . some guy always did . . . 'maybe this one is for me?' "

From the first landing until long after the island was secured, all the odds, paced by nature and the enemy, were hard against the pilots at Henderson. [The Army P-40's made some air kills, but were generally useless as intercept fighters because of their rate-of-climb, low operating ceiling and lack of proper oxygen equipment. Their most valued contributions were many low-altitude bombing and strafing missions in support of the ground troops.] They were fighting against the cream of the enemy air force—first-line Jap pilots who averaged 500 to 800 flying hours. Some of these had previous combat. Most Marine and Navy pilots who opposed them had less training and very few had combat experience.

The enemy planes, particularly the Zero and the twin-engine Mitsubishi bombers, were superior in many ways to the Wildcats and the Dauntless dive-bombers. More important, the Japanese had strong reserves of pilots, planes, and material. It was many months before that was true of the Allied force at Henderson Field.

Yet, the scoreboards showed that the Marine pilots were somehow beating down those high-piled odds. They averaged six to eight kills for every pilot they lost in air combat. The reasons for this success were not unaccountable but esoteric.

The weird, devil-take-the-hindmost scramble at Guadalcanal produced a blood brotherhood in its exact sense. Pilots, gunners, ground crews, generals, Seabees, and infantrymen blended into a nondescript melting pot of common courage.

There were other factors, too. Marines have always been calculating, inveterate gamblers with their own lives. The greater the risk, the more often they gambled. And, on the ground and in air, there were first teams on both sides of the fence. The man who thought and moved first, came back.

In the little, chaotic world around Henderson Field, they called the fighter pilots the "Quick Thinkers" along with the usual banter of "bird-men" and "fly-boys." The infantrymen, watching the daily air battles over-head from their foxholes, agreed that those "stick-jockies" really had it. By night, the pilots listened to the unholy noises of night battle along the perimeter and swore they had it easy and that the foot soldiers were the boys who did the work. And so as the melting pot at Guadalcanal simmered out the dross and the dead, each day the mutual respect of the air and ground teams increased for one another.

The first mission of VMF 223 was to rake the fleeing Japanese who survived their own first big push against the Marine perimeter on August 21, in the Battle of the Ilu River (originally called the Tenaru because of early confusion about the island's geography). It was the first ground support mission by Marines for Marines since those in Nicaragua.

That same day, 4 fighters of 223 intercepted 6 Zeros off Savo Island. In the dogfight, Major John Smith made the first Marine air kill in the Solomons. That Zero was the first of a run of 19 planes to be shot down by this raw-boned, cold-eyed Oklahoman, whose quick, vicious kills made him the first major American air ace of the war.

He was hard-pressed for top honors in that first month at Cactus by the Midway veteran, Marion Carl, and a second lieutenant Frazier, both of his own squadron, and the skipper of VMF 224, stocky Major Bob Galer.

Carl led the parade of kills on August 23 against enemy carrier planes, during the Battle of the Eastern Solomons, off Malaita. He downed 2 bombers and a Zero, as did a lieutenant named Ken Pond. Hamilton of VMF 212 (up on temporary duty) shot down 2 Zeros while Frazier of 223 dropped 2 bombers. In all, the Marines downed 16 planes with a loss of two pilots.

When they weren't on fighter scrambles, the F4F pilots were covering the ceaseless strikes of the dive-bombers whose mud- and oil-smeared SBD's rambled the skies like pregnant blue guppies.

The fanciest targets for the SBD's were the battleship, cruiser, and destroyer components of the Tokyo Express which plied up and down the Slot to Cactus, escorting the bulging Japanese transports and supply ships. The Jap landing barges were just good target practice. The dive-bombers did everything else in the book—sub searches, spotting missions, and close support attacks—but they preferred the juicier diet of the Express and its transport brood.

Mangrum's bombers went out on the 25th after a small fleet—a light cruiser, 5 or 6 destroyers, and 4 transports. His 8 dive-bombers, 3 of them Navy, turned that collection into a shambles, with the main killing by Lieutenant Baldinus, who scored a direct hit on a *Jintsu*-class cruiser. In the attack, two SBD rear-gunners, Pfc's Macias and Eades, each shot down an enemy float plane with their .30-caliber guns.

The methodical Japanese of the 11th Air Fleet never varied their schedules. Between 1000 and 1400, Henderson Field counted on Condition Red, and invariably got it. Fighter Command met the attacks by keeping up a small fighter barrier patrol. When the alert was given, the field was cleared of planes and more F4F's were scrambled to join the battle.

Down the Japs came on the morning of August 30 and were met below New Georgia by 8 Wildcats and 7 P-40's. In the low-altitude regions, the Army pilots downed 4 and lost 2 MAG 23's fighters shot down 14 planes. Major Smith got 4 in a brisk dogfight, bringing his score to 9.

The balance of MAG 23's flight echelon arrived late that afternoon, led by Colonel Wallace. It consisted of 19 fighters of VMF 224 commanded by Galer and a dozen SBD's of VMSB 231 under Major Leo

R. Smith. Guadalcanal's naval air force then totaled 61 planes and 74 pilots, though not all of them were in a state of high operating efficiency.

Infantry activity around the airfield perimeter was comparatively quiet during the first week in September. The enemy, at first uncertain whether the Marine attack was a raid or a landing, was now moving in reinforcements for a wholesale offensive.

On September 9, a similar lull in the air action ended and the Japanese command sent heavier formations against Henderson. Two dozen bombers and their Zero escorts bored down each day to batter the field, the supply ships, and the supply areas along the beaches.

The raid on the 9th lost 4 Zeros and 5 bombers to Geiger's fighters, in trade for 2 pilots, one of them Marion Carl, who then had 11 planes. Carl returned safely five days later with the help of native guides.

On September 10, the enemy air force returned with 27 bombers and 30 Zeros for cover. They did some damage in the perimeter, but it cost them 5 bombers and 3 Zeros. That performance was repeated on the 11th by 46 planes and on the 12th by 42 planes. The Japanese lost 13 bombers and 5 Zeros on these raids, which were jumped first by a few Marine fighters, led on both occasions by Major John Smith, who raised his personal tally to 16 planes.

This air crescendo was augmented at night by heavy shelling of the Marine positions by the Tokyo Express and by increased activity just outside the perimeter.

This activity developed quickly on the night of September 12 into the Battle of Bloody Ridge. The main attack was knifed against a position held by the First Raider Battalion south of the airfield. The target was Henderson Field. Day and night the battle raged bitterly until it broke off early on the 15th. The Marine Raiders who in this action helped save Henderson Field were commanded by Colonel Merritt (Red Mike) Edson, the almost legendary infantry leader and former Marine aviator who won the Medal of Honor.

During the air battle for Bloody Ridge, the Wildcat pilots broke up raid after raid on perimeter positions. Because of the proximity of the fighting, they frequently operated from the field under sniper fire.

The mid-September crisis was not the climax in the battle for Cactus, merely a frightening prelude of what would happen again in the black days of October and again in the final fury of November. Navy and Marine air reinforcements had arrived dramatically just as the mid-September battle spiral started upward. Their aid helped blunt the combined enemy assault. There would be no such aid in the following months.

At September's end, those at Air Command, Cactus, felt a sort of benumbed satisfaction that they had come off well in these early rounds. Three of the Marine fighter pilots had become the country's leading aces. They were Smith with 19 meatballs (tiny Rising Sun flags) on his plane, the gaunt Carl with 16, and Galer with 13. Medals of Honor were later awarded Smith and Galer for their scores and the expert audacity with which they led their squadrons. Carl twice received the Navy Cross.

The first over-all tally (kept like all the early records, earnestly penciled on dirty sheets of scrap paper) showed 171 victories over the enemy air force by Henderson-based planes. VMF 223, John Smith's Rainbow squadron, was credited with 93½ planes, of which 50½ were twin-engined bombers and 41 were Zero fighters, plus a Kawanishi four-motor flying boat and a twin-tailed, double-engined bomber of dubious lineage. Galer's VMF 224, with less combat time, had piled up 6 float planes, 9 Zeros and 21½ Betty bombers. Navy's Fighting Five had accounted for 22 assorted kills and the AAF's 67th Pursuit, 4 Zeros.

These airmen in their blue ball caps, shoulder holsters, and filthy odd-lot flying gear looked and felt much unlike the giant-killers that headlines called them. They were sick. Dysentery racked their bowels and stomachs. Malaria shivered and burned them. The tasteless, clammy food, Jap rice, and hardtack seemed only to nurture the gnawing of the hunger rat in their bellies. And sleep—sleep was a dream just beyond their fingertips. In their tired minds, behind their sunken eyes, they caressed the thought of a quiet night's sleep as if it were a lush treasure. But there was no break. The work and the weariness went on for those who flew and for the quiet, earnest men who kept them in the air.

The fighter pilots abided by the legend that there were only two types in their midst—the old and the bold. Four of them would spiral upward to take on forty, and shrug their shoulders at the odds. But they wouldn't dogfight a Zero. The F4F's weren't built for it. In the squirrel-cage air battles, the Marine pilots tried working together in two-plane sections. (It was this system which Jimmy Thach, the Navy commander, later refined into the formidable Thach Weave.) And when they had to go it alone, the fighters used all the stock tricks of attack and devised new ones. Generally they bored up or down, through the enemy formations, shooting up what they could on fast passes. This roller-coaster action gave them little time for accuracy, but that, plus the lack of armor and self-sealing fuel tanks in the torchable Japanese planes, was enough.

The Dauntless SBD's and the few Navy TBF's at Cactus developed their own slugging tactics as the days wore on. They flew their shuttle missions against the Express offshore and a rapidly increasing number of land targets of opportunity. Weather, ship-based flak, rollicking Zeros, and gadfly float planes were their biggest headaches as the daily sorties in their logbooks mounted. But like the pernicious mosquitoes of Guadalcanal, the bombers never stopped coming.

In the regrouping of September 22, Lieutenant Colonel Albert Cooley arrived in advance of his MAG 14 to take over as bomber commander, while the fighters were merged under Colonel Wallace.

Cooley's first orders from Geiger were to extend the range of his striking force and hammer at the enemy float-plane base at Rekata Bay on Santa Isabel and their installations at Gizo Bay. It was a likely plan, immediately carried out, but, as October would prove, a bit premature.

After the Battle of the Ridge, September passed rather mildly, in a Guadalcanal sense. Not until the 27th did enemy air aggressiveness again assert itself. Three waves of bombers and Zeros came down that day. The Navy and Marine fighters went up too late to keep Henderson Field from a pounding but shot down 11 of the retreating planes.

The Cactus F4F bumblebees had a field day on the 28th. Fifty-five bombers and Zeros came over. Twenty-four were spared the tedium of a return trip north.

The Days of October

Even the laconic, impersonal language of the Navy communiques issued in Washington gave an inkling of the black clouds that were massing alarmingly on the horizon of Guadalcanal's defenders:

No. 141. "On October 1, . . . Navy and Marine Corps dive-bombers and torpedo planes attacked four Japanese destroyers to the south of the New Georgia group . . . one destroyer was hit and damaged and when last seen was dead in the water.

"On October 2 . . . the Japanese again attacked Guadalcanal with a small group of bombers, heavily protected by fighters. Our intercepting fighters shot down four." (Both Smith and Galer, shot down in this action, returned unharmed.)

No. 142: ". . . On October 3, small groups of Japanese bombers, preceded by about 30 Zeros, attempted to raid U. S. installations on Guadalcanal. AA shot down two while nine more of the attacking Zeros were shot down by seven Navy Wildcat fighters." (Marine pilots of 223 and 224 got them all. Carl, one; Ken Frazier, two; and Lieutenant Colonel Harold "Joe" Bauer shot down four Zeros.)

"During the night of October 3-4, Navy and Marine Corps dive-bombers attacked an enemy cruiser and several destroyers which were engaged in landing troop reinforcements on Guadalcanal. At least one hit was scored on the cruiser. One of our planes was shot down, but the crew was saved." (The attack was led by a Navy Lieutenant Eldridge; he and Commander Bullet Lou Kirn, another Navy SBD skipper, were noted bomber leaders.)

Communique 142 carried a quaint understatement of fact when it said, "The enemy continued to land small detachments of troops on the island under cover of darkness." After the first ten days of October, those small detachments added up to nearly 10,000 enemy troops including regiments of their crack, undefeated Sendai or Second Division. They may have seemed small to the communique readers, but the men on Guadalcanal thought otherwise.

No. 146: ". . . During the night of October 5-6, Navy and Marine Corps dive-bombers and torpedo planes from Guadalcanal attacked six enemy destroyers which had been located by our search planes. One destroyer was sunk and another damaged.

"During the night of October 7-8, the enemy continued to reinforce his troops on Guadalcanal.

"During the evening of October 8, Navy and Marine Corps dive-bombers and torpedo planes, assisted by fighters, attacked an enemy surface force northwest of Guadalcanal . . . one cruiser and four destroyers . . . covering landing operations on northwestern tip of the island. The cruiser received one torpedo hit and was further damaged by bombs. Four enemy planes were shot down . . . two of our planes were lost . . ."

No. 148: ". . . On October 9 . . . Marine Corps aircraft attacked a Japanese force of two light cruisers and four destroyers in the area north of New Georgia Island. A direct hit [by Second Lieutenant W. H. Fuller of VMSB 141] damaged one of the cruisers and when last seen she was down by the bow. The second cruiser was also attacked and minor damage was reported. Three of the enemy seaplanes which attempted to fight off our attack were shot down.

"Navy and Marine Corps search planes bombed enemy aircraft installations at Rekata Bay and strafed seaplanes on the water.

"On October 11 . . . four waves of Japanese bombers with fighter escort totaling about 35 bombers and 30 fighters attempted to bomb our positions at Guadalcanal. Army, Navy, and Marine Corps fighters intercepted and forced the bombers to drop their loads in an open field. Eight enemy bombers and four Zero fighters were shot down. One U. S. fighter was lost." (It was the biggest raid to date on Henderson, but lost its target as towering cloud masses moved in over the field. VMF 223 and 224 found the raid in the cloud layers and shot down 11 flamers. The Airacobras picked off one bomber.)

No. 149: ". . . during the morning of October 12, Navy and Marine Corps torpedo planes and dive-bombers left Guadalcanal to locate the retreating enemy ships [survivors of the night sea battle off Cape Esperance in which the Japanese suffered heavily in their first contact with the Navy off Guadalcanal since early August]. At about 10 o'clock, two enemy cruisers were overtaken south of New Georgia island. A torpedo hit was obtained on one cruiser and several bombs exploded near by . . . it was left burning in the water. During the afternoon of the 12th, an air group from Guadalcanal attacked an enemy cruiser and destroyer. A direct bomb hit severely damaged and stopped the cruiser. A direct hit and several near-misses set fire to the destroyer . . . she was left in a sinking condition."

No. 153: ". . . On October 13th . . . during the afternoon the airfield at Guadalcanal was twice bombed by enemy aircraft. Three enemy planes were shot down and one U. S. fighter lost." (Twenty-four bombers with 15 Zeros escorting came down on the early raid and got in without warning. Henderson scrambled its fighters, but they were unable to reach the bombers' altitude on time. Two hours later the same conditions prevailed when 15 bombers and escort Zeros finished their runs before the interception was made. The raids buckled and holed the steel matting on Henderson, damaged several planes, and burned out 5,000 gallons of precious aviation gas.)

A new menace sounded off at dusk on the 13th, when, for the first time, heavy Japanese artillery opened up on Henderson Field. The backyard of battle since its taking, Henderson had been the bull's-eye for the day and night bombers and the naval shellings. Now it had a new heckler on its hands, Pistol Pete. This or these heavy artillery pieces whanged away at the field and other perimeter positions sporadically and without warning for months to come, and though Pistol Pete was the object of intensive searches and raids, its fire-and-run technique kept it in constant operation.

The early morning of the 14th passed tensely after the shelling as flurries of action gave credence to the feeling of anxiety prevailing inside the Cactus beachhead.

Ninety minutes past midnight, Louie the Louse, a naval spotting plane, released his flare over the field. It cast a garish, unholy glare on the upturned faces of the Marines huddled in their foxholes. Then came hell, unvarnished, as an enemy naval armada standing off in Sealark Channel bombarded the airfield and the Lunga Point area with uncanny accuracy for nearly two hours. Battleships, cruisers, and many destroyers salvoed broadside after broadside into the quivering earth of Guadalcanal in a Fourth of July display that was like the arsenal of the underworld exploding.

Jap bombers took over when their fleet withdrew. When the Marines rose out of their foxholes at dawn, a barrage of artillery fire opened up and they ducked back into the earth.

That morning Henderson Field was found to be so badly rubbled it was hardly worth saving. Only 4 of the command's 39 remaining SBD's could be flown. The five top officers of VMSB 141, which had arrived the night before, had been killed in the shelling, as were more than a score of others.

However, the F4F's based on Fighter One, the small grass airstrip to the east of the main field, had suffered comparatively little.

Geiger surveyed his battered remnants and pronounced them in sorry shape to withstand the expected invasion. The Japanese at Rabaul, certain that Air Command, Guadalcanal, had been cut to pieces and even those pieces destroyed, sent down two final softening-up raids to precede the invasion convoys. At noon, two dozen bombers dropped their loads without a loss. One hour later, 15 bombers and 10 Zeros passed over the field, but this time were intercepted and Wildcat pilots shot down 9 bombers and 3 Zeros.

Down the Slot came the 2 convoys—6 transports escorted by destroyers and a support force of a battleship, 3 cruisers and 4 destroyers.

Feverish effort by the ground crews readied the SBD's which made two attacks on the transports, sinking one and damaging another.

It was late in the afternoon of October 14, when, in the weird light of coming dusk, a lumbering twin-motored PBY Catalina eased in over the shambles of Henderson Field. The darting, bloodshot eyes of the tired gun crews watched it barely clear the headless stumps that had been coconut trees. The plane spanked the end of the runway and then moved on furtively as if afraid to lose speed. Downfield, the Cat groaned painfully to the touch of a brake and hurried off the strip.

It was the Blue Goose, Geiger's personal plane, back from another ferry run to Espiritu, this time with two 2,000-pound torpedoes, one slung under each of its long, ungainly wings. The pilot was "Mad" Jack Cram, a wiry, eager Major.

Before reporting in to the "Old Man," he got the word on the local havoc from bemoustached Major Joe Renner, an operations officer. Renner spoke with the clipped, haggard tension of a man who hadn't slept for 72 hours:

"They've got our backs moulded into the wall. We've had a permanent Condition Red all day. No sirens now unless at least 15 Jap planes come in. The F4F's can't meet all the raids. We haven't enough gas or ammunition to send them up each time.

"What did you bring up this time? Torpedoes? What in the hell good are they now? Everyone of the TBF's got smashed up in the shelling last night. Good Lord, what a show that was! They must have had the whole bastardly fleet out there! It was like kicking a wounded guy in the groin time after time to see if he'd yell 'Uncle.'

"They frisked the place like a pickpocket. There were BB's out there in the channel with a flock of cruisers and destroyers in support. The insolent stinkers just stood off and plastered the place like they were in a free shooting gallery. Some of them walked searchlights up and down the shore, picking out the targets. The rest of them went over the place like a fine-toothed rake. If they ever try to break through what's left today . . . God help us, Jack . . . it'll be bad."

At dawn, activity along the front line remained sporadic, but ten miles up the coast a search plane found five enemy transports busily unloading troops protected by a heavy destroyer screen.

The runway at Henderson was rent and torn. There were 19 shell craters in the straightaway. Renner did the best he could, marking out a weird path for the pilots around the craters with flare pots.

He finally got one started at 0430 by running in front of the plane, flagging the pilot to the take-off position. The first SBD crashed in the middle of the field.

Renner took the next pilot in his jeep and drove him carefully down the runway, pointing out each of the bad spots in turn by flashlight. Somehow, this SBD got off the deck, but the pilot was barely airborne when he found his wheels were frozen in place. He tried working the dive flaps. They were glued tight. Shell fragments had punctured his hydraulic system.

Quietly, the pilot turned and headed for the shadowy transports. He laboriously climbed the circle for altitude, then pushed over in his dive. The rushing air played queer tricks with no flaps and the wheels down. He corrected, jinked through the flak barrage from the destroyers, and jerked the release toggle for a direct hit on the first transport.

More lone SBD's followed, doing what damage they could.

An enemy photo plane appeared first, to make certain of the devastation at Henderson. What he saw must have convinced him, for on his third pass he came screaming down from 11,000 feet and flat-hatted across the airfield. Everyone within two miles cut loose at him. Even a heavy howitzer fired a few hopeful rounds. The plane crashed in flames at the edge of the strip.

At 0700, an umbrella of 30 Zeros took up station at 15,000 feet over the landing area. Geiger stopped the lone strikes and ordered all hands to prepare for a coordinated attack with all that was left.

Major Cram, who had been arguing for an attack in his PBY, was given permission to make a torpedo run on the transports under cover of the SBD mission. Of him, an officer at Geiger's command post later said:

"If ever I saw a man with sheer guts, it was Jack Cram. He knew it would probably be his last flight, but he jumped at the chance. As long as he had to, he was going out in a blaze of glory."

Renner did his coordination by jeep. The communications system had been obliterated the night before. Cram rode with him.

The Army fighter squadron promised to have four planes ready to fly. Major Duke Davis' squadron would furnish the balance of the fighter cover. (Davis' VMF 121 had arrived several days before.)

Colonel Al Cooley said he could have twelve SBD's ready at 1010. On the way back to the Blue Goose, Renner told Cram, "This will be the most screwed up show in history . . . but there's no other choice. If it works, miracles are still with us."

That a PBY had never before made a daylight torpedo attack or that he had no co-pilot didn't faze Cram. Neither did the fact that he knew little or nothing about using torpedoes. Before Renner dropped him off, he learned how to use them in a five-minute instruction course from a fighter pilot whose brother was a torpedo bomber pilot.

The Goose was first off. Cram nursed it into the air, climbing toward the rendezvous area for the 8 fighters and 12 SBD's two miles east of Henderson and away from the Zeros. Behind him Duke Davis' Wildcats were airborne and the last of the SBD's was clawing for altitude. They had all taken off through an artillery barrage raking the field.

While they watched, the 30 Zeros on station were relieved by 30 more. The Japanese pilots seemed to watch incredulously this strange parade from Henderson, but they stayed on station over the convoy.

Then to the west at 9,000 feet the lurking SBD's exploded into action. The lead plane rolled over on its back, wings gleaming dull in the sunlight. As it whipped down on the transports, the mud-brown Zeros peeled off for the kill.

In the PBY, Cram hunched forward, then shoved the yoke to the fire-wall. The surprised Cat went over on its nose in an almost vertical dive towards the first transport, a mile away. Never built to go over 160, the Blue Goose hit 270 mph indicated in the dive. Cram fearfully watched the needle climb while the huge umbrella wings shrieked and groaned, flapping like an ancient crow's.

Afraid of what would happen, Cram hauled slowly back on the yoke. The Cat held together. He leveled out at 1,000 feet and went whistling past the first DD before they spotted him. Dead ahead, the Japs were living and dying like frantic ants as the bombs from the SBD's gutted their ships.

The Cat screamed past the first and second transports at 75 feet. Flak from the destroyers flailed the plane like a steel whip. It bucked and shuddered from the impact. At point-blank range, Cram lined upon the third transport, sighting off his bow. Holding the yoke steady with his left hand, he jerked the release toggle so viciously he almost tore it out of the instrument panel.

The first torpedo splatted in the water and bored into the hull of the transport. A second later he yanked the toggle and the second torpedo porpoised, then followed the first one into the side of the ship. Just as he pulled out of the run, flak from one of the destroyers sheared off the PBY's navigation hatch.

Five Zeros broke off from the dogfight and went after the flying boat. Cram started to pull up, saw the Zeros and stood the PBY on its left wingtip in a turn that headed him back to Henderson. As he passed his target transport, it was settling in the water.

The Zeros played tail chase, making pass after pass, in their eagerness to smash down the waddling Goose. Cram roller-coastered it up and down and back and forth to make it as poor a target as possible. The Zeros ventilated the plane conscientiously during the 12 miles back to the airfield. The Blue Goose barrelled in over the tree stumps at the end of Henderson moving too fast to land and with one Zero still on its tail. It went on to Fighter One.

Lieutenant Roger Haberman was bringing his smoking F4F into the landing circle with his wheels down when he saw Cram's situation. Wheels still down, Haberman kept casually in his turn, wound up on the Zero's tail and shot it down. Cram pancaked somehow, he and his crew still intact and the Catalina everything else but.

He was awarded the Navy Cross for the attack.

B-17's, up from Espiritu Santo, hit the convoy of ships again at noon, scoring hits on a transport and a destroyer. Twenty-seven Mitsubishi bombers hit Henderson at noon. There was no interception. Geiger's pilots were to busy with the convoy to bother.

By nightfall, two of the transports had been sunk, another was beached and burning, and the remaining two had been hit. When they tried to escape, the SBD's struck again, firing one and hitting the other.

That night, between air raids and another shelling of the airfield, Geiger counted up his losses for the day. They were not bad—three SBD's, one F4F, and one Airacobra—but the Japanese had managed to land thousands of troops and supplies. They were coming ashore faster than the weary Marines could kill them off.

Geiger's almost ludicrously little air force was back at it the next day, eking out its usual missions and seven strafing runs on the positions of the newly-landed enemy troops at Kukumbona. They flew in spite of an almost total lack of aviation gas to keep the planes in the air. The ground crews drained wrecked planes and searched out forgotten little caches of gas drums—anything for a few gallons to fill the thirsty wing tanks.

SCAT, the transport feeder line, helped meet the crisis by flying in plane after plane loaded with bombs and barrels of gas and oil. These Douglas R4D's were a thin, defenseless artery, but they were the only constant lifeline the Cactus forces had in those days when the enemy controlled the air and sea approaches to the island.

General Geiger's frantic call for reinforcements brought in 19 Grumman fighters of VMF 212 led by Joe Bauer, the Lieutenant Colonel who had shot down 5 planes while "visiting" the Canal. Bauer was regarded by his cohorts as the finest fighter pilot the Air Arm ever produced. He was destined to be among those around whom the sad adage grew: "the best of them don't come back." But not before he scored again, heavily.

As his planes went into land, Bauer spotted 8 Japanese dive-bombers battering a U. S. destroyer offshore. In a lone attack, he flamed 4 to bring his personal score to 11. For these kills and his "extraordinary heroism and conspicuous gallantry as squadron commander," he was posthumously awarded the Medal of Honor.

The Last Act at Cactus

When the Japanese failed to follow up their three-day blitz, Air Command, Guadal took advantage of the unaccountable lull to refurbish itself, count noses and scores, and welcome the newcomers.

Seven SBD's arrived the day Bauer did, to help plug the gaps of attrition and evacuation. The survivors of VMF 224 were sent south along with VMSB 231. The redoubtable Mangrum and the remainder of his VMSB 232 had long since gone, as had Smith's VMF 223. MAG 23, on October 16, turned over its tactical command of Henderson to MAG 14 and, except for some ground personnel, pulled out with its haggard remnants. Its scoreboard showed 244 planes of the Rabaul Air Fleet permanently out of business, at a cost of 23 fighter pilots lost in combat. Thirty-two Army and Navy pilots operating under MAG 23 were listed as killed in action, eight of them by naval gun fire.

VMF 223 led the list. It had garnered 110½ planes. Smith was the leading ace of the Pacific with 19. Carl had 16.

Major Galer sparked his squadron's total of 60½ kills. Though shot down three times himself, Galer kept going back up until he earned 13 meatballs and his Medal of Honor.

Fighting Five, Navy Commander Simpler's squadron, had a total of 38 when it was evacuated. The Army 67th Fighter unit earned a total of 8.

Even the bombers sported the coveted meatballs on their fuselages. VMSB 231 and 141 had shot down three each, the Navy's VB-71 and VT-8 were credited with two each. VMSB 232 had added one.

Five more assorted kills were on the Henderson tally. They had been seen going down in flames, but in the confusion of the dog-fights no one claimed credit for them.

The balance of the 244 aerial kills belonged to the two new units —Davis' Flying Circus and Bauer's 212. (Bauer's first five kills were marked up for 223 with which he had been on duty at the time.) These two squadrons, paced by cigar-smoking, exuberant Joseph Foss, who became the first five-time ace in the Pacific, took another large chunk out of the enemy air force in the weeks ahead.

In the bomber command, two new squadrons came in as replacements—Major Joe Sailer's VMSB 132 and Major Robert Richards' VMSB 142. They, with VMSB 141 and VMSB 131, the Air Arm's first torpedo squadron, took over the bombing routines.

Incomplete records for the torpedo and dive-bombers credited them with sinking many types of enemy ships. Of these, the Marines sank 14 warships and 20 cargo or transport vessels, and damaged 49. Their sea-going damage also added up to more than 200 enemy small craft sunk and 140 damaged. There was no way of accurately reckoning the damage they had done to enemy land-based troops and installations, but it was later found to be extensive.

With the arrival of the new squadrons, the face of Henderson Field itself changed. The Pagoda, well-holed in the naval shellings, was bulldozed out of existence. The Air Command moved into a tent area on the banks of the Lunga, further away from the field. The makeshift grass-covered strip, Fighter One, was in use. Fighter Two, to the west of the big field, was under construction. The plight in supplies and operating conditions eased up a little.

In the first ten days after MAG 14 took over, its pilots shot down 90 enemy planes as the high odds continued. This score looked well in the headlines, but it did not stifle the undertones of impending disaster which were audible. The Solomons situation forced the admission in Washington that the defenders of Guadalcanal were even further from final victory than they had been in the first days of the landing. The possibility of defeat was even hinted.

Eight days after the mid-October blow-off, the Japanese launched a heavy attack along the Matanikau River in a desperate drive to retake Henderson Field. The early losses were heavy and continual rain almost nullified air operations.

The attack reached a climax on October 25, known as "Dugout Sunday." That day provided a new peak in the South Pacific air offensive. Both the bombers and the fighters were on deck only long enough to refuel, rearm, and take off again.

Seventeen Zeros and 5 bombers were shot down within easy sight of the watching ground troops. Foss got 4. Lieutenant Jack Conger ran out of ammunition during one series of dogfights. Rather than lose his opponent, he hauled back on his stick and sent his Wildcat sawing up into the Zero. His engine and left wing hit the Zero and it went down. So did Conger, his chute swinging only twice' before he hit the water. Earlier, four F4F pilots—Conger, Drury, Stout, and Faulkner—strafed 3 destroyers and badly damaged them.

Intensive enemy naval action, mainly by destroyers in the vicinity of the Canal, forced Geiger to dispatch asking ComAirSoPac for a strike from other bases against the ships. Mud had made Henderson Field inoperative for his 12 available bombers. Down south they scraped the fields bare and sent up seven fighters and three SBD's.

Eight SBD's and 3 P-39's finally were airborne, and in three separate attacks, they damaged both a heavy and a light cruiser.

Marines and one Army regiment fought incessantly for four days along the entire perimeter and were finally successful in preventing any major break-through to the airfield. In the fighting, the prize Japanese Sendai division and its support units were decimated and ceased to function as an offensive force. Immediately, in spite of three months of constant fighting, the First Marine Division launched an offensive back across the Mantanikau to push the enemy once and for all out of striking range of the airfield. But as the Marines moved to the west, the enemy landed more troops to the east.

Then the weary horror began winding up again. It was to be their third and last midmonth nightmare, one that would test them to the far limits of endurance.

Geiger was relieved on the 5th by General Woods.

On the afternoon of the 7th, Woods sent out an assorted striking force of bombers and fighters to hit a Jap task force of 10 destroyers and a cruiser sighted in the north. It gutted the cruiser with two torpedoes, one 1,000-pound bomb hit and one near-miss. One destroyer was hit by a torpedo and another took two direct bomb hits, while the fighters strafed 4 of the DD's. The F4F's nailed 10 enemy fighters, the Army planes 5. Our losses were 4 fighters. Three of the pilots, one of them Foss, later returned.

In the dingy weather the Japs still came on. Search and Coast-watcher reports on November 12 totaled up to a staggering enemy armada between Rabaul and Tonolei Harbor at Kahili and those on the move in the Slot. More than 100 heavy surface vessels, including 2 carriers, 4 or possibly 8 battleships, 11 cruisers, and over 60 destroyers and transports were ready for the final push. Numerically our available naval forces were small by comparison and our air strength was equally so.

U. S. transports were rushed to Guadalcanal in hope of landing needed reinforcements and supplies before the Japanese fleet moved in for the attack expected on Friday, the 13th.

On the 11th, Jap dive-bombers hit the American transports in Sealark Channel (now better known as Iron Bottom Bay). Marine planes downed 5, losing four pilots. Later the same day the bombers hit Henderson. Marine pilots shot down 6.

On the 12th, at 1415, 25 enemy torpedo bombers with Zero escorts came in low and fast against the naval concentration in the Channel. AA batted down 8; the fighters, led by Foss, downed 17 bombers and 6 Zeros with the loss of a P-39 pilot and four planes. Only one enemy plane escaped.

The anticipated heavy naval shelling on the night of November

12-13 turned into a furious sea battle off Savo Island, in which both sides lost heavily and the American ships were forced to retire.

Morning search planes from Henderson found the enemy battleship *Hiyei* dead in the water off Savo and covered by a Zero fighter screen. The F4F's downed eight of the Zeros, and throughout the day Marine and Navy torpedo and dive-bombers hacked away at the dying steel carcass of the battleship. Though still afloat at nightfall, only an oil slick remained of the BB next morning.

Pursuing its dogged pattern, an enemy task force stood offshore and pounded Henderson Field for nearly an hour on the night of the 13th until chased off by PT boats.

The air force sustained minor damage from the shelling. Shrugging it off, they wound up for their greatest day's work of the campaign as the enemy invasion force moved down the Slot between New Georgia and Santa Isabel.

The daring, relentless Major Sailer tracked down the night task force with 5 SBD's escorted by 6 F4F's. They caught up with the 5 heavy cruisers and 4 destroyers north of Vella Lavella. Sailer bored in close and dumped his bomb on the bow of a heavy cruiser. A lieutenant named Kelly, of VMSB 141, followed up with a direct hit on the cruiser's bridge.

Dooley, a captain in VMSB 131, led a second attack of 6 Marine and Navy torpedo planes against the ships. They made 3, possibly 4, direct torpedo hits.

The fated convoy steamed closer to Guadalcanal. Its transports, sardined with troops and supplies in a fashion that only the Japanese would dream of, were covered by 2 cruisers and 9 destroyers. If it reached its destination even 50 per cent intact, it could well have been the Sunday punch on the well-bruised jaws of the Henderson Field defenders.

Instead, the airmen turned the convoy into a nautical abbatoir in one day of frightful slaughter. After two light attacks by search planes, Joe Sailer's 25 Marine SBD's and TBF's hit the convoy off New Georgia. They battered the first group of 5 transports. One 8,000-ton ship received two direct 1,000-pound bomb hits. Another transport got four. Major Richard's division of SBD's scored six hits on another transport and two on a light cruiser.

Throughout the day, the hard-jawed Woods threw every plane in his command at the convoy. B-17's hit one transport in their attack. Army B-26's from the Fijis joined in. The Navy squadrons from the carrier *Enterprise* joined the mad shuttle run, and in the third attack from Henderson with Marine planes, ten bomb hits were scored on eight transports. Foss and Bauer and all available fighter planes rode cover over the bombers, drove off intervening Zeros, and then made one strafing pass after another at masthead height through the writhing convoy. The sea was littered with frantic enemy troops who had been blown or jumped overside in the attacks. The decks of the transports, packed like anthills with troops, ran red. The slaughter in the area was so sickening that some of the usually impersonal fighter pilots vomited after their strafing runs—and went back for more ammunition.

By midafternoon, 4 transports were dead in the water and 3 burning well. The remaining 4 still came on.

Back at Henderson, General Woods kept the attacks going with a fury of ground action. Messmen, musicians, line troops, and office clerks joined the regular ground crews in refueling and rearming the planes. Gas was passed from field drums to wing tanks by chain gangs. The crews loaded the smaller bombs into the racks on their bare backs and mauled the heavy torpedoes by hand.

Sailer went out for his third attack of the day, leading four SBD's. They hit one transport twice and buckled the deck plates of a light cruiser with another bomb. Five other Marine pilots sank another transport with four direct hits. Navy bombers, fighting off a Zero attack, scored three hits on the third of the moving transports.

It had been a great victory. As one of Woods' officers put it: "Today we've probably killed more enemies of the United States than any other day in its history."

He couldn't have been far from wrong. Readjusted estimates put the total enemy dead at over 20,000. At war's end, the enemy high command admitted it had lost 11 transports in the action, and that only 10 percent of the supplies ever reached their Guadalcanal garrisons.

Soon after the battle, Admiral Halsey, then ComSoPac, dispatched the following message to Guadalcanal:

"To the superb officers and men on land, on sea, in the air, and under the sea who have performed such magnificent feats for our country, in the past few days—you have written your names in golden letters on the pages of history and won the undying gratitude of your countrymen. My pride in you is beyond expression. No honor for you could be too great. Magnificently done. God bless each and every one of you. To the glorious dead—hail heroes!—rest with God!"

The enemy's debacle had cost Henderson five pilots and four gunners. Among them was the well-loved Joe Bauer. He went down after a dogfight with a Zero and was sighted in the water by Foss.

Foss returned to Henderson and guided out Major Renner and his rescue plane, the J2F. For four days Renner combed the area around the Russell Islands, without success. Bauer was never heard of again.

The seaborne struggle was joined again on the night of the 14th when heavy U. S. and Jap forces tangled off Guadalcanal, with the enemy losing heavily. His three-day losses were 16 ships sunk, and 12 heavily damaged.

After the mid-November conflict, the enemy was quiet for a while. Then he tried sporadically to reinforce his island garrison, but unsuccessfully. At long last, the tide of battle at Guadalcanal had turned. The last major Japanese effort to recapture the island had failed.

Actually, the Japanese later admitted that the disastrous defeats in October and November had heightened the value of the Solomons in their eyes. They stopped vacillating long enough to order the Eighth Area Army out of Java to Rabaul. These 50,000 troops, augmented by local forces, were to be hurled at Guadalcanal on February 1, 1943. This action and the reinforcement problem in the Solomons delayed their major drive in New Guinea. Then Allied strategy caught them off base again with a drive across New Guinea's Owen Stanley mountains. On Christmas Day, 1942, Tokyo ordered

Rabaul commanders to cancel plans to reinforce Guadalcanal. Instead, they were to evacuate the forces still there and to establish a final defensive position in the Munda–Kolombangara area of the New Georgia group. It was this area which became the routine target for Henderson-based planes in the months ahead.

There were several flurries of heavy enemy action before Cactus was finally written off their books. During these sporadic attempts, first to reinforce and later to evacuate their dwindling Guadalcanal garrisons, the Marine squadrons and their cohorts concentrated on the ancient battle pattern of "seek and destroy."

Operating like an insatiable mongoose against rodent remnants in a barnyard, Air Command, Guadalcanal, took a heavy toll of enemy sea-and airborne traffic in the closing months of the battle at Cactus. After a brief lull, the ground forces, were exerting constant pressure to the east and west against the remaining Japanese troops. Finally, the infantry concentrated in a last westward drive to Point Cruz and beyond.

The First Marine Aviation Engineers came ashore on November 11 to give impetus to the program for improving and expanding the overcrowded Henderson airbase facilities. Joining the Seabees, the engineers helped to hard-surface the runways, put in drainage systems, lay out the badly needed dispersal areas, and build the auxiliary fields.

Following their November 14 defeat in the naval battle off Tassafaronga, Japanese surface forces appeared again three days later and were hit by Henderson planes 150 miles off Guadalcanal. The SBD's, TBF's, and fighters crippled 4 ships and shot down 10 of the covering float planes.

The pattern of the Cactus Shivaree changed in early December when, after four months of jungle nightmare, the remnants of the First Marine Division were relieved by Army troops. Before embarking, General Vandegrift, in his message to all hands, paid high tribute to "the pilots, Army, Navy, and Marine, whose unbelievable achievements have made the name 'Guadalcanal' a synonym for death and disaster in the language of our enemy. . . ."

The airmen heard the tribute, watched the line Marines depart, remembered Vandegrift's Tulagi message about God favoring the strong and bold of heart, and kept right on flying eight and ten hours a day, mauling Japanese between Bougainville and Kokumbona.

Eleven destroyers prowling in the Slot on December 12 were routed by Marine dive-bombers. Five of the enemy DD's were badly damaged in the attack during which Sailer, of VMSB 132, was shot down and killed.

The new airfield which the Japanese had skillfully constructed under the concealment of coconut trees at Munda on New Georgia received its heaviest working-over on Christmas Eve. During the bombing and strafing attack, 14 intercepting Jap planes were shot down and 10 more destroyed on the ground.

On December 26, General Woods turned over his command to Brigadier General Francis P. Mulcahy and the advance staff elements of the Second Marine Air Wing. It was a topside change, not radically affecting Marine Air Arm operations on Guadalcanal. The Forward Echelon, First Wing, continued to serve under Mulcahy, as did its tactical groups and squadrons. The combined ground elements were under Army direction, while General Mulcahy commanded all Allied air activity.

During January, Mulcahy's fliers were involved in a series of actions which highlighted his persistent and expanding pattern of bomb, strafe, and search missions designed to wipe out remaining enemy resistance in the Guadalcanal area and choke off naval attempts to supply or relieve it.

The daily air pattern droned on in a manner not unlike the communiques which reported it:

January 1: " . . . Dauntless dive-bombers dropped bombs in the vicinity of Kokumbona where Japanese headquarters on Guadalcanal are believed to be located . . ."

January 2: ". . . At 8:20 A.M., medium bombers and dive-bombers escorted by fighters bombed the Japanese airfield at Munda on New Georgia Island. Hits were scored on antiaircraft emplacements and other installations.

"At 6 P.M., Dauntless dive-bombers escorted by Wildcats and Lightnings (P-38's) attacked a detachment of Japanese destroyers 30 miles northwest of Rendova Island in the New Georgia group.

The destroyers were protected by 10 enemy fighters and one dive-bomber. One of the destroyers was left burning badly and another appeared to be sinking."

January 5: " . . . During the darkness of the early morning, a U. S. task force of surface units successfully bombarded the Japanese airfield at Munda . . . as the task force retired, it was attacked by Japanese dive-bombers. Four Wildcats intercepted and shot down four of the enemy dive-bombers and probably destroyed two more."

January 11: ". . . a force of Dauntless dive-bombers escorted by Wildcat fighters was attacked by 12 Japanese Zeros between Santa Isabel Island and New Georgia Island. Four Zeros were shot down and two others possibly destroyed. One Wildcat failed to return."

January 15: ". . . during the morning a force of dive-bombers escorted by F4F's and Airacobra fighters attacked 9 Japanese destroyers 140 miles northwest of Lunga Point on Guadalcanal. Twelve enemy Zeros intercepted . . . 8 were shot down. One of our dive-bombers was forced down and 5 of our fighters failed to return. The dive-bombers pressed home the attack and seriously damaged 2 of the enemy destroyers . . . .

"During the evening a force of dive-bombers with Wildcat and Airacobra escort attacked an enemy cargo ship 37 miles northwest of Munda. Two direct hits and four near-hits were scored and the ship was left burning. Our Wildcats and Airacobras drove off enemy Zeros which attempted to intercept and shot down 7 of them. One U. S. fighter failed to return."

The kills that afternoon were the last spree for Foss, Marontate, Loesch, Haberman, Freeman, and Presley, the high-scorers of the Flying Circus flight of VMF 121. Davis' squadron total in 63 days of combat reached 132 planes shot down against a loss of 14 Marines. Foss, with 3 Zeros downed on the 15th, set a new American record of 26 planes destroyed in aerial combat, for which he received the Medal of Honor.

Lieutenant Eugene Marontate, second highest VMF 121 scorer with 13 kills, failed to return from the air battle of the 15th. It was presumed he crashed into a Jap plane.

The toll of the American death trap around Guadalcanal showed considerably on the seemingly endless reserves of the Japanese toward the end of January. There was little enemy activity during the day. Instead, now that their bases on New Georgia and Bougainville were in better condition, Japanese night air actions increased, mainly as a cover for the wholesale evacuation of the remaining Japanese troops. Under the cover of darkness and foul weather, enemy fast destroyer transports ran a shuttle into the Cape Esperance and took out many thousands of troops and naval forces.

Mulcahy's planes made several successful contacts with the destroyer and barge evacuation traffic, but on too small a scale to stop it.

Then on February 9, 1943, six months and two days after the landing at Gaudalcanal, organized resistance was declared at an end. Radio Tokyo, with its usual whimsy, said flatly that their Imperial Army had been "transferred because its mission had been fulfilled."

Hardly true of the beaten Japanese, the "mission fulfilled" phrase was applicable to the living and dead of the Marine Air Arm, who with their Army, Navy, and New Zealand allies, had established the aerial beachhead over Guadalcanal and held it.

The Marine fighter and bomber squadrons and their support echelons exacted a savage toll of things Japanese during the half-year of battle for Guadalcanal. Japanese commanders at Rabaul admitted losing "about 1,000 planes" during the period, and by far the largest share of them had fallen to the Marine fighter squadrons. Small bomber squadrons of the Air Arm accounted for more than 400 Japanese ships of all types sunk or damaged.

The Cactus Shivaree had been weird and costly, but not unworth the price, for as it ended, so did the defensive phase of the Solomons war for the Allies.

☆ **5** ☆

SPEARHEAD IN THE SOLOMONS

WITH the end of the Cactus shivaree, the Marine Air Arm was given a new and different role, that of spearheading the Allied drive up the island chain. Its squadrons were to carry a major load in the year-long offensive and its ground echelons were to play a dominant role in the campaigns which finally put an end to any semblance of Japanese air strength over the Solomons.

There was little delay in the triphibious drive through the Solomons. Before the Guadalcanal campaign closed, the offensive to the northwest had begun. The enemy, by plan, was holing up along the Munda–Kolombangara front in the New Georgia group an intensifying airbase development back up the line to Rabaul. The purpose of the new Allied drive was to keep the Japanese back-pedaling and on the defensive.

The first major invasion objective was the airbase at Munda. Backing its defense were installations at Vila on Kolombangara; airfields at Ballale, Kahili, Kieta, Kara, and Buka; and seaplane bases in the Shortlands, Rekata Bay, and Soraken. This network of Japanese air defenses was fed by five fields in the Rabaul area and provided the air umbrella for nearly 50,000 enemy troops still in the islands.

Diamond tip on the Marine air spearhead was a new and excellent weapon—the Chance-Vought Corsair, or F4U. The first plane to better the Zero's performance in Pacific combat, it looked like a blue ball bat with inverted gull wings. The Corsair was originally built for use aboard Navy carriers, but was thought to be unsuitable for flat-top duty. Turned over to the Marines for land-based use, the F4U proved to be the major nemesis for any type of fighter plane the enemy produced. In the hands of Marines, it became the most versatile fighter craft in the naval service, doing five-way duty as a land-based fighter, a carrier-based fighter, a fighter-bomber both on land and off carriers, and a night fighter. Soon known to the enemy ground and air forces as "The Whistling Death" for the clean, sharp sound it made in its dives, the Corsair became a Pacific legend of offense.

A Marine Corsair squadron (VMF 124) saw combat for the first time on February 13 when its planes escorted B-24 bombers to attack shipping in the southern Bougainville area. Corsairs continued to escort the high-level bombers to Bougainville until ineffective bombing and high plane losses forced the B-24's to operate at night. But it was not until the summer months that the F4U generally replaced the F4F as the Marine fighter plane.

As the air campaign picked up in tempo, the island marathon was on again. Army and Marine troops invaded the Russell Islands, 30 miles northwest of Guadalcanal, on February 20. Covered by Marine fighter patrols and other Henderson-based elements, the landing met no opposition. The infantry consolidated positions on Banika and Pavuuvu.

Advance elements of Marine Air Group 21 landed at Banika on March 13 and began development of an airbase with the aid of the Seabees. The base eventually had so many Stateside comforts, including a free hamburger stand and steam laundry, that it was known as "Boomtown." Under the command of Colonel Raymond E. Hopper, MAG 21 readied a 2,000-foot coral airstrip on which the first emergency landing was made May 7. By early June, two Marine Corsair units were in operation off Banika.

March passed as the quietest period of the Solomons' air war as the enemy shifted emphasis again to the New Guinea theater. Only eight enemy planes were downed in the month with no losses in air combat to Allied fighters. Meanwhile, Strike Command took quick advantage of the absence of enemy fighter patrols to intensify its milk-run shuttles and expand its range of operations.

Munda was the prime target. In four months it was raided over a hundred times, with more to come. Of the price and effectiveness of these raids, an enemy gunnery officer at Munda, Lieutenant Commander S. Yunoki, IJN, later said:

"The dive-bombers and torpedo bombers made very serious attacks. Food and ammunition dumps were constantly destroyed. Runways were badly damaged by raids, but were usually fixed again within 48 hours."

Though lack of larger bombs and the planes to carry them made it impossible for Marine and Navy airmen to annihilate Munda and the other enemy airfields, the persistence of their attacks and their unusually high degree of accuracy, made the bombing efforts a temporary but continuing success.

Vila Field on Kolombangara received its share of the daily heckling including the 1,000-pound "daisy cutter" bombs. These exploded just above the ground and scythed a large area around with small, sharp fragments. The "daisy cutter" was so effective that Radio Tokyo protested vehemently against this "inhuman" weapon and made dire and mysterious threats of retaliation.

In a move to help choke off the enemy's supply and water support traffic, 42 Marine TBF's saturated the waters around southern Bougainville with shipping mines. This ticklish mission on the night of March 20 was the first of its kind in the South Pacific.

The Japanese, who had been heavily reinforcing their major bases at Rabaul and Kavieng, on New Ireland, briefly reopened the battle for control of the air. They sent down two raids against the new American positions in the Russells on April 1, losing 20 planes to 6 for the Allies.

Goaded by the easy Allied air successes and the Navy's cruiser-destroyer task force raids, the enemy struck back vehemently on April 7. Early that afternoon, ComAirSols got word from the Coastwatchers that a giant raid had formed up over Bougainville and was closing on Guadalcanal. Sixty assorted planes were scrambled to meet the incoming armada of 160 Zeros and Aichi dive-bombers. Among the interceptors was a four-plane division of Wildcats led by 22-year-old James 'Zeke' Swett, a first lieutenant who had yet to see an enemy plane in combat.

At 1530, the Japanese raid swept through the thin cloud cover over

Cape Esperance and headed for the shipping concentration in Sealark Channel. Contact was immediate. A dogfight fanned across the sky as the Aichi dive-bombers broke out of the formation, in their usual tight patterns, and headed for the ships.

Swett's division peeled off at 15,000 feet and closed on the rear of the Aichis. Less than 15 minutes later, Swett had catapulted himself into a world's combat record and won the Medal of Honor by destroying seven bombers and a possible eighth.

Swett told the story of his killing spree with the same dispatch that he went through it:

"I got on the tail of the first one and gave it a squirt. He jettisoned his bombs and burst into full flame.

"I skidded and mushed in behind No. 2 while my tracers laced him. He smoked, burned, and went down.

"I had trouble getting the third one boresighted. Then I relaxed and the plane flew itself into the saddle. As the Aichi nosed over in his bomb run, my first burst smoked him. When he pulled out, I was still on his tail. A few more bursts and he exploded. Just as I pulled away, one of our 40mm, AA gun crews on Tulagi drew a bead and wrecked one of my port guns. They almost blew it out of my wing." •

Swett, ducking over Florida Island to check his damage, spotted five more bombers lumbering north toward the protection of a big cloud area, and away from the dogfight over the Channel.

He swung into position below and behind the Aichis which were strung out Indian file, three-quarters of a mile apart. Then he gunned the F4F and began his fish-tailing run up the string.

He hit the first plane before its rear-gunner saw him. As tracers flamed its gas tanks, the bomber nosed over gently and hit the water afire.

Crossing over on Victim No. 5, the Marine squeezed out two quick bursts that went home. The Jap plane gushed smoke, burst into flames, and crashed. Pouring on the power, he closed the next gap, but was too eager. He got so close that the Aichi's slipstream jolted his aim. But he dropped back, fired, and the bomber followed its predecessors' pattern of oblivion.

The seventh kill was the easiest of the day. A quick flurry of tracers from the side and the Jap burned like wildfire and sputtered out in the sea. Swett, with his guns still firing went for the last of the five planes.

This time there was no surprise advantage. As he closed, the Jap rear-gunner laced lead right into Swett's face. Machine-gun slugs and tracers streamed through the greenhouse in front of him, shattering its glass in his face. Blood spurted from a deep gash in his nose. In the confusion, Swett failed to push the trigger button and overshot his target.

With blood smearing his vision and oil streaming from the Wildcat's engine, Swett jockeyed the plane back into position. With his first burst of fire, the enemy rear-gunner fell over his guns. Swett held the trigger down until the last of its ammunition hammered into the dive-bomber. Pluming heavy black smoke, it disappeared into the clouds.

Swett, afraid of being caught alone by Zeros, turned his battered plane back toward Tulagi. Over the harbor, his engine conked and he moved out to sea for a water landing. As he passed low over Tanambogo, a battery of our .50-caliber AA guns tried frantically to finish off what the enemy rear-gunner had started. Tracers ribboned by the plane for many seconds, but did no further damage.

Swett crash-landed on the water, but was trapped in the sinking plane as his parachute straps caught and held. Only after the F4F passed the 15-foot mark on the way to the bottom, was he able to wrench free and rise to the surface. Dazed from the shock and with blood running freely over his face, Swett managed to inflate his life raft and climb into it. Then, as if in final insult, a small picket boat pulled in close to the raft with a machine gun and rifles trained on its occupant.

"Are you American?" the crew shouted nervously.

He could only answer, "You're goddam right I am!"

"Oh, one of them Marines," the coxswain said. "OK, pick him up."

That afternoon, 38 enemy planes were destroyed with a loss of only one of our pilots. In addition to Swett's 7, the Marines accounted for 21.

Through the balance of April and May, the air forays were few and indecisive as both sides built up their reserves against future events. These slightly subdued periods were not, however, without their bits of drama, some of which seemed beyond even the fictions of war or Hollywood.

One of these was the constant parade of aerial castaways who, having failed to return from missions, were listed as MIA (missing in action) and at least tentatively committed to the realm of the departed. During the early months on Guadalcanal, a goodly number of airmen like Leslie, DeBlanc, Meents, Hurst, Lundin, Smith, Carl, and Amerine went down at sea or in the jungle behind enemy lines and worked their way back to Henderson in a matter of hours or days. Some had harrowing experiences, like Amerine, who had to crush a skull and rob his victim on the way back.

The Coastwatchers and their skillfully organized network of friendly natives brought scores of others back right under the noses of enemy patrols. Still more returned in planes flown by men like Major Michael Sampas, who became so adroit in rescue operations that he was commended for saving the lives of 39 pilots, 61 aircrewmen, and over 200 others in less than three months.

William Coffeen, a flying Marine staff sergeant, stepped out of a Navy "Dumbo" patrol plane at Guadalcanal one afternoon after being missing in action for 72 days. Bearded like a prophet, with a parakeet perched on his bony shoulder, Coffeen recounted his Crusoe-like tale to Staff Sergeant Harry S. Bolser:

"Our Corsairs were escorting some torpedo bombers on a mission up the Slot. Between Kolombangara and Choiseul, my engine started smoking. I lost altitude rapidly, so I bailed out and hit the water in a few seconds. I jerked the toggle on my Mae West, but it had been punctured. My life raft inflated, but the paddle was missing.

"Thirty minutes later a storm broke. High waves flipped my raft around like a toothpick until it overturned. Into the water went my medical supplies and emergency rations. All I had left were my clothes, a hunting knife, and a pistol.

"At dusk, as I paddled with my hands, sharks swished around the raft. That night I slept sitting up. Near sundown on the second day,

I reached the shore of a small island. I was thirsty, hungry, and exhausted. I ate two coconuts and drank their juice. That night I curled up in the raft in a coconut grove and tried to sleep, but the hordes of mosquitoes made it impossible.

"On the fifth day, I shoved off for a larger island I could see in the distance and made it at dusk. Next morning, I set out for another island. It took me all day to get there, but it was the same story—no food, no life, no fresh water. I had diarrhea and my left arm and right foot were infected.

"Next morning my arm was swollen twice its normal size. I cut open the source of infection and bathed it in salt water. I tried drinking coconut milk that morning, but couldn't get it down my throat. I decided to move on again.

"I paddled for a day and a half to a house up the coast. Its only occupant was a hen which I couldn't catch. I did get some eggs and oranges which kept me going for the next six days, when I set out for another island. There I found fresh water, my first in 27 days. That night I was barely able to move, but next morning I paddled out again.

"Near dusk on the fourth day at sea, when I had barely enough strength to move my arms, a heavy storm blew up. As it carried me out to sea, I remember screaming. Then I passed out.

"When I came to, I was in the arms of a husky native. He said the big wind had blown me ashore.

"You Merican or Jap?" he inquired.

"You Merican! Ah, you good," he smiled.

"The date was May 15. The native wouldn't believe I had been lost for 32 days. He said no white man could live that long on the sea and in the jungle. He wasn't far from right.

"Three days later, I was able to walk and went by canoe to the native village where they fed me and bathed the ulcers on my body. I got malaria, but they gave me quinine and the attack passed in five days. I stayed with the natives for 40 days until a Dumbo rescue plane picked me up."

Sergeant William Henze, a rear-gunner in an SBD, displayed the same fortitude as Coffeen, but he was not as fortunate.

When Henze's pilot was killed by AA fire during a dive on a Munda target, Henze inserted the rear control stick as the SBD darted crazily about the sky. He managed to level the plane off and radio for help. Major Ray Vroome swung his Corsair close to the dive-bomber and gave instructions to Henze, who had never flown a plane.

Another pilot joined up on the Corsair and the SBD and the three planes followed island landmarks back toward Guadalcanal. Near the Russell Islands, the SBD ran low on gas and Henze had no means of switching tanks from the rear seat. Henze elected to jump and Vroome's radio went dead just as Henze put the plane into a steep dive rather than a climb. As the gunner jumped, one of his legs hit the SBD's stabilizer and was amputated below the knee.

Henze applied pressure to the main artery until he hit the water where he floated face down, unconscious. He was given up for dead, but the salt water had stopped the flow of blood until natives picked him up and administered first aid. Henze was flown by PBY to the hospital at Tulagi two days later. He recovered but returned to the States to die of malaria.

Awarded the Air Medal posthumously, Henze, through his own unfortunate experience, helped save the lives of many gunners. A program was instituted immediately to give adequate rear-seat flying time to dive-bomber aircrewmen.

Rat Race Over No Man's Land

The aerial sparring of April and May developed gradually into a battle of annihilation as the actual drive on Munda began. Time and new arrivals slowly tipped the balance to Allied favor as the Japanese Air Force lost heavily in each sortie. [*Major General Ralph Johnson Mitchell, a balding, hawk-faced veteran of two decades in the Air Arm, traded commands with General Geiger on April 21. Mitchell, who was to spend 27 energetic months in the forward areas of the Pacific, took over the First Wing. Geiger returned to Washington to become Director of Marine Aviation again. Brigadier General Field Harris, a somber Southerner, as commander of the For-*

ward Echelon of the First Wing, was tactically in command of Marine elements in the Munda drive. Harris, who was awarded the equivalent of four Legions of Merit for his Pacific combat leadership, was also Chief of Staff for ComAirSols during the period.]

Twenty Zeros appeared near New Georgia on May 13 after their installations at Munda and Kolombangara had been shelled during the night. A large fighter screen from Henderson intercepted and batted down 16 of them. Fifteen of the kills were by pilots of VMF 124 and 112, the Wolf Pack squadron. Captain Archie Donahue was credited with four kills. Three were shot down by tobacco-chewing Kenneth A. Walsh, once a flying corporal and now a first lieutenant who became one of the high-scorers of the mid-Solomons' battle.

In the neutralization raids on northern bases, Marine fighters of VMF 112 and 124 and Navy bombers caught a destroyer, a corvette, and cargo ship near Buin, on June 5. They burned the corvette and the AK and were given a probable on the destroyer. The fighter umbrella beat off an interception, shooting down 15 planes and losing 5. Of the kills, Lieutenant Walsh was credited with 2 Zeros.

A larger engagement near the Russells on June 7 resulted in the loss of 23 Zeros and 4 Allied pilots, and in two bizarre incidents.

After going to the rescue of a New Zealand P-40, Lieutenant Sam Logan was forced to bail out of his plane at 18,000 feet. While Logan descended in his chute, one Jap Zero made repeated firing runs on him. These failing, the enemy pilot made a screaming pass at Logan, trying to butcher him with the propeller. In spite of the Marine's frantic efforts, the Jap's propellor severed part of his right foot. Before the Zero could do any more aerial surgery, it was driven off by an Allied plane.

In spite of his injury, and while still dropping, Logan applied a tourniquet to his foot, injected morphine and swallowed sulfa tablets. He was rescued at sea.

The experience that afternoon of Lieutenant Gilbert Percy made headlines in Stateside newspapers which read:

MARINE FIGHTER PILOT SURVIVES IN MIRACLE JUMP:
LEAPS 3,000 FEET AND LIVES AFTER CHUTE FAILS

In the middle of the dogfight, Percy had five Zeros shooting at him from behind. He managed to get one before the others blasted off his wingtip and aileron and gutted his plane's gas, oil, and hydraulic systems.

Percy went over the side at 3,000 feet. He jerked the ripcord, but the parachute failed to open. When he stopped pinwheeling through the air, Percy stiffened out, arms rigidly at his sides and feet together. Knocked out by the impact when he hit the water, he came to, well under the surface. Inflating his Mae West, Percy bobbed to the surface only to find he had no use of his legs and that he was barely able to stay conscious.

Anxious to get medical aid in a hurry, Percy used his only means of locomotion and back-stroked toward an island a mile distant. Seven hours later he made its off-shore reef and fainted. At dawn, he floated to the beach and pawed his way up the sand. Three natives reached him by canoe, but were unable to move him because Percy couldn't stand the pain. So one stood guard over him until a motor launch with two doctors appeared. Lieutenant Percy spent a year in the hospital recovering from a broken pelvis, two broken ankles, and serious internal injuries.

Through June the tempo quickened as both air fleets lashed out in a rising frenzy.

As the fighter scores went up, the bombing pace increased. Marine SBD and TBF squadrons aided by those of the Navy and Army high-level bombers stepped up their raids to neutralize the enemy airbase chain up to Bougainville.

For the bombers, it was a deadly but monotonous business. And as they came back down the Slot from these shuttle runs, the crews bellowed out their ire in a ditty labeled "On the Road to Munda Bay" (to the tune of "On the Road to Mandalay"):

> Verse 1
> Take me somewhere east of Ewa
> Where the best ain't like the worst,
> Where there ain't no Doug MacArthur,

And a man can drown his thirst;
Where the Army gets the medals
And the Navy gets the queens,
But the boys that get the rookin'
Are United States Marines.

Chorus
Hit the road to Gizo Bay,
Where the Jap fleet spends the day.
You can hear the duds a'clunkin
From Rabaul to Lunga Bay.
Pack your load up to Rekata,
Where the float-plane Zeros play,
And the bombs come down like thunder
On the natives cross the way.

Verse 2
In the air to old Lambeti,
Losing Corsairs all the way,
You can hear the pilots cussin',
You can hear the gunners pray.
On the road to Munda Bay,
Where the Haps and Tonys play,
And the flak comes up like thunder
Out of Vila cross the Bay.

At night they sang it again at "Hotel de Gink" or in their fox-holes while Jap bombers raided Henderson by the bright of the moon.

The New Georgia invasion schedule called for simultaneous landings at Rendova Island, across Blanche Channel from Munda, and at Viru Harbor, Wickham Anchorage, and Onaivisi. Marine Raiders landed secretly at Segi Point on Southern New Georgia June 21 to move in on Viru from the rear. [The Raider landing there met no opposition and work was begun at Segi on an interim airfield. VMF 214 began operating off Segi field on July 24 but after the opening of Munda, Segi was not used extensively by Marine or Navy planes.]

Early on the morning of June 30, the main landing was accomplished at Rendova without major incident by the 43rd Army Division, accompanied by the staff of the Second Marine Air Wing. [*Commanded by Major General Mulcahy, the Second Wing staff comprised the major portion of ComAirNewGeorgia during the invasion phase of the campaign.*] Elements of the Marine Raider battalions and the Army units comprising the Northern Landing Force hit their beaches under air and fleet cover.

Two Japanese air attempts to reach the Rendova transport area were brushed off by the fighter cover. Then, in midmorning, as the invasion fleet pulled out of Blanche Channel, the Allied air umbrella of 170 fighters pounced on Japanese torpedo planes attacking the transports. That interception touched off an epic air battle which ended with 100 enemy planes destroyed of the 130 which had appeared.

The troops moving against Munda took five weeks to capture the field while the air battles raged overhead. The Japanese defenders, well intrenched and skilled in jungle warfare and the art of night infiltration, took heavy casualties for every yard of ground they gave. The fighting on the land and in the air resembled the savagery of the French and Indian wars.

Even the jungle-wise Raider units of the Northern Landing Force failed to meet with their usual success. They went ashore at Rice Anchorage on northern New Georgia on July 5 to advance on the Bairoko–Enogai area and prevent reinforcement or retreat of the Munda garrison.

Strong air support was unable to destroy the heavy enemy positions at Bairoko, and the Raiders were forced to retreat after driving a patrol into the village. They received further air support in their withdrawal and were dropped rations and medical supplies by SCAT transport planes during the action.

Several days previous to their drops at Bairoko, SCAT planes made their first supply drops to troops in the jungle south of Munda to pioneer air delivery service in the South Pacific.

An account of that first supply drop July 19 was given by an observer on the mission:

"We took off from Henderson in Douglas R4D's. Knowing we would be without fighter protection until near the target area, the three-plane section flew about 10 feet off the water, rising only to clear the dozens of small islands on our course. We were so low that the passage of the planes left three white wakes in the water behind us, like the paths of motor boats.

"Near the target area, eight new Zealand P-40's appeared over the Sky Train, scissoring back and forth as we closed in.

"Within a mile of the drop area, our plane pulled up and the crew could have picked coconuts as it moved inland, dead on the tail of the lead plane, flown by Lieutenant Colonel Harry Van Liew.

"As Van Liew's transport passed over the target, a few hundred yards behind the front lines, 14 black bursts of heavy AA fire exploded off his left wingtip but did no evident damage. Then our Douglas bounced like some giant's hand was trying to shake it apart. It was more flak necklacing us, without effect.

"Our plane made six runs over the dense jungle of the drop area. Each pass took us over enemy lines and within spitting distance of chopped-up Munda field, where a big gun was pumping AA at the formation.

"Because of our low altitude, the Jap ground troops had a rare target practice. Even over the sound of motors we could hear the crack and chatter of small arms banging away at us. One escort pilot suddenly roared a curse over the radio as the tail of his plane was hit by AA. He politely excused himself, rolled off, and strafed the gun position.

"From the navigator's blister, you could see colored chutes and cargo containers pop out of the third plane, open for an instant, and hit the trees.

"As we came in for our last run, the entire drop area was littered with colored parachutes. They had all gone right into the infantry's lap. We heard later that not one pound of the nine tons of cargo fell into Jap hands." [During late July and early August, the Marine transport planes successfully dropped 100,000 pounds of food, am-

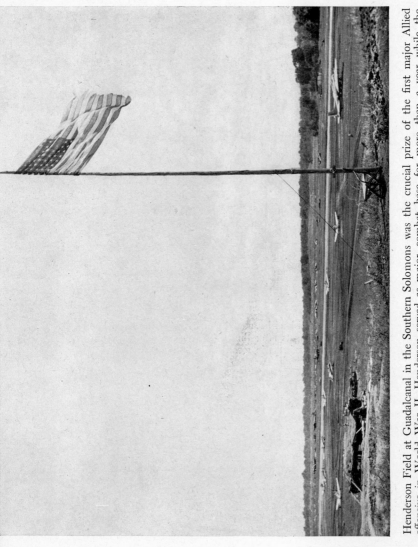

Henderson Field at Guadalcanal in the Southern Solomons was the crucial prize of the first major Allied offensive in World War II. Henderson served as major combat base for more than a year while the Marine aerial spearhead battled the cream of the Japanese air force for control of the air.

Dauntless Divebombers of a Marine squadron drone up the Slot in the Central Solomons enroute to their morning mauling of Vila airfield on Kolombangara.

Munda Field on New Georgia island became a jump-off point for Allied bombing of Northern Solomon's targets after the Seabees had rennovated its strip and taxiways in record time.

Battle casualties from Bougainville wait to be loaded aboard a SCAT transport at Barakoma Field on Vella Lavella for a flight to base hospitals.

ijian jungle troops received their food, mmunition and medical supplies by SCAT r cagro drops during their weeks of uerilla warfare deep in Japanese territory n the island of Bougainville.

Lieut. Col. John L. Smith

Captain Kenneth A. Walsh

Lieut. Col. Gregory Boyington

Major Robert E. Galer

Captain Richard E. Fleming

Captain James E. Swett

Lieut. Robert M. Hanson

Major Joseph J. Foss

Lieut. Col. Harold W. Bauer

Captain Henry T. Elrod

Solomon's Skytrains fly a tight formation enroute to Green Island with loads of high priority cargo in their famed role as SCAT, the aerial lifeline of the South Pacific combat forces.

Marine Mitchell Bombers, with bomb bay doors still open, leave the target area over volcanos near Rabaul after an aerial strangulation mission. Black puffs of Japanese antiaircraft fire burst harmlessly around them.

Mitsubishi Zeke Fighter

Val Divebomber

Betty Medium Bomber

munition, and medical supplies to ground troops in New Georgia.]

Enemy planes continued to attack the New Georgia beachheads. Out of 70 bombers and fighters sent down on July 15, the enemy lost 45. Eight VMF 122 planes made the first interception and shot down 14 planes in as many minutes. Two more divisions of Corsairs jumped the survivors and got 16 planes.

The main source of these counterattacks was the enemy field at Kahili. Their bases at Munda, Vila, and Ballale were inoperable due to bombings. Three heavy missions were directed against Kahili during the early morning of July 17. Escorting Corsairs destroyed 38 enemy interceptors. The bombers sank a light cruiser, two destroyers, two cargo ships, a patrol craft, and a tanker.

In the final drive on Munda airfield, the small bombers blistered enemy strong points, wiping out pillboxes, supply dumps, bivouac areas, and machine-gun nests. Bairoko, too, received its share of attention from the SBT's and TBF's. On July 21, 132 planes pounded that area in six separate attacks.

The ground campaign ended formally on August 5, when Marine tanks and flame throwers spearheaded the Army infantry capture of Munda airfield. The enemy's bitter resistance had cost him heavily— 358 planes, several thousand ground troops, and 40 ships sunk or damaged. [Marine squadrons were credited with a startling ratio— as high as 25 Jap planes destroyed in the air for each Marine loss.]

Unfortunately, the capture of the airfield did not mean the elimination of all the forces defending it. More than 3,000 Japanese troops escaped. Nor did the seizure of the field end enemy resistance in the air.

At its capture, Munda airfield looked like a slash of white coral in a Doré drawing of hell. It lay like a dead thing, between the shore of Blanche Channel and the torn, coffee-colored hills of Bibilo and Kokengolo. The Seabees performed their usual wonders despite Jap snipers and bombers, and in ten days the field was ready for operations of a sort.

Two Marine squadrons came in first. They began operating on August 14 under conditions which they labeled "slightly informal."

The lack of adequate ground crews, fuel, spare parts, and oxygen, the rugged condition of the field, plus a lack of night-fighter defense put their first month of operations in the category of the equally primitive conditions at Henderson Field just a year before.

The enemy's 11th Air Fleet and its seemingly inexhaustible complement of skilled pilots and planes were now showing signs of wear. The Corsair had proved a match for the Zero-type fighters, and so did its new, rugged Navy counterpart, the Hellcat (F6F), then making its initial appearance in the Solomons. But the air defense of Munda still was proving a desperate and costly business. The end was not in sight and Allied pilot and plane reserves were running thin.

Early Allied offensive plans had envisioned the Solomons campaign as a war for airfields which might necessitate the eradication of the enemy from each of his many island bases, one at a time. This tedious process was discarded with the taking of Munda and dropping of plans for a large-scale invasion of Kolombangara. Island-hopping was the new technique which was to prove that while the Japanese island bases were "unsinkable carriers," they couldn't maneuver.

The next step in the campaign to choke off enemy airpower at Kahili, its vital source in the Solomons, was the invasion of Vella Lavella. This island lay across Vella Gulf from Kolombangara and its 10,000 defenders. Vella Lavella, in contrast, had negligible defenses.

It was invaded on August 15 by an Army combat team and a Marine defense battalion. Naval forces and air cover watered down possible strong points of interference. The only immediate opposition to the landing came via the air.

This new penetration closer to Kahili brought violent reaction from the Japanese air force, and there ensued a series of milling air battles as fighters from Munda defended that base, the beachhead at Vella Lavella, and closed on Kahili itself.

It was during this period and the early phases at Munda that Marine fighter squadrons piled up kill-scores reminiscent of the pace set by Smith, Carl, Galer, Bauer, and Foss over Henderson Field.

For example, the Munda spree netted the Hellhawk squadron

(VMF 213) a total of 7 aces and 102 planes with a loss of only 8 pilots. On its roster were three of the ranking fighter pilots of the South Pacific: Lieutenant Wilbur 'Gus' Thomas, with 16½ kills; Lieutenant Edward O. Shaw, with 13; and Captain James N. Cupp, with 12 victories.

Ranking ace for the moment was Ken Walsh, who fought precisely as would be expected of a Brooklyn-born Irishman. With 10 years in the Corps and 2,000 flying hours in his log book, Walsh had a penchant for tackling any odds. He had 3 planes riddled under him, but shot down 20 before he left the Solomons.

His citation, read at the White House when he received the Medal of Honor, was an indication of his expert ability:

"For extraordinary heroism and intrepidity above · and beyond the call of duty as a pilot in VMF 124 . . . determined to thwart the enemy's attempt to bomb Allied ground forces and shipping at Vella on August 15, 1943, First Lieutenant Walsh repeatedly dived his plane into an enemy formation outnumbering his own division 6 to 1 and, although his plane was hit numerous times, shot down two Japanese dive-bombers and one fighter. After developing engine trouble on August 30, during a vital escort mission . . . Walsh landed his mechanically disabled plane at Munda, replaced it with another, and proceeded to rejoin his flight over Kahili. Separated from his group when he encountered approximately 50 Japanese Zeros, he unhesitatingly attacked . . . and destroyed four hostile fighters before cannon fire forced him to make a deadstick landing off Vella Lavella where he was picked up . . ."

As Walsh had found, late August provided ample excitement for the fighter pilots, both on defense and offense. Captain William Crowe and Lieutenant Thomas Mutz were separated from their Vella patrol and climbed to meet an oncoming Jap raid of 130 twin-engine Bettys and fighters. They jumped the back of this armada and rode it down to its target at Vella Lavella. Fighting through a screen of friendly flak and enemy tracers, Crowe and Mutz downed four planes between them before pancaking their riddled Corsairs at Munda.

Out of a black storm front that hung over Kahili on the afternoon of August 26, plummeted a lone Marine fighter plane, upside down. Lieutenant Alvin Jensen flipped it over as he went in on the field. His wingmen had been lost in the swirling thunderhead.

Jensen leveled off below the treetops and roared down the mile-long strip weaving violently, his tracers biting into the packed planes and startled gun crews. In ten seconds, aerial photos later showed, Jensen destroyed 12 Mitsubishi bombers, 8 fighters, and 4 dive-bombers. He was awarded the Navy Cross for his lone mission.

At Munda, muscle was being built into the air force as squadron after squadron of bombers, fighters, transports, and patrol planes moved into the revetments and hardstands even before the Seabees had time to complete them.

Bomber take-offs at Munda made the air control officers wince. Planes couldn't get away singly; there wasn't time. They pelted down the field in tandem with as many as nine planes in motion at once. Some were bound for air-support missions at Bairoko or Vella La-vella. Others pounded Kolombangara and Choiseul. But in the main they were bound for sprawling Bougainville and its airfields. Day after day, General Moore [Brigadier General James T. Moore of the First Wing relieved General Mulcahy as ComAirNewGeorgia] passed the order: hit Kahili, hit Ballale, hit Faisi, hit Kieta, hit Kara, hit Bonis, hit Buka—hit them singly, hit them together, hit them day after day, and never mind the weather.

But the enemy did not sell Kahili cheaply. It was their key airbase in the Solomons. Planes, mostly fighters, were jammed along its length. From its flanks and tiny, near-by Ballale island spouted the heaviest antiaircraft fire in the Solomons.

Kahili had all the resilience of a sponge rubber wall. Each time the raids came north, a batch of Kahili fighters were shot down. The next day, its supporting fields fed in a new swarm of planes which would add to the growing Allied losses before they too were shot down and replaced.

Since the early raids in February, Kahili had been regarded as the place where the bold, not the old, pilots visited. Because of Kahili, by early September the air war for control of the Solomons was still in a costly, indecisive stage that had all the markings of a stand-off.

Then there appeared the man who was to be the scourge of the Japanese Air Force in its latterly days in the South Pacific. He and his squadron had the answer to Kahili. It was a new tactic in the theater—pure aggression in the Marine frontal-assault sense. The tactic: the fighter sweep. The man: Major Gregory Boyington, a rugged, boisterous veteran of General Chennault's Flying Tigers in China and Burma.

At 31, Boyington looked and fought like a battle-wise bulldog. He had left the Marine Corps to join the Flying Tigers. Flying the shark-nosed P-40's, he shot down six planes, then resigned to rejoin the corps when America declared war. His first tour with VMF 121 in the Solomons had been a washout. He didn't see an enemy plane.

In August, when Marine air resources were running low, Boyington, at his own loud insistence, was given a collection of pool pilots —some of them remnants of other units, but mainly green replacements—to form into a squadron. The normal training period for this exacting business was from six months to a year. Boyington, whose off-hour antics made many a general and colonel boil, did it in six weeks.

Though the other Marine fighter squadrons were holding their own, Boyington and his Black Sheep [Variously called "Pappy and his Clowns," or "Boyington's Bastards," the squadron finally compromised on calling themselves "The Black Sheep" though their insignia retained the black bar of bastardy across its shield] hit the combat area with the tumult of a small hurricane.

On his first mission, Boyington shot down 5 planes while escorting bombers to Ballale. The Black Sheep followed his lead and in one month destroyed 57 enemy planes in combat, with 2 losses of their own for a better than 25-1 average. In that time, their clowning on the deck and cunning in the air captured the imagination of the Air Arm from Espiritu up to Munda, and Boyington was on his way to becoming a living legend.

At night, his pilots lay in their sacks or smacked at the fox-hole mosquitoes while they sang their own version of the Yale "Whiffenpoof Song":

To the one-arm joint at Munda,
To the foxholes where we dwelt,
To the predawn take-offs that we love so well,
Sing the Black Sheep all assembled,
With their canteens raised on high,
And the magic of their singing casts a spell.
Yes, the magic of their singing,
And the songs we love so well,
Old Man Reilly, Mrs. Murphy and the rest,
We shall serenade our Gregory
While life and voice shall last . . .
Then we'll pass and be forgotten like the rest.

At 0400, one morning, Boyington was routed out of his bunk by an Operations officer wanting four volunteers to strafe Kahili. The squadron's tour was officially over, but Boyington and three wingmen went on the mission. He lost the other planes in a storm front and went after Kahili alone. He was too wide on his first pass and, in the half-light, circled and came in again at 30 feet. This time he blew up three bombers. Pulling out, he swung his Corsair over near-by Tonolei Harbor, found a destroyer, and strafed it thoroughly. Finding he still had ammunition left, he hunted down the coast of Choiseul until he found an enemy troop barge and sank it.

When he returned to Munda, Boyington was certain that the answer to Kahili was the fighter sweep. It would be a costly gamble, one which called for incessant patrols over Kahili, fighting one battle after another until the Japanese decided that their losses were too great to continue an inelastic defense. If the enemy refused to give way, the Allied fighter squadrons might be so depleted that it would be months before they could again build up to full offensive strength.

Boyington and five of his Black Sheep went after Kahili several days later when their bombers failed to rendezvous because of weather. Fifty Zeros rose to meet them, and in the dogfight, Boyington shot down three in thirty seconds.

That day, he received permission to start the fighter sweeps. Twelve of the squadron went up to try their luck, but the canny Japanese refused to take off. Boyington and his wingmen circled

Kahili for 20 minutes yelling ancestral imprecations and challenges over their radios. Twenty enemy fighters took the bait and climbed up. The Corsairs shot down 12 without loss.

On another sweep, they prodded the enemy into a fury with their radioed insults and 50 Zeros were suckered into combat. VMF 221 shot down 16 while the Black Sheep got 12. Boyington led a few more sweeps. His personal score rose to 20 planes, 6 of which dated back to China and the AVG. In late October, the Black Sheep squadron went south for a rest. Behind them were Kahili and enemy air power in the Solomons. Both had their backs broken.

Where the fighters left off, the day and night bombers took over and ground Kahili and its satellite bases into coral dust as the date for the invasion of Bougainville neared.

The Munda and Barakoma planes averaged four bombing attacks a day against the Kahili network during the weeks prior to the invasion of Bougainville. These shuttle raids often mounted as many as 100 planes in an attack.

These strikes were so commonplace to the veteran SBD and TBF squadrons that they grew bored in spite of the daily quota of incidents and opposition inherent in the missions.

Throughout October, mopping-up and expansion were at a fever pitch in the Central Solomons. New Zealand troops, which had taken over from the Army, concluded their ground actions at Vella Lavella on October 9. The enemy evacuated 400 of the surviving defenders by night to save them from a last-ditch trap.

Vila Field on Kolombangara was occupied without firing a shot on October 10. Again, enemy evacuation efforts were successful. This time more than 10,000 troops on Kolombangara were moved out by night barge traffic and destroyer-transports. In each instance, however the enemy suffered losses in night naval actions and from bombing and strafing.

Marine squadrons moved up from the burgeoning base at Munda. Two fighter units began operations on October 17 from Barakoma field on Vella Lavella's southeastern coast. MAG 14 took over the small airbase on Ondonga Island, a few miles up the New Georgia coast from Munda, which served Army, Navy, and New Zealand planes. Colonel William O. Brice was named Air Commander, Ondonga. [Brice had commanded the Navy and Marine Corps Air Center at Auckland, New Zealand, before taking over MAG 14.] The headquarters of ComAirSols moved from Guadalcanal to Munda on October 20 and Henderson Field became a rear base after 14 months of intensive operation.

Two more intermediate landings under heavy air cover closed the gap. New Zealand and Marine ground troops landed in the Treasury Island group on October 27. Personnel of a forward echelon of the First Wing, under Major B. V. Leary, landed with the assault forces to establish a radar station and a Fighter Command. No serious opposition was encountered and both Mono and Stirling Islands were occupied. Work was begun immediately on an airfield at Stirling.

The Second Marine Parachute Battalion landed in rubber boats at Voza on Choiseul Island in a large-scale diversionary raid the night following the Treasury landings. The parachutists met a large enemy force at Sangagi on October 30 and routed it, doing considerable damage under heavy Marine and Navy air cover. This threat created such a furor that jittery Radio Tokyo announced that 20,000 Marine had landed on Choiseul.

Then, as the final hours of October ticked off, the Allied war machine in the South Pacific rolled ponderously into a new invasion action.

They called it "Cherry Blossom."

☆ 6 ☆

THE BATTLE FOR RABAUL

SOON after dawn broke over the Northern Solomons on the morning of November 1, 1943, U. S. Marines invaded Bougainville—the last and biggest Japanese stronghold in the Solomon Islands.

"As the night mists cleared from the Empress Augusta Bay, the seaborne invasion force took form on the water below. For four hours before dawn, our Marine Ventura night fighter had patrolled over the task force without encountering enemy night bombers.

"Now the troop-packed transports were pointed in an arrow at Cape Torokina, on Bougainville's southwestern coast, and at the closely adjacent Purata Mission. Hovering around the line of transports at dawn was the naval force of cruisers and destroyers which started shelling the beachhead at 0601.

"When the mist cleared along the shoreline, this site of the second great Marine invasion in the Solomons looked very much like the first one at Guadalcanal. It had the usual coconut trees and a flat shoreline which extends inland for miles in plateau fashion. Back from the small white patch of beach, the terrain moved into jungle which seemed to congeal into a slimy green wave.

"Not a single Japanese plane appeared to challenge the landing during its vulnerable first daylight hour. During that time we had undisputed control of the air, with dozens of Navy and Marine Corsairs, Army P-39's, and New Zealand P-40's maintaining high, medium, and low cover over the shipping and ranging far out around the perimeter of the invasion area.

"At 0630, the lead transport bent the arrow formation and turned

left to parallel the beach. By this time the incessant naval barrage
lifted its line of fire and began shelling further inland. Finally, landing craft hovered close to the transports as Marines climbed into
them from cargo nets.

"A formation of Marine torpedo planes bombed the beachline.
Douglas dive-bombers followed. Immediately after, the first wave of
Lieutenant General Vandegrift's Marines hit the beach at Bougain-
ville."

So wrote a Marine correspondent covering the first phase of the
"Cherry Blossom" operation from the air.

During the early hours of the landing, brief but severe resistence
was encountered from the Japanese defending Purata and the Torokina area.

The enemy made halfhearted attempts to reach the invasion area
by air during the day, but were brushed off by Allied fighter cover
which shot down 25 planes. A light enemy naval task force of 12
ships closed on Empress Augusta Bay during the early morning of
D-plus-1. It was routed with a loss of 5 ships.

By November 2, the assault phase of the invasion was over and
immediate objectives had been taken. In the weeks that followed,
the campaign progressed with an amazing lack of opposition from the
sea and air. Marine fighter pilots had looked forward to the invasion
of Bougainville as an aerial smorgasbord which would fatten up their
kill scores. They expected far greater opposition there than the violent
reactions of the Japanese Air Force over Munda and Kahili.

The largest of the Solomons, Bougainville is only 255 air miles
from the bastion of Rabaul. There, on New Britain, the enemy had
600 fighters and bombers which might have disputed the invasion
at Torokina and assisted counteroffensives by the 50,000 Japanese
ground troops defending the island.

The Japanese land-based Air Fleet at Rabaul comprised nearly 300
naval planes which were supplemented regularly by 300 carrier planes
from the Combined Fleet. [Japanese Army planes which had been
active during the evacuation of Guadalcanal were withdrawn from
Rabaul just prior to the invasion of Bougainville and 250 were sent
to Wewak, New Guinea, the headquarters of their Fourth Air Army,

where they were utilized in opposing the campaigns of MacArthur's troops.]

However, the enemy naval air forces at Rabaul refused to do major battle over Bougainville and confined their constant attacks to night bombing. Presumably the Jap planes were being saved for the defense of Rabaul itself. Their aggressive spirit had certainly been broken.

The 16-month battle for control of the air over the Solomons from Guadalcanal to Kahili had proved a death-trap for 2,000 of their first-line planes and pilots. Their network of airbases on Bougainville was now battered and inoperative. The pace and fury of Allied landings at Vella Lavella, the Treasuries, Choiseul, and Bougainville made the Japanese fearful of another imminent landing, perhaps even at Rabaul.

Though the Japanese day activity was nominal, their night bombing and strafing attacks did provide fodder for a new type of Marine squadron in the Solomons—the night fighters.

These shadow stalkers, with radar as their guide weapon in the night skies, were precise, scientific, aerial killers. An informal kind of night fighting had been attempted when men like Major Joseph Renner over Guadalcanal and Major Boyington over Munda tried using their day fighters to shoot down night intruders by moonlight or searchlight. Several Army pilots in P-38's were successful in shooting down night bombers with the aid of searchlights over the southern Solomons. But that method, at best, was haphazard. [*The first night fighter defense in the Pacific occurred when half a dozen Brewster Buffaloes from MAG 21 at Ewa were sent to the island of Kaui, T.H., prior to the Battle of Midway in June, 1942. These planes operated as night fighter patrols for five weeks without making contact and returned to Ewa.*]

During the early phases of the Munda campaign, VMF (N) 531, the first Marine night fighter squadron to see action, arrived in the Solomons and began experimental combat operations off Banika field in the Russells. It was a six-plane unit, flying the cumbersome PV-1 Venturas which the Navy had been using as a medium search and attack bomber. The Ventura's radar unit or dome was installed in a false fuselage nose. The plane carried an average crew of three:

the pilot, a radar man who also doubled as a gunner, and a top turret gunner who joined in frontal firing and protected the plane against attack from the rear.

The basic control unit of VMF (N) 531 and other night fighter squadrons was the GCI or Ground Control Intercept station. Either ship- or shore-based, it was handled by a fighter director and could operate, if necessary, as an independent radar and control station. Enemy night intruders were picked up on the GCI screen as bogeys or unidentified aircraft. Then the IFF (Identification Friend or Foe) homing signal was checked. If there was no reply, the bogey was considered an enemy plane. Its speed, altitude, and direction were radioed by VHF (Very High Frequency voice channel) to the plane in the air, which was then vectored (directed) as close as possible to the intruder.

When the night fighter was within two miles of his quarry, the intruder was picked up by the plane's smaller radar unit. Its radar man then guided the pilot in closing the gap until visual contact was made.

Visual contacts by the pilot could be made even on black, moonless nights by using stars and clouds to outline the enemy plane. Once the intruder was sighted, the night fighter closed in for further recognition. If its silhouette and exhaust pattern indicated it was not a friendly plane, he opened fire with the .50-caliber guns mounted in the nose, aided, when possible, by the twin .50's of the turret gunner.

Commanded by Lieutenant Colonel Frank Schwable, who had been trained in night fighting techniques by the British, VMF (N) 531 had rough going during its early months in the Solomons. Air and naval commanders were hard to sell on the potential effectiveness of the new weapon. Schwable found it difficult to get facilities on forward fields and the cooperation of ship- and shore-based commanders in utilizing the services of his unit. In addition to constant troubles with the operation of the GCI station, the radar gear, and communications, Schwable and his squadron had a minimum of ground crew, spare parts, and margin for error. Their six planes were replaceable only in the United States.

Several weeks after the Marine squadron began its patrols, it was joined by VF (N) 75, a naval night fighter unit, flying Corsairs. The faster F4U's had a higher operating ceiling and on some occasions were assigned high-cover patrols while the Venturas handled medium- and low-cover missions.

Until the appearance of these two squadrons, the enemy operated freely at night, with little to fear from antiaircraft fire and with in- creasingly serious effects on Allied ground and naval morale.

Although Schwable's squadron flew incessantly, covering the land- ings at Treasury and Bougainville, its first kill was not made until November 13. Captain Duane Jenkins, patroling through scattered clouds under a full moon, was vectored out to intercept a flight of six Jap bombers headed for a naval task force off the Solomons.

Coming out of a cloud bank, Jenkins spotted the enemy formation to his right and 1,500 feet below. Easing down, he crept in on the rear plane. His first burst set the Betty's starboard engine aflame. The other bombers broke off and hightailed for home as Jenkins followed his first bomber down in a shallow dive, raking its fuselage. A mass of flames, the Betty exploded as it hit the ocean.

Jenkins was killed in action several weeks later, after making his second kill. Fighter-directors put him on the track of a third intruder and then watched, helplessly, as the radar "blips" or tracks of the 2 planes merged in mid-air. No traces of Jenkins or his crew were found. It was presumed he had crashed into the enemy plane, thus destroying them both.

VMF (N) 531 moved its base of operations from the Russells to Barakoma Field and then to Bougainville. Schwable relinquished command of the unit with 72 missions and 4 kills credited to him. His successor, Lieutenant Colonel John Harshberger, finished his tour with 4 victories and 98 night missions. The squadron's total kill record in the Solomons was 12 planes. That was not startling by com- parison with day squadrons' scores, but it was an unusual perform- ance in the new night fighter technique and was warmly acclaimed by ground, sea, and air units.

In one sense, the Bougainville campaign was unlike any of the preceding invasions in the Solomons. Instead of a prolonged operation to wipe out all enemy resistance on the huge island, the ground forces were committed to capturing a small six-by-eight mile beachhead in the Cape Torokina area. This foothold was to provide a forward airbase which would bring the major Japanese installations at Rabaul within range of the fighters and light bombers.

The combined efforts of three Marine air commanders—Major Generals Roy S. Geiger, Ralph J. Mitchell, and Brigadier General Field Harris—were major factors in the precision progress of the Bougainville operation and the subsequent move on Rabaul. [General Geiger, air commander at Guadalcanal, took over both the air and ground forces ashore at Bougainville after General Vandegrift was recalled to become Commandant of the Marine Corps. Geiger's command, the First Marine Amphibious Corps, was composed of the Third Marine Division under Major General A. H. Turnage, the Army's 37th Infantry Division, and the First Marine Raider and Parachute Regiments. Also under Geiger was Brigadier General Field Harris, serving as Commander, Aircraft, Northern Solomons. Harris, with his Forward Echelon, First Marine Air Wing, hit the beach on D-Day with the assault troops and directed all air cover and air support missions at "Cherry Blossom." On November 20, Major General Mitchell became Commander, Aircraft, Solomons.]

It was during the first weeks of the Bougainville occupation that the Marine version of precision close air support for infantry had its first major workout. Air infantry support had been used sporadically and effectively during the Guadalcanal and New Georgia campaigns, but not in the planned, scientific manner that utilized the full possibilities of immediate, direct, and close-bombing support for the ground troops. [An accepted version of Marine close air support reports it as: "That direct support given by aircraft to front-line infantry units which are in combat with the enemy. This support is normally in the form of strafing, rocket firing, or the dropping of demolition, personnel, or fire bombs on enemy troops and material which are in immediate contact with our assault units. The purpose of close air support is identical to the purpose of close support by any other weapon. It is to destroy enemy personnel, emplacements, or material which may be holding up the advance of our infantry or *causing casualties to our assault troops.*"—Marine Corps Gazette, *September, 1946.*]

Several months before the invasion, three air officers and enlisted men were attached to the Third Division for air liaison duty. These officers, under Lieutenant Colonel John Gabbert, were Marine aviators familiar with the techniques of light-bomber aviation and general infantry operations. The enlisted men had received special training in using portable radio gear and in aviation communications.

An intensive air support school under Gabbert, the Division Air Officer, was attended by officers from each infantry regiment and battalion headquarters. The main objectives of the experiments of the Division were: improved means of target designations, exploration of the precise effects of bombs and their various type fuses, and the determination of safety margins necessary for the protection of friendly troops.

Colonel Gabbert used himself as a target for live bombs to determine an exact rule-of-thumb for the effect of their explosions on friendly troops. Without a foxhole or natural cover of any kind, Gabbert, in several experiments, squatted in an open field while planes dropped bombs of various weights at measured distances from him. He also utilized static explosions, standing at measured distances from bombs which he set off by hand. When he had completed his tests, Gabbert had proved that the "yard to a pound" norm was correct. A 100-pound bomb could be dropped 100 yards from prone friendly troops without endangering them.

The first instance of close air support at Bougainville was on the morning of the invasion by Marine torpedo and dive-bombers. As the landing craft headed for the beach, one division of planes hit assigned targets on Torokina Point, while others dropped strings of 100-pound bombs and strafed in the jungle and swamp area immediately behind the shore. The infantry reported that this air effort was "excellent," but not in sufficient strength and urged the use of heavier bombs.

The Third Division made its second call for air support on November 9, asking that 18 torpedo bombers be on station over Piva Village the following day to soften up Jap positions prior to an infantry attack. Twelve planes reported at the requested time and contacted the air liaison party. Friendly front lines were marked with colored mortar smoke and the bombers went in, laying their explosives within 120 yards of the Marines. The target area was well covered by the first attack. The infantry push was immediately successful as the Japanese had abandoned their positions, leaving behind much equipment.

During the next few days a number of close support missions were ordered and carried out with excellent results. The torpedo bombers based at Munda were called upon to aid the infantry in an assault on "Hellzapoppin" Ridge. This particular assignment came close to failure. It was not until the second day of the support mission that heavier bomb loads than previously used were dropped accurately within 75 yards of our troops and the path opened for the infantry.

It had been the practice of some ground commanders to withdraw their troops several hundred yards to the rear while the close support planes bombed. This tactic was dropped when they found that the Japanese moved up and occupied abandoned positions before friendly troops could return. The enemy's own trick of withdrawing from their own front lines during an Allied bombing attack and then quickly moving back in was obviated by the use of dummy runs. By mixing up their live and dummy runs by prior plan with the troops, the TBF's and SBD's were able to keep the Japanese down and immobile while friendly troops carried out their advance.

The last calls for air support by the Third Division were made on December 25 and 26 while straightening out the final lines of the perimeter at Hill 600A. The TBF's made two attacks on Christmas Day and one on the 26th against targets in the jungle which varied from slit trenches to splinter-proof emplacements. Following the third strike, infantry patrols found the target area abandoned although it showed evidence of having been occupied by 800 enemy troops.

Although the Bougainville infantry-support missions were of the rudimentary type, they were considered by Marine air and ground commanders to be "well worthy of the designation—close support."

Supplementing their fighter cover, night fighting and close-support missions, the Marine Air Arm in the Cherry Blossom operation carried out the numerous other requisites of a tactical air force serving the infantry.

The first Marine photographic squadron (VMD 154), flying the naval version of the B-24 Liberators, provided initial photo intelligence prior to the invasion. As the fighting progressed, infantry observers flying in SBD's and TBF's over the front lines added further data. The light bombers served as flying artillery-spotter platforms and protected the ships in the unloading areas from heavy enemy gunfire by remaining on constant patrol over suspected artillery emplacements. Munda-based bombers flew 750 such infantry missions until the SBD's on the new Torokina strip took over the duty.

SCAT transport planes made their usual quiet and significant contributions to the success of the Bougainville campaign in their specialties: air supply drops, evacuation of wounded, and delivery of badly needed cargo.

The Marine and Army wounded in the early weeks of fighting were taken out of Bougainville either by seaplanes (the Navy's PBY Dumbos) or by destroyer to Vella Lavella where they were reloaded into the R4D transports and flown to rear-base hospitals. SCAT planes moved into the strip at Torokina the day it opened and took over the air evacuation task. During the entire campaign, SCAT transports of MAG 25 and the Army's 13th Air Force carried out 1,217 casualties and delivered 840 tons of high priority cargo, including parapack air drops at Choiseul and to advance assault elements at Bougainville. [During the first stages of patrol activities outside the perimeter, knife-wielding jungle experts of the First Fijian Infantry Regiment cut across the Crown Prince Range and established a raiding base and tiny airfield at Ibu on the eastern side of Bougainville. SCAT planes flew regular air-drop missions to Ibu to keep the Fijians supplied with rations, ammunition and medical supplies.]

Experts of the Marine air-ground team summed up the Bougainville campaign, by far the largest Pacific undertaking up to that time, as "a long stride in the evolution of the part which aircraft was to play in the support of the amphibious advance" and advised many minor refinements in the Air Arm's role. In spite of the short campaign and lack of major air opposition, the air show at Bougainville had proved to be a competent, well-rounded affair that was satisfactory in itself and an excellent harbinger of deadlier precision teamwork in the future phases of Pacific campaigning.

Humbling a Fortress

With the Bougainville perimeter barely secure, the Allied Air Force reared back without a pause, and stuck its head into the lion's mouth—at Rabaul. All prior air beachheads in the Solomons paled in contrast with the struggle that followed until the lion choked to death.

The Japanese captured Rabaul Town on January 23, 1942, from a small Australian ground and air force. Ensuing months were concentrated on developing the area into a land, sea, and air fortress. As headquarters for the Southeastern Fleet and the Eighth Area Army, Rabaul became the key structure of the enemy's empire in the South Pacific, and the major staging and supply base for their activities in New Guinea, New Britain, and the Solomons.

Simpson Harbor, in Blanche Bay at Rabaul, was one of the largest natural harbors in the Pacific. It was almost landlocked and capable of handling 300,000 tons of shipping. Utilized by the Southeastern, the Eighth, and the Combined or roving Third Fleets, Simpson Harbor was the base for enemy naval elements regularly composed of 10 cruisers, 20 destroyers, 10 submarines, and 20 small craft. Two hundred and twenty large transport and supply ships of the Southeastern Army forces were based there along with 500 small boats and barges. [Enemy troop strength in the Rabaul-New Britain area in the fall of 1943 was approximately 100,000 men of whom 76,0000 were Army forces.]

Located in the shadow of six volcanoes, Rabaul was hedged by five airfields: Laukani, Vunakanau, Rapopo, Keravat, and Tobera. [The first two fields were captured from the Australians and expanded. Laukanai, immediately south of Rabaul on the coastal flats of Crater Peninsula, handled 90 fighters and 10 bombers; Vunakanau was a concrete strip, with revetments for 90 fighters and 60 bombers, located nine miles south of Rabaul; Rapopo, 14 miles southeast of Rabaul at Lesson Point, had a concrete strip and revetments to accommodate 94 bombers and 10 fighters; Keravat, 14 miles southwest of Rabaul passed from Army to Navy control, but because of drainage problems was never operational; Tobera, also a concrete field and capable of handling 75 fighters and 2 bombers, was 12 miles southwest of Cape Gazelle. These airbases were manned by the 10,000 men and 600 planes of the 11th Air Fleet, a part of the Southeastern Fleet.]

This Rabaul air network and its heavy complement of planes was the immediate target on which General Mitchell put his finger. Once enemy air power there was equalized, or eliminated, the light bombers could begin working on the airfields, the shipping concentrations, and finally the ground installations.

The answer to the forbidding Japanese air strength at Rabaul was the same as that at Kahili—the fighter sweep. It was five times the gamble it had been over southern Bougainville, but General Mitchell wasted no time in feints or preludes. He picked as sweep leader the expert, Major Greg Boyington, whose Black Sheep were back in the Solomons, operating off Barakoma field.

Major Rivers Morrell, a Guadalcanal veteran, brought in VMF 216 to begin defense operations at Torokina on December 10 as the Seabees completed their short steel-matted strip ahead of schedule.

On the morning of December 17, the Torokina taxiway opposite the field was sardined with a double line of nearly 100 Allied fighter planes—Marine Corsairs, Navy Hellcats, and the slow, gaudily painted P-40's of the eager New Zealanders.

The lead plane, an F4U, pulled out of line and on to the apron. A green light blinked from the tower. The splay-legged Corsair rocketed down the field and out over Empress Augusta Bay. It was Boyington, off on the first sweep to Rabaul.

That first mission proved a disappointment, as the Japanese continued their coy reluctance to fight. The P-40's tangled with 30 or 40 fighters a few minutes before the main sweep formation arrived. Six were shot down and 2 Allied planes lost, but Boyington failed to lure upstairs another 40 enemy fighters on the taxiways at Lakunai.

Boyington on his return argued vigorously that the first formation had been entirely too big, complex and unwieldy. He outlined his own tactical ideas on Rabaul sweeps: they should consist of 36, not more than 48, planes; the number of squadrons and plane-types participating should be limited to cut down the possibilities for confusion; the sweep leader should be where the first contact is expected to be made, whether in the high, medium, or low cover; the fighting should be kept in a compact area and not degenerate into small dogfights over a wide area; a two-plane section was an unbeatable combat unit regardless of whether the planes happened to be of the same type or squadron. Finally, Boyington insisted that aggressive action was paramount and that all fighters stay in the battle unless a very good reason required otherwise.

The second mission to Rabaul was to escort B-24's on a shipping strike. Again the Japanese fighters only picked at the bait. Four of them were shot down and 4 Allied planes were lost, 2 in a midair collision.

December 23 provided the first real air battle at Rabaul and a new technique which gave the answer to the enemy's refusal to employ its fighter strength.

The first mission of the day was a heavy-bomber strike to be followed an hour later by a fighter sweep. The bombers were late and Boyington's stacked-up fighters arrived just as the B-24's were retiring from the target. The fighters caught 40 intercepting Zeros flat-footed. In the ensuing fight, 30 of the 40 enemy planes were destroyed. The Black Sheep browsed through 12 of them, Boyington getting 4. His personal score was now at 24 and the 26-plane record of Foss was in danger for the first time in a year. As the clamor and tension rose, Mitchell sent Boyington a message of congratulations.

The Black Sheep commander made his next kill during a sweep over Rabaul on the 27th. Then spurting oil filmed his greenhouse. Three times Boyington wound back his hood and hunched up out of his cockpit trying to wipe away the oil in the middle of a whirling dogfight. He failed and came back to Torokina, downhearted, with the comment, "What difference? I couldn't have hit an elephant in the backside with a bull fiddle."

Bad weather kept the sweeps out of Rabaul for several days, while

Boyington, record-conscious for the first time, chafed at the delay. He was on his third and last tour, with only a few days left to beat the Pacific record.

He went back to Rabaul for the last time on January 3. It was a morning full of tension on the field at Torokina. Boyington, bareheaded, stumped in and out of the ready tent in his grimy flight suit. There was none of his usual banter. Knowing the strain he was under, everyone kept out of his way.

Under the eyes of war correspondents, Boyington fireballed his plane down the runway. Airborne, he circled slowly until the formation joined up. Then he led it off to Rabaul.

Hours later, planes from the sweep came straggling back, alone or in small groups. They reported that it had been a hell of a fight, but had no word on Boyington. More planes landed. Then Matheson and Chatham of Boyington's own division passed the word that they had seen him shoot a Zero down in flames. That tied the ace-of-aces record. They saw nothing further except that Boyington and his wingman had then gone off after a flock of Zeros.

At dusk, pilots of the Black Sheep squadron flew in under a storm front and searched the Rabaul area until long after dark. That night, the islands heard the news that Boyington, the indestructible, was missing. Continual searches for days, then weeks, confirmed the report. Both pilots were given up for lost months later when the Japanese failed to report their capture.

A year went by and only the Black Sheep remembered Boyington's promise—whatever happened, he'd see them at that bar in San Diego, after the war was over.

He did just that.

Held as a secret captive and not posted as a prisoner of war, he was freed from Omori, near Tokyo, after the war had ended. On his return, Boyington told his story:

"Captain George Ashmun was my wingman that morning. Halfway up to Rabaul, my engine started spewing oil over the greenhouse. I throttled back, leaned out and wiped it off with my handkerchief. When we got over Rabaul at 20,000 feet, the weather was good. Sixty to eighty Jap fighters were rising to meet us from their airfields below. When they reached about 12,000 feet, I told the boys to wait a second, and get set. I took one quick look around and hollered, 'Let's get the bastards.'

"Ashmun and I picked out two Zekes flying at 15,000. He took one and I the other. I made an overhead run on mine. He was a dusty brown color. I closed to 400 yards and fired one short burst. That was pretty far out for me, I'd rather get in to about 100 yards. But the Zeke flamed and went down. It surprised me.

"As I pulled out of my run, Ashmun yelled: 'You got a flamer, Skipper!' [It was the plane Chatham and Matheson had reported.]

"George and I circled for a few seconds, then picked a large formation of Zeros and dove. We caught them at 12,000 feet, but before we could open fire, we were surrounded by Zekes. We scissored, weaving back and forth over one another. We cut across three times and in those few moments, we both got flamers. [His 27th kill.]

"Suddenly George started nosing down, with smoke pouring out of his plane. I kept screaming, 'Dive, for God's sake, dive!' But he was hit, apparently, because his plane kept gliding down at the same 45 degree angle.

"It was the old story of the Nips piling in on the guy who can't fight back. About ten of them ganged up on him in a sort of aerial 'Banzai' charge. I got behind that procession and kept kicking the rudder back and forth, firing short bursts into the mob. Ashmun's Corsair burst into flames, with smoke pouring out of his wing tank and fuselage. Then one of the Nips in front of me went down in flames. [His 28th victory.]

"All the way down while I was trying to chase them off Ashmun's tail, the rat race was complete, with a flock of Zekes riding right behind me. When George's plane smashed into the water, I leveled out low and gave it full throttle.

"I went about half a mile wide open when my main gas tank burst into flames. Right then I didn't have a Chinaman's chance. I flipped over on what I hoped was my back. The fuselage burned like an inferno. It was like looking into an open blast door. I grabbed my safety belt in one hand and the rip cord ring in the other. If I'd had a third hand, I would have grabbed the hood. About two or three hundred feet over the water, I kicked the stick forward and catapulted out.

"Thank God, the chute worked. I felt one tug and then slammed into the water without even time to swing once. I hit on my side, so hard that the impact crushed the canteen on my belt and even the one in my back pack.

"I spent the next 15 or 20 minutes duck-diving while four Zekes expended their ammunition strafing me. One would make a pass and pull out while another came in, firing, from the other direction. Their 20mm stuff was kicking up all around me. I finally got so tired, as they closed in, that all I could do was lay my head on the water . . . and hope. Finally the Zekes gave me up for dead and went back to Rabaul.

"After treading water for two hours to make sure they didn't sneak back, I reached down for the raft danging between my legs. It wasn't hit, so I popped it and crawled aboard to examine the damage.

"My scalp was dangling down over my eyes. My left ear was about chewed off. My throat was cut open and the left ankle torn up. My hands were full of shrapnel holes and my left leg hurt badly. It must have hit the stabilizer when I bailed out. Generally, I was pretty much of a mess.

"I had hope all the time that Dumbo would pick me up. There was a strong wind and a slight storm which was blowing me toward St. George Channel and New Ireland where I knew that Black Angel Boske, the Coastwatcher, would be waiting to take care of me.

"Just at dusk when I felt very safe, a submarine broke surface right alongside my raft. I thought it was one of ours until I saw the tarpaulin on the conning tower with the big red meatball on it. Then the little yellow men with funny hats climbed out through the hatch. I remember thinking. 'Oh, oh, Boyington, here we go!'

"They pulled me aboard and cruised on the surface all the way to Rabaul because it was dark. On the way in, they treated me well and gave me some cigarettes and matches. One of them spoke English and asked my name. I had to tell him. It was stenciled all over my flight gear.

"When we docked in Simpson Harbor, they took me off the sub, blindfolded me, and tied my hands tightly in front. They led me at the end of a rope, limping a bit painfully, for about half a mile to a small building where they started questioning me. They kept at it for 24 hours. Every time they didn't like an answer I gave, they'd cinch up on the rope around my wrist until I was ready to pass out.

"It was ten days before they allowed my wounds to be treated. By that time I stunk to high heaven. I smelled so bad I don't know how they could stand being in the same room with me.

"During the six weeks I was at Rabaul as a prisoner of the Jap navy, they slugged me on the jaw every day. Everything had to be done on the double, no matter how weak you were. When you didn't move fast enough to suit the little slobs, they'd slam you over the head with boards or beat your legs with rifle butts.

"On February 17, they took six of us to Truk in a transport plane on our way to Japan. We landed at Truk right in the middle of our first naval carrier strike. They shoved us into a concrete slit trench at the end of the field just as a Hellcat fighter roared over and blew up our DC-2.

"Our slit trench was at the foot of a hill, just 50 feet short of the aiming point for a target near by where several dozen Jap planes were parked. Those Navy torpedo planes kept coming in over the hill and dropping their bombs as they passed over us. One 1,000-pounder exploded 15 feet away and shook the trench apart, but didn't hurt any of us. Things were so beat up at Truk by that raid that they couldn't get a plane in there for ten days to take us out."

[*Boyington was taken to the secret naval intimidation camp at Ofuna outside Yokahama where he was beaten regularly and on three occasions whaled with baseball bats. Thirteen months later he was transferred to a camp at Omori, where he was rescued.*]

Enemy air power at Rabaul held out for six frenzied weeks, as other Marines set an even wilder pace after Boyington vanished. [*The Black Sheep squadron finished its second combat tour five days after Major Boyington disappeared. Its two-tour record was 94 planes destroyed in combat. Of these, 92 were Jap fighters. The squadron was credited with the probable destruction of 32 more planes in combat, damaging 50 others, and destroying 21 on the ground. The Black*

Sheep sank 4 small ships and 23 barges and strafed 125 enemy ground installations in the Northern Solomons, New Britain, and New Ireland for a total of 4,195 combat flying hours and more than 200 missions. Its losses were 12 pilots missing in action and 6 wounded.]

Crack Marine squadron in the New Britain melee was VMF 215, the Fighting Corsairs, commanded by Major Robert Gordon Owens and paced by three of the highest-scoring Allied fighter pilots in the South Pacific air war.

India-born First Lieutenant Robert M. Hanson earned his Medal of Honor and title of the "One Man Air Force" by shooting down 20 Japanese fighters over Rabaul in a 17-day period.

"Butcher Bob," as he was called by his squadron, had downed 5 planes in two tours before he went up to Rabaul. He had been shot down in one engagement over Bougainville while driving off 6 torpedo bombers attacking a convoy on D-Day.

Then, on January 14, he fought the first of a series of six air battles which made him the fastest of the super-aces. Seventy Zeros attempted to intercept a light-bomber mission attacking shipping in Simpson Harbor. Hanson picked out 5 enemy fighters and shot them down in flames in quick succession.

His next five missions to Rabaul netted him 1 Zero, 3 Zeros, 4 Zeros, 3 Zeros, and 4 Zeros. Then, with 25 enemy planes to his credit and on the threshold of bettering the existing fighter record in the Pacific, the boyish and zealous Hanson crashed to his death in a strafing run at Cape St. George only a week before he was due to return to the States.

Lieutenant Hanson's quick rise to fame and his sudden death left him little-known to the public which heard only, in the reading of his Medal of Honor citation, that "He was a master of individual air combat" and that "His great personal valor and invincible fighting spirit were in keeping with the highest traditions of the United States Naval Service."

Such was his epitaph at the age of twenty-three.

Captains Donald N. Aldrich and Harold Spears found the air battles over Rabaul as much to their liking as had Hanson. Aldrich tied Lieutenant Walsh's record of 20 planes shot down, and Spears got 15 Japs before returning to the States, where he was killed in an operational accident.

The combined total of 60 planes shot down by Hanson, Aldrich, and Spears was a major factor in the four new Marine air records established by VMF 215 in the South Pacific. It was credited with:

1) 137 Japanese planes shot down in 18 weeks of action
2) 87 planes shot down in one month
3) 106 planes destroyed in a single, six-week tour
4) 10 aces in the squadron.

[VMF 215 was the first Marine squadron to be awarded the Navy Unit Commendation.]

Once their planes had been brought to battle by the bomber-fighter sweep technique, the Japanese at Rabaul fought back with all the unyielding vigor they had evidenced at Kahili. In the early weeks of the New Britain campaign, all available Jap fighters were sent up for interception of the Allied raids.

At first the number of Zekes and Tojo and Hamp interceptors (these latter two were new and improved planes) ranged from 50 to 200. The Jap fighter planes tried to remain in formation during the interception, but as their own numbers decreased and Allied plane strength rose, the Japanese were forced to resort to individual tactics.

The Japanese later admitted (in U. S. Strategic Bombing Survey interrogations) that they had a healthy respect for both American fighter tactics and planes. The most difficult maneuver the Japanese encountered was the "scissoring" or Thach weave performed by Allied planes flying escort for bomber missions.

On their own missions, U. S. bombers flew tight-knit, unwavering unit formations as inseparable as those for which the Japanese were noted. Allied fighters covering the strikes had an inviolable rule: "Stay in formation and protect your bombers." Pilots who violated that creed to engage in separate fighter combat were severely disciplined by strike commanders regardless of any kills they might have made.

One new tactic which the enemy introduced into the South Pacific air war was the use of aerial burst or phosphorous bombs. Carried on the underbellies of fighter planes, the Japs used them by making a fast pass at an Allied formation, usually from head-on. The Zeros pulled out of their high-speed runs sharply, flipping the bombs at the Allied bombers. They exploded, throwing out white-hot streams of phosphorous to sear the bombers as they flew through the tentacles, and to break up the American formation to make its component planes better available to fighter gunnery.

The burst bomb made few kills and failed to break up Allied formations, so it was eventually discarded.

The typical Japanese pilot preferred to make his gunnery run on bombers from a frontal approach and against fighter planes from the rear. However, the inferior speed of the enemy fighters usually precluded a successful run on the rear of the Corsairs and Hellcats and they were forced to use the suicidal head-on approach.

The enemy's evaluation of Allied plane types was that the twin-engined P-38 and the slow P-40 were the easiest to shoot down, once an initial combat advantage had been gained over them. The Corsair, because of its superior speed and heavy armor and armament was regarded as the best Allied fighter plane, while the F6F, though not as fast as the F4U, was considered to be highly maneuverable and well adapted to combat.

In spite of the severe opposition, bad weather, and the constant midday cloud cover over Rabaul, Allied fighter planes, at a price, beat down the size of the enemy air force and its will to fight more quickly than had been anticipated. During January, 1944, Mitchell's airmen flew 28 major day missions and five large night attacks against Rabaul installations. Of the 740 Allied planes available, Mitchell's groaning ground crews worked around the clock to keep 480 planes ready for combat at all times.

The relentless Allied air drive against Rabaul reached its zenith during the first weeks of February, when more than 3,000 sorties thundered over the base that was the anchor of the enemy's hopes in the South and Southwest Pacific. Then, on February 19, Marine fighter pilots met their last major opposition from the Rabaul fields. Fifty Zeros rose to meet the incoming raid. Twenty-four were shot

down at the cost of one Allied pilot. That battle marked the final
death throes of what had been the once mighty air strength of the
Japanese in the Bismarck Archipelago.

With excellent timing, a large American carrier task force hit
Truk on February 17 in the raid in which Boyington had been caught.
The damage was so severe that Japanese Admiral Koga, Commander-
in-Chief of the Combined Fleet, ordered all naval planes and pilots
still at Rabaul to return immediately and reinforce the defenses at
Truk. [On February 4, 1944, two Marine photographic planes of
VMD 254 carried out the first successful photo-reconnaissance of
this secret base since 1941, returning with aerial photos which were
instrumental in the success of the first American carrier raid on Truk.
The two unescorted planes (PB4Y or B-24 type), piloted by Major
James R. Christensen and Captain James Yawn, battled freak tropical
storms during most of their daring 2,000-mile mission and escaped
aerial interception over Truk.]

Koga's order left the fortress of Rabaul without any semblance of
organized air defense after February 25. A few Army and rebuilt Navy
planes operated after that date until they too were destroyed. But
on the February date, the air battle for Rabaul was over.

In their 65-day campaign, Marine, Army, Navy, and New Zealand
fighter pilots were credited with shooting down 695 of the 863 Japanese planes estimated to have been lost. The balance were destroyed
on the ground.

The complete collapse of enemy air power at Rabaul and in the
South and Southwest Pacific by March, 1944, marked the end of the
air war in that area. In the long, bitter battle to destroy enemy air
strength from August, 1942, to March, 1944, the Marines shot down
1,520½ planes or three-fifths of all the Japanese planes lost in air
combat in the South Pacific.

With the annihilation of its air umbrella, Rabaul and the rest of
the Bismarck Archipelago were ripe for further invasions which would
complete the Allied strangle-hold of the area.

First step was the invasion of the Green or Nissan Islands, which
lie between Bougainville and New Ireland. New Zealand infantry
landed on Green Island on February 15, under strong air cover pro-

vided mainly by planes of the First and Second Air Wings. [One hundred and ten combat veterans of the Forward Echelon, First Wing, under Brigadier General Field Harris, went ashore on D-Day at Green to direct the air cover for the landing phases and develop the position as an airbase.] During the assault phase, in which light resistance ashore was encountered, the planes of VMF 212 shot down only six enemy aircraft.

On March 6, Lagoon Field, a 5,000-foot coral strip on Green, was completed, and one week later VMF 222 and 223 arrived to take over local defense of the area.

Encirclement of Rabaul was completed on March 20 when the Fourth Marine Regiment (Reinforced) landed without opposition at Emirau Island, in the St. Matthias Group, only 75 miles from Kavieng. Again, the air-ground team in the landing was implemented by elements of the Forward Echelon, First Air Wing, under Colonel William L. McKittrick, who was designated as Air Commander Emirau.

MAG 12 arrived at Emirau on April 5. Major General James T. Moore took over the Air Command and relieved Brigadier General Houston Noble, USMC, as commanding general of the island. In the meantime, Major General Mitchell had been replaced as Com-AirSols by Army Major General H. R. Harmon. Mitchell then took over as Commanding General, Marine Aircraft, South Pacific, (MarAirSoPac) which had been established February 1, 1944, as the senior Marine air echelon in the South Pacific. It was composed mainly of the First and Second Wings.

In the months that followed, there were a series of moves and command changes which concentrated the strength of Marine aviation at the northern airbases. The First Wing moved its Headquarters March 10 from Espiritu Santo to Guadalcanal and from there to Bougainville on June 8. In late April, 1944, General Harris became ComAirSols and was relieved at the end of May by General Moore.

In mid-June, the Navy's ComSoPac command was disbanded and control of its units passed to General MacArthur in the Southwest Pacific area. ComAirSols was also deactivated and replaced by ComAirNorSols. This new but similar organization was commanded by

Major General Mitchell, who had served as ComAirSoPac from April until June. The Second Wing moved its Headquarters from Efate to Espiritu Santo on July 3, preparatory to an operation in another theater. The First Marine Air Wing, as a command and with a variable number of squadrons, remained in the South Pacific area until the end of the war.

The pressure of Allied air activity against the Bismarck Archipelago was seriously threatened during March, 1944, when Japanese infantry remnants in the Northern Solomons gathered to make a wholesale counterattack on the Bougainville perimeter. The enemy admitted that from fifteen to twenty thousand troops were engaged in the abortive efforts, after having laboriously rounded up their scattered forces, moving them at night with few motor vehicles over battered roads, or by barge and jungle trail and carrying their few heavy artillery weapons piecemeal through the jungles from Buka and Kahili.

The immediate objective of the desperate attacks was to retake the Piva bomber and fighter strips which were less than a mile from the defense perimeter. A further thrust would make the original field at Torokina beach untenable and eliminate Bougainville, key link of the Allied air chain in the Northern Solomons.

Beginning on March 7, the Japanese closed on the perimeter in force and began shelling the airfields with such accuracy that the Piva fighter field was temporarily abandoned. While their fields, revetments, and camps were under constant shell fire, the Bougainville fighter and light-bomber pilots retaliated by harassing the enemy artillery positions and their troop concentrations with considerable success.

A major Japanese attack against the perimeter began on March 10. Army troops on the perimeter piled up Japanese dead along the barbed-wire front lines by the hundreds. Before the enemy broke off the attacks in late March, they had suffered casualties numbering 10,000 dead and wounded. Of these, 5,000 later died of wounds, according to the commander of their forces, General Imamura.

After the dispersal of the remaining Japanese infantry on Bougainville and with the opening of the airstrips on Green and Emirau, the

Marine Air Arm in the South Pacific settled down to the hard task of aerial strangulation of the by-passed islands.

The first light-bomber strike on Rabaul was a disappointment. Cloud cover prevented sighting the target area. Two days later, a second mission was unable to find the target and dumped its load on the lighthouse and radio installations at Cape St. George on the southern tip of New Ireland.

Marine bombers finally got through on January 9 and put the airfield at Tobera temporarily out of commission while their fighter cover shot down 21 enemy interceptors.

Two more heavy raids failed to get at their targets. But on January 14, the break came when the dive-bomber and torpedo planes struck shipping in Simpson Harbor while their fighter escort took on 70 enemy interceptors. A light cruiser, a destroyer, and seven cargo vessels were damaged by the bomber attacks. The Marines accounted for the cargo ships with nine direct hits. Twenty-nine Zeros were picked off by the fighter cover and five by the bombers.

The SBD's and TBF's caught eight cargo ships in the harbor on the 17th. The torpedo bombers bored in at masthead level and the SBD's dive-bombed. Three of the AK's were sunk, two left in sinking condition, and three damaged. Thirteen Allied planes were shot down in the raid and 18 enemy interceptors were destroyed.

Throughout the balance of January, the light bombers went to Rabaul with milk-run regularity, flying as many as three missions a day. The novelty of hitting Rabaul wore off sharply in February as the heavy shipping disappeared and its fighter defense ended. [Airborne rockets were used for the first time by Marines when VMTB 134 loosed the five-inch type against shipping in Simpson Harbor on February 17. In late April, 1944, VMF 114 (Death Dealers) made one of the first experiments with the Corsair as a fighter-bomber in destroying a 450-foot bridge on New Ireland.]

Participating in the early phases of the systematic harassing of Rabaul was VMB 413, the first Marine medium bomber squadron. It started deviling the Japanese in March, 1944. Flying PBJ's off Stirling field in the Treasury Group, the squadron concentrated on precision night heckling.

Taking over where the day units left off, VMB 413 earned the title of the Flying Nightmares. One of their planes appeared over Rabaul just as the Japanese began their evening meal. It dropped several bombs and retired. Minutes later, it came in again, hundreds of feet lower. More bombs dropped and it circled away. This pattern was repeated until, on its last run, the plane strafed the target area.

As the sound of its motors died away, the Japanese heard the second plane coming in on schedule to repeat the maddening process which went on night after night.

In spite of AA fire and tropical storms which took a regular toll of the squadron, it maintained the pattern of attack which was recognized in a letter of commendation from the Commanding General, 13th Army Bomber Command, to which it was attached:

"You have . . . developed the dangerous, tiresome mission of night heckling to the highest perfection it has attained in the 14 months I have been working under ComAirSols."

Three more Marine medium-bomber squadrons joined VMB 413 during the strangulation campaign and concentrated their strikes against targets on New Britain, New Ireland, and Bougainville. [The Seahorse squadron (VMB 423) flew 1900 sorties against by-passed targets for the Australian Second Army Corps which was engaged in mopping up the thousands of Japanese still on Bougainville in the summer of 1945. The unit flew 120 infantry-support missions for Australian troops during one four-month period.]

By midsummer of 1944, Allied commanders felt that Rabaul, despite its potential strength, was lost to the Japanese and the Allied offensive by-passed it completely. For the rest of the war, however, it was subjected to a rigid aerial and naval blockade to continue its neutralization and weaken the will of its garrisons.

Though a vast assortment of planes and services were engaged in this neutralization campaign, Rabaul was a major and unwanted problem child of Marine Aviation until the end of the war. Its squadrons flew 14,718 sorties, more than half the total number of all Allied sorties against the New Britain stronghold.

Thirty-three Marine squadrons, a major portion of the Air Arm's strength in the Pacific, were involved in the Rabaul attack and neutralization phases. These units dropped 7,142,000 pounds of bombs for a third of the total Allied tonnage rained on that section of New Britain. The Marine array included 16 fighter squadrons [and one VMF (N) unit]; 8 dive-bomber squadrons, 5 torpedo plane squadrons, and 4 medium-bomber units. These were aided by a complex assortment of Army, Navy, Australian, New Zealand, and Royal Indian Air Force units.

The Marine airmen, pilots, and ground crews who were shackled to the dull rigors of aerial strangulation in the South Pacific resented their fate thoroughly and perhaps not without reason. As a land-based force they had proved second to none in spearheading the Solomons campaigns and the Rabaul offensive. They could agree that circumstances, fate, and the old adage of "turn about, fair play" had something to do with their morbid fate, but it made them none the happier.

Hour after hour, day after day, month after month, the routine was the same, as the Marines performed their tiresome chores of strangling the by-passed bases which were now far in the backwash of the Pacific war. The only saving grace of this deadly pace was their wry, ironic sense of humor. Over Guadalcanal, they had sung and cussed, feeling in the pits of their stomachs that they might not be around another day. Over Rabaul or Kavieng and later in the Central Pacific, it was the other extreme. Yesterday, today, and tomorrow had no meaning or identity.

As they lived in the skies that had become a prison, the fliers let off steam that produced no great epics nor Battle Hymns of the Republic—just the salty epithets of the hour and the unmetered parodies that lamented their fate. Among them, was this melody of the milk runs, "ComAirSols Never Cries for Me," (to the tune of "Oh, Susanna"):

> Oh, I went up to Kavieng,
> My maps upon my knees;
> The soup was thick, the night was black,
> No wingtips could I see.

The lights went on, they shot at me;
I swore and heaved a sigh;
We stayed up there for two damned hours—
ComAirSols, don't you cry!

Oh, AirSols never cries for me,
Though I go to Kavieng each night
And bomb the enemy.

It's off to Kavieng I go,
With a hundred-pound G-P's;
There's a Nick a'closin' on my tail,
I'm shaking in my knees.

The weatherman he says its clear,
So clear I could do stunts,
And off to Kavieng I go
Through fifteen different fronts.

Oh, SoPac only starts to pray,
When I'm sixteen hours past
My scheduled ETA.

Oh, ComAirSols, he says the blips
Upon my screen are fakes;
So off to Kavieng I go,
Escorted by ten Jakes.

We tune in on the A. S. George,
Gaze in the crystal ball;
When Geisha girls smile in the scope,
We know we're at Rabaul.

We bomb Rabaul from dark to dawn,
And start some twenty fires;
Unless they see the blaze at Green,
We're just a bunch of liars.

This life's a mighty pleasant thing.
If I depart too soon,
Please write my epitaph to read—
"No hits, twelve runs, no moon."

At war's end, the Marine airmen still in the South and Southwest Pacific heard what they had long believed: they had bombed Rabaul too often. In the opinion of the Strategic Bombing Survey, "Our air attacks on these by-passed positions were often continued longer and in greater weight than was reasonably required or justified." [The USSBS units covering Rabaul and the Central Pacific were headed by Brigadier General Lewie G. Merritt, USMC.]

That hindsight reckoning was little consolation for the epidemic of dry rot they had been through, but the Marines knew they had accomplished a major share of the damage which the USSBS determined had been done at Rabaul by Allied air attacks:

1) Elimination of enemy air power by destroying more than 800 planes and forcing the withdrawal of its air defense

2) Elimination of enemy naval power by sinking 20 fleet vessels of all types, damaging 23, and forcing evacuation of Navy units by February, 1944

3) Destruction of 154 large cargo vessels, 70 small cargo ships, 517 barges, and 4 submarines in Rabaul waters; demolishing port installations and making 60 percent of Simpson Harbor and 40 percent of Keravia Bay unnavigable because of sunken wreckage

4) Inflicted at least 4,700 deaths on the enemy garrison

5.) Knocked out 94 AA weapons and coastal guns

6) Demolished or burned out all important surface installations

7) Destroyed 6 radar units and a central Army radio station

8) Destroyed 884 vehicles of all kinds

9) Destroyed considerable quantities of all types of stocks, including two-thirds of the Army's food supply

10) Weakened the over-all health of the command by destroying all of the original hospitals and more than 15 percent of the area's medical stores.

Surviving Japanese denied that Allied raids had any serious effect on their morale, although they had been seriously inconvenienced by them. This testimony was heartily disagreed with by one Father Mueller, an Australian and head of the Sacred Heart Mission station, who arrived in Rabaul in 1940 and was subsequently interned in a stockade.

Mueller said, "From what we could see, your raids had a terrible effect on the Japanese. Our Sisters here behaved much more courageously than they did. Once the Japs cleared out and left us here for three weeks. They retreated into the hills and left everything behind them. Their officers kept face, but their soldiers were down and out. The Japs aren't too intelligent and they couldn't always identify the Allied planes. So they waited until the first bombs were dropped, then they knew they must be enemy planes. Only a few days before the end of the war, they told us it would only be a short while longer and Japan would rule the world."

It was Mueller, along with other prisoners, who verified the story that all captured Allied pilots were tortured. On Japanese treatment of Chinese, Indian, and Allied pilot captives, the USSBS investigators documented instances of torture, execution for trifling offenses, ceremonial cannibalism, medical malpractice, and burials alive by the Rabaul garrison.

At the end of their long trail of destruction, the survivors of the First and Second Marine Air Wings heard the testimony of General Hitoshi Imamura, 60-year-old commander of the Southeastern Army Forces at Rabaul. It was a prejudiced tribute, but not too unlikely: "We lost the Solomons campaign because of your strong air force."

7

THE FORGOTTEN WAR IN THE CENTRAL PACIFIC

MAJURO, MARSHALL ISLANDS, APRIL 3, 1945—The LCI called 'Hogan's Goat' warped laboriously into her berth beside the rusty steel floating pier that juts from a palm-shaded coral beach into the blue Majuro lagoon. There was a moment's pause, and over her rail climbed, slowly and with much effort, seven nearly naked little men.

"They were Japanese prisoners from the atoll of Wotje, once an 'unsinkable carrier' in the heart of Nippon's Central Pacific mandate. Now, still unsunk, but a carrier no longer, Wotje was a mummified corpse of an island, torn by shells and scorched by fire. The prisoners were starving. Their muddy brown skin, eaten by ringworm, was stretched taut upon fleshless bones. Their necks were thin, dried-weed stalks and their eyes glittered deep in their skulls. Their black hair bushed up, stiff and dry and lustreless, like the fur of some dead animal.

"On the dock, a Corsair pilot of Major General Louis E. Woods' Fourth Marine Air Wing stared in disbelief as he watched the seven climb like feeble spiders over the rail. 'Ye Gods!' he exploded, 'Is that what we've been peckin' away at for a year?' " [—*From a story by Lieutenant Harold H. Martin, USMC.*]

His reaction was a summation of the forgotten war that was fought over the atolls of the Central Pacific. It occupied the planes and patience of a goodly portion of the Marine Air Arm for 18 months.

The Marshall Islands, in the Central Pacific, are a series of coral

145

outcroppings within the equatorial latitudes that are cooled by the trade winds and sopped by rain. Some 1,900 miles west-by-south from Honolulu, their two rough groupings, Ralik on the west and Radak on the east, cover a sea area one and one-half times the size of Texas. Yet their total land mass is only 74 square miles. They came into the possession of the Japanese by the mandate provisions of the Versailles Treaty and were lightly garrisoned from the 1920's until 1940. The two exceptions were Roi and Kwajalein, completed as military bases in the 1930's. Both are parts of the Kwajalein Atoll.

Because of prolonged disagreement in the Japanese High Command over whether the Marshalls or the Marianas should be the first line of Empire defense, it was not until the eve of war that the atolls of Wotje, Maloelap, Majuro, Mille, and Jaluit were hurriedly developed as feeder bases for Roi, headquarters of the 24th Air Flotilla.

It was the intent of the Japanese strategists to use the Marshalls, with the captured additions of Wake and Midway to the north and the Gilberts to the south, as a screen to protect their southern drives through the Philippines, New Guinea, and the Solomons. As the eastward extension of the Caroline Islands, which harbored their mobile carrier striking force at Truk, Marshall-based forces were to harass or cut off, if possible, the sea and air communications between the United States and Australia.

Once their gains had been consolidated behind this barrier, the Japanese hoped to push south from the Marshalls through the Gilbert and Ellice islands into the Samoan and Fiji groups. This move would seal off Australia and New Zealand, which could then be exploited at will. It was further expected that powerful Japanese sea and air task forces, staging through the Marshall bases, would be able to raid advanced Allied positions and seriously oppose American counter-operations in the Pacific.

The Allies recognized the danger inherent in this threat and counter-moved accordingly. Five thousand officers and men of the Second Marine Brigade sailed from San Diego on January 6, 1942, for Samoa. Their mission was to prevent the enemy from driving south and establishing a rigid blockade of east-west shipping between the United States and Australia and New Zealand. Thirty days after it had been formed, the Brigade completed its 4,500-mile journey in Samoa's Pago Pago harbor. A network of defense installations for the main island of Tutuila mushroomed and, by early March, its first airfield was complete.

First air defense for this forward outpost were the planes of Marine Air Group 13. Grumman Wildcat fighters of its VMF 111 took off on their initial patrols March 19, and by mid-April were conducting daily search and patrol missions of the area with the aid of a naval scouting squadron. [*MAG 13 had been commissioned as part of the First Air Wing at San Diego March 1, 1942. One week later its forward echelon sailed for Samoa.*] Outer-barrier defense of the Samoan group was enlarged in mid-April when fighters of VMF 211 were stationed at Palmyra, Line Islands, which is 1,400 miles northeast of Samoa and in a direct line with Pearl Harbor. [*This was the rear echelon of the squadron which fought at Wake Island.*]

With the transport routes covered by Samoa in the south, the Allies moved their convoys safely into New Zealand. The expected Japanese thrust at Samoa never materialized and activity in that sector of the Southeastern Pacific was static during the balance of 1942 and early 1943, with one exception. Marine units from Samoa occupied the atoll of Funafuti without resistance on October 2, 1942, moving their perimeter 280 miles northwest into the Ellice Islands. The Samoan-based offensive was so long in getting underway that it was not until March, 1943, that VMF 441 was ordered to Funafuti as its garrison air force.

In the interim, another finger had been poked out at the barrier in the Marshalls. On March 17, Marine planes of VMSB 133 began operating off tiny Johnston Island, 700 miles southwest of Pearl Harbor and almost directly north from Samoa.

First harbinger of the advance in the Central Pacific was the arrival of Brigadier General Harold Campbell, USMC, in late August, 1943, to command the Aircraft Defense Force, Samoan Area. One week later the forward echelon of the Fourth Marine Base Defense Aircraft Wing left Pearl Harbor for Tutuila. Brigadier General Lewie G. Merritt arrived in early October as Wing Commander. [*The 4th MBDAW was activated in August, 1942, at MCAS, Ewa, Oahu under the command of Colonel Claude Larkin. Its slow development resulted from its squadrons being used as replacements in the Solomons.]*

In the fall of 1943, as the tide turned in the South Pacific theater, the American offensive began inching its way up to the Central Pacific. VMF 441 was moved up to Nanomea, northernmost of the Ellice Islands, within flight distance of the Japanese bases in the Gilberts. On Armistice Day, General Merritt set up Fourth Wing Headquarters at Funafuti in final preparation for the Central Pacific thrust. [*The Fourth Wing then comprised two Air Groups: MAG 13 with VMF 111 and 441 and VMSB 151 and 241; and MAG 31 with VMF 224, 311, 321; scout bomber squadrons 331 and 341, and the transport unit VMJ 353.]*

Then, on November 20, 1943, while the South Pacific Marines were consolidating their positions on Bougainville, Marines of the Second Division stormed the bloody northern beaches of Betio Island, Tarawa Atoll, site of the airfield and principal installations in the Gilberts. Seventy-six violent hours later, Betio's Japanese garrison of 4,000 was dead. American casualties in taking this square mile of level hell were nearly 1,000 dead and 2,500 wounded. Makin, uppermost island of the Gilberts, was secured by the Army's 27th Division on November 22 against nominal resistance. Apamama, some 60 miles south of Tarawa, was occupied against light resistance by a platoon of Marines landed from a submarine. Several further minor landings were made and the Gilbert Islands were safely in American possession.

The Fourth Wing island-hopped again in late December to begin housekeeping in the debris at Tarawa. Its scout bomber squadron 331 was sent forward to the airbase at Makin, just two hours' flying time from either Jaluit or Mille in the Marshalls. An early combat action of the Marines scored on December 21 when planes from Makin sank a 6,000-ton enemy freighter in a raid on Jaluit.

With the loss of their Gilbert bases, Japanese commanders in the Marshalls made feverish preparations to withstand a momentarily expected invasion. They anticipated landings at one or more of the secondary bases prior to a later assault on the main centers at Roi and Kwajalein. American strategy operated to the contrary, on the thesis that the entire Marshalls area could be effectively neutralized by capturing the key bases first. Accordingly, the many-pronged invasion began February 1, 1944, with simultaneous assaults on Roi-Namur, Kwajalein, and Majuro by troops of the Marine Fourth and the Army Seventh Divisions.

At the end of the third day, all atolls were secured against opposition that varied from meager to strong. These units and other troops of the Fifth Marine Amphibious Corps, under Major General Holland M. Smith, continued the landing series, occupying Engebi, the airbase at Eniwetok on the 17th and its main island two days later. These major beachheads were supplemented by a large number of landings by small troop units during the months of February, March, and April. Many of these secondary invasions were supported by carrier aircraft or shore-based planes of the Fourth Air Wing. [VMF 311, flying from Roi field only a week after its capture, covered several of the earlier infantry operations. Dive-bombers of VMSB 151, operating from Engebi, supported the landings at Wotho, Lae, and Ujae Atolls in mid-March. The longest recorded sustained flight for Corsairs under combat conditions was established by planes of VMF 113 while covering a landing at Ujelang Atoll. The F4U's were airborne for 9 hours and 40 minutes.]

In early March, Merritt's command moved up from Tarawa to Kwajalein atoll, deploying its squadrons to the captured airbases. From them, land-based Marine units began the prolonged aerial siege against Japanese installations and garrisons on the by-passed islands in the Marshalls' area. [Two new Air Groups had joined the Wing: MAG 22 at Eniwetok and the transport group, MAG 15, with two squadrons based at Apamama. MAG 13's planes operated from Majuro while MAG 31's three fighter units and one night-fighter squadron, VMF (N) 532, were stationed at Kwajalein. VMF 111 was based at Makin in the Gilberts.]

The landings at Eniwetok and Engebi wiped out the Japanese stragetic position in the Marshalls. However, the enemy still held his four new bases at Mille, Wotje, Maloelap, and Jaluit. These had been swept clean of their aircraft and cut off from normal sources of communications and supply. Though isolated and without fear of invasion, the enemy commanders on those four atolls hoped that by keeping their air facilities operative, the day would come when their bases might serve as staging points for Japanese air and sea operations against American holdings in the Marshalls and Gilberts. During the remainder of 1944, despite the aerial siege, Japanese garrison forces on these atolls worked diligently to keep the airfields open and to strengthen their defenses. [*In their strategic role as an outlying screen, the enemy bases in the Marshalls were never adequate because they lacked offensive air power. Even their defensive air strength was nominal because their naval air power was siphoned off into the Solomons air war.*]

The Marine siege targets—Wotje, Maloelap, Mille, and Jaluit in the central and lower Marshalls—were never garrisoned or built to peak strength. When the strangulation operation began against them, the four enemy atolls shaped up as follows, according to enemy data gathered by the U. S. Strategic Bomb Survey: *Wotje:* 160 miles from Kwajalein with 3,000 troops on a land area of three-quarters of a square mile, a well-gunned and built up airbase commanded by Rear Admiral Nobukazo Yoshimi, IJN. *Maloelap:* 75 miles southeast of Wotje and 210 miles from Kwajalein; 3,000 troops, main island of Taroa is one-half mile roughly square, maximum food stocks, well-defended. *Mille:* 165 miles south of Maloelap, 195 miles from Makin; reef forms 90 islands with Mille at southwestern tip, the largest, four miles long, half a mile wide; 3,000 personnel on this southern anchor of the Marshalls' defensive zone; 100 assorted guns in concrete, coral, or coconut log revetments. *Jaluit:* 125 miles west of Mille, 210 miles from Kwajalein; five islands in the chain, 33 miles long and 18 wide, used as bases—Tiniet, Emidj, Enybor, Ainemann, and Jaluit; 2,200 personnel; Emidj had main system of defenses and had been used as a seaplane base; well-integrated and dispersed defense, food stocks, and communications. Climate on all four main target atolls is continuously hot and rainy. Barely above sea level, the atolls had considerable vegetation and several thousand native civilians who were anti-Japanese.

To thwart Jap hopes and to eliminate any future threat the atolls might hold for the northern convoy route, American planes were committed to their continued neutralization. The aerial siege was further expected to humble the enemy garrisons to the point of surrender and eliminate the necessity of costly invasions.

There were a few flurries of air action in the first phases of the campaign against the by-passed atolls which gave rise to the hope among the Marine garrison squadrons that the Japanese might decide to battle it out as they had so often in the South Pacific.

Mitchell medium bombers hit Ponape in the outer fringes of the Carolines on March 26. Their escort planes, Corsairs of Major Loren D. Everton's Whistling Devil Squadron, intercepted 12 Zeke fighters rising from the Ponape field. Everton raised his South Pacific score to 14 by downing 3, while his wingmen splashed 5, damaged 3 probables, and burned another on the airstrip.

Ten Betty bombers raided Eniwetok at night, killed 3, wounded 21, and escaped untouched. When they raided again on April 14, pilots of VMF (N) 542 found them in the dark, shot down 2 and turned back the attack.

These flurries ended aerial combat in the Marshalls except for a stray snooper plane at rare intervals.

Then the disappointed Marines of the Fourth Air Wing turned to the exasperating chore of grinding down enemy resistance on the by-passed atolls. They were aided by Army planes until June and by auxiliary strikes flown by Navy land-based planes until the end of 1944. There were sporadic carrier raids and task-force shellings, but the major responsibility for maintaining the neutralization pressure rested with the Marines.

The perpetual motion of the milk-run raids in the South Pacific jungles was trying enough on the restless combat energies of any air unit. But in that theater there were, at least, trees to be seen, and mountains, and islands big enough to get lost on for a month. By comparison, the Marines on the atolls felt they were prisoners on a pinhead. Alternately baking and steaming in the equatorial weather, blinded by the aching glare of the cloud-white coral and the brilliant blue of the skies, the air Marines moved through the doldrums of their daily existence.

For days and weeks and endless months, they flew back and forth, bombing and strafing the low-slung atolls. Often they hit the same target twice in a day. On one flight, the weather might be CAVU (clear and visibility unlimited). On the next day they might be fighting their way in and out of sudden hazardous tropical storms. They bombed and strafed and strafed and bombed a narrowing assortment of targets—runways, buildings, gun positions, power plants, radar stations, blockhouses, dugouts, and gardens. At times, they varied the monotony of their loads by scattering surrender leaflets and canned salmon to enemy survivors and the natives. Slightly miffed, they stopped the psychological salmon warfare when one of the emaciated prisoners reported he would not eat American Salmon because it was of such low grade.

Throughout the months from March to September, while the war and the glory moved on into the Western Pacific, a dozen or more Marine squadrons—Corsairs, Dauntlesses, and Hellcats—mauled the atoll targets. They micrometered their precision bombings to a point where a hit was not registered unless the bomb struck inside a 30-foot circle. On more than 11,000 sorties in the period, they rocked the enemy islands with 3,300,000 pounds of bombs and serrated them with millions of rounds of machine-gun ammunition.

Antiaircraft fire during the first months was blistering in its accuracy against the low-altitude attacks of the Marines. Thirty-six planes were shot down in six months. Of their crews, 17 pilots and 3 enlisted men were lost while 16 officers and 5 rear-gunners were rescued in spectacular operations by the flying boats and destroyers circling the targets for just that purpose.

Their grinding attrition took its toll. Where flak fire had been "intense and accurate," the reports now read "light and inaccurate." The primary targets had been sought out and obliterated, while fire bombs scorched the remains. Tiny fishing craft and scrawny parties working in the dawn and dusk were ripped by machine-gun fire from the search planes which scoured the atolls between raids for any signs of life or movement. By night, the tiring Japanese were kept awake in their dugouts by patrol bombers making their watchman rounds and raids.

Far to the west, the invasion timetable had called off landings at Saipan, Tinian, Guam, and Peleliu. But the "rock-happy" squadrons of the Fourth Wing stuck to their milk runs over the atoll circuit. The turnover in personnel was slow and the strain of their drudgery in the forgotten war increased space as the airmen learned the truth of the wry island adage that dive-bombers do not make headlines, Their contributions went virtually unnoticed, even that of Major Elmer "Iron Man" Glidden. This lantern-jawed commander of the Ace of Spades (VMSB 231), one of the oldest squadrons in Marine Aviation, reeled off a consecutive string of 77 combat dives against the atolls in his SBD. With him as rear-gunner on all these strikes was Master Technical Sergeant James A. Boyle. Glidden's total in the Marshalls, added to the 27 he made in the early days at Midway and Guadalcanal, set his record at 104 twisting, weaving runs down at the barking, red muzzles of the flak guns. It was the only record of its kind in naval aviation, but it passed almost without kudos because the front lines were thousands of miles away.

Cigar-mauling Brigadier General Louis E. Woods, called "Bullets and Beans" by his men, took over as boss of the forgotten war in late August. [Woods relieved Brigadier General Thomas J. Cushman, who, in turn, had replaced Merritt in mid-May.] Woods stepped up the crescendo of the bomb ballet as the summer passed into fall. Tonnage totals reached new peaks during the intensive pounding through December. There was a change of pace in these months as the venerable Dauntless SBD's were replaced in the squadrons by Corsair fighters. [Months later, the VMSB units switched again, this time to the SB2C, Curtiss Helldiver bombers.] The Wing concentrated its efforts on exploiting its new weapon, the VMBF, or fighter-bomber squadrons.

The fighter-bomber technique was the notable innovation produced by the cat-and-mouse war in the Marshalls. Marines used the enemy targets for experimental purposes in developing new tactics and weapons and improving old ones and, incidentally, turning the surviving Japanese crews into some of the most accurate AA gunners in the Pacific. In the spring, the Corsairs had accompanied the bombers as fighter escorts, to strafe targets ahead of bomb runs.

Soon, with fighter protection obviously unneeded and strafing runs hardly worth the trip for the Corsairs, the fighter squadrons tinkered with the idea of using the fast F4U as a bomber. This was in direct opposition to the standard dive-bombing technique which required slowing down even the none-too-fast SBD's in their final dive to get needed accuracy for pin-point bombing.

Major William E. Classen's Devildog (VMF 111) squadron made the first experimental run when eight of its Corsairs struck heavy AA positions on Mille with 1,000-pound bombs from their belly racks. Results were considered good, as four hits were made in the target area without the use of bombsights. Subsequent tests were devoted to determining the type of dive angle that could best be used and the maximum effective bomb load for the Corsairs which had never been designed for the purpose.

Classen reported: "This type of bombing is an art, not a science," he said. "It's like playing a violin. In the last analysis, you can't tell a man how to do it. He's got to experiment until he works out his own individual technique."

His pilots reported their own tactics: "Keep the whole target in view just above your engine cowling. When it disappears under the cowling, release the bomb. Release at the point where you've either got to drop it and get the hell out of there, or fly right through the target."

Squadron tactics with the fighter-bomber varied. Classen's pilots often worked the glide approach rather than diving. The bomb-carrying F4U was covered by wingmen on both sides who kept the AA positions inactive while the bomber came down in a high-speed approach and released at 100 feet. Wingmen continued to strafe until the bomber retired out of range.

Most Corsair squadrons eventually concentrated on using the F4U as a dive-bomber. Their efforts on live targets proved that the Corsair could be safely and accurately employed as a dive-bomber up to and including 70-degree dives.

The F4U readily handled 2,000 pounds of bombs on its wings or under the fuselage, either as one bomb or as a mixed load of 500- and 1,000-pounders. Full use was made of their six wing guns during the last stages of the dive because the Japanese ground gunners would not stay at their stations in the face of such fire.

In improving the striking power of its own fighter squadrons, the Fourth Marine Air Wing was so successful with its fighter-bomber technique that it was adopted in toto by all of naval aviation and contributed materially to the increased potency of carrier warfare in the later stages of the Pacific war, as did the Wing's experiments with Napalm bombing.

The fire bomb, a fluid mixture of gasoline and a jelly substance called Napalm, was used for the first time late in July in the Tinian campaign, but its initial use was complicated by difficulties with mixing, fusing, and release mechanisms. Marine Corsairs, late in 1944, explored the difficulties and potentialities of the fire bomb on frequent raids, and their hazardous trials in the Marshalls demonstrated its effectiveness against personnel, brush-covered areas, and light installations.

At year's end, the Fourth Wing was still hammering at the slowly dying bases from Kwajalein, Eniwetok, and Majuro with more than a dozen squadrons, aided now by a Mitchell medium-bomber unit (VMB 613), which pushed its PBJ landplanes on long, dangerous overwater shipping searches. Woods, now a Major General, continued to command the Fourth Wing long after its policy of daily air strikes against the Marshall bases was cancelled in late January because all available targets had been destroyed.

Postwar interrogations of the enemy survivors on Wotje, Maloelap, Mille, and Jaluit provided singular testimony to the efficacy of the near 7,000,000 pounds of bombs, rockets, and Napalm which the Marine squadrons had laid on their atolls. [*The combined tonnage for all services in the Marshall Islands' siege was 12,900,000 pounds. Pin-point techniques used by Marine planes were credited with destroying the major portion of the defensive systems on the four atolls and contributing extensively to enemy problems by continued destruction of their living quarters and food and medical supplies. The radio facilities on all bases except Jaluit were kept inoperative and the airbases were all but wiped out by the persistent raids. Prisoners gave a lion's share of the credit for the over-all atoll damage to the* "little planes" or the "small ones." Next to the SBD, the Corsair fighter-bomber was rated by the Japs as the most effective aerial weapon.]

After the carrier planes had wiped out the atolls' air defense, and the Army high-level bombers had destroyed a large portion of the massed areas of light construction, the Marine aerial strangulation proved viciously effective. More than 6,500 Japanese of the original garrison force of 13,000 died either in the bombing raids or as a direct result through the loss of food and medical supplies. The aerial blockade resulted in the deaths by starvation of 3,900 enemy troops at Mille, Wotje, and Maloelap. Japanese morale, originally high, dropped off sharply during the fall and winter months of 1944 and stayed low as the food and medical situation got worse.

Some enemy enlisted personnel surrendered before the end, and greater numbers would have had it not been for fear of being shot by their own troops. The senior medical officer on Wotje admitted that he had collected American propaganda leaflets which carried pictures of tempting meals and stared at them while eating the atoll delicacy of boiled rats for dinner. Both at Wotje and Jaluit, no attempt was made to treat enlisted men suffering from major wounds unless they held key jobs. Otherwise, it was frankly stated, they were left to die.

Japanese prisoners admitted that in the final months of the siege, cannibalism became an active pursuit on some of the atolls and that guards had to be posted over freshly buried corpses to prevent grave robbing for the sake of food.

It had been the mission of the Marine squadrons to smash the by-passed atoll installations and garrisons beyond all hope of recovery. The postwar survey (by U. S. Strategic Bombing Survey groups) was grisly proof they had succeeded. Enemy garrisons on Wotje, Mille, Maloelap, and Jaluit were virtually impotent. The offensive power of their bases had been annihilated and their defensive strength was nil because the daily life of the "feeble spiders" who remained had become only a struggle for existence against insurmountable odds.

Fourth Wing in the Marianas

Final segment of Admiral Nimitz's 1944 plan for the Central Pacific campaign was Operation "Forager," involving the capture of Saipan, Tinian, and Guam islands in the southern Marianas.

As was true of so many Pacific invasions, the seizure of these bases was to advance American airpower along the road to Tokyo, since they would provide fields from which all of the enemy home islands could be brought under heavy air bombardment. Further, their capture would seal off enemy bases in the Carolines to the south and possibly bring the elusive Japanese Navy to battle. The bases at Saipan and Tinian were to screen the giant naval and air centers to be built at Guam, the former Navy and Marine base which the enemy had captured in the first days of the war.

Troops of the veteran Second and Fourth Marine Divisions, supported by the 27th Army Division, hit the western beaches of Saipan, capital of the heavily fortified Marianas on June 15. There was no enemy air opposition during the early assault phase because enemy airbases within range had been neutralized by carrier raids and land-based heavy bombers. However, Admiral Shigetaro Shimada, Japanese fleet commander, launched a mighty two-pronged air assault on the invasion area and its supporting fleet on June 19, to crush the American forces in a huge vise as carrier planes struck from one direction and land-based bombers from another. The abortive effort turned into the spectacular "Marianas Turkey Shoot" for the carrier planes and into the Battle of the Philippine Sea, in which the Japanese task force was hard-hit.

Ashore, the line Marines fought a bitter, 25-day battle over rugged terrain before securing Saipan, 1,500 miles from Tokyo.

Marine Air Arm operations in the Saipan campaign were small, and centered on the activities of the VMO (Observation) squadrons flying artillery-spotting missions and the air-evacuation flights of the transport units attached to the Fourth Wing.

Tiny "Grasshopper" Stinson Sentinel planes of VMO-2 landed from carriers on a narrow roadway outside the town of Charon-Kanoa and began operations at dawn of the third day of the assault. During its first days ashore, the eight-plane squadron moved its base frequently because it was continually under enemy artillery fire.

Commanded by Captain John Ambler, the OY-1 pilots moved up to Aslito, main enemy field, right after its capture and eventually were the first planes to fly from three other captured fields. As the eyes of the artillery, the Grasshoppers flew from dawn to dusk on low-altitude patrols behind enemy lines, carrying with them air observers from one of the infantry units. Their usual scouting altitude was 200 feet, though more often they flew only a few feet off the ground as they searched ravines, caves, canefields, and camouflaged positions. Most of their missions were flown within easy range of enemy small arms so that the cloth fuselages of their planes and wings were well-punctured by bullet and shrapnel holes. Six of Ambler's eight planes were cut up by enemy fire, but the pilots escaped unharmed.

VMO 4 did not fare so well. Five of its planes were wrecked and two pilots killed during the Saipan-Tinian campaigns. Its commanding officer and one pilot were seriously wounded by enemy bombs which killed three men and destroyed two planes. Six remaining pilots in the unit flew 700 hours to complete 400 missions during the operations, one of which was spotting a submarine and directing the destroyer gunfire which sank it.

With ten days of rest after the costly Saipan assault, the two Marine Divisions crossed a two and one-half mile strait to land at Tinian. There, in a rapid eight-day operation against strong resistance, the weary Marines pushed surviving Japanese defenders into a pocket in which they were destroyed with the aid of air and naval bombardments. At Tinian, the two VMO squadrons continued their missions, concentrating in the last phases of the Tinian push on scout and observation missions for the fast-moving infantry units.

Near the south end of Tinian, Captain Ambler, whose squadron had spent 760 hours in combat flight, discovered two Japanese tanks racing toward a ridge position held by 400 enemy troops. Target information was radioed to the artillery batteries which knocked out the tanks, the 400 Japanese, and the strongpoint.

The third phase of "Forager" unfolded when troops of the Third Marine Amphibious Corps, under Marine Major General Roy S.

Geiger, made two simultaneous landings on Guam's western beaches the morning of July 21. Marines of the Third Division and the First Provisional Brigade, with the 77th Army Division in support, drove through stubborn opposition in the cities, canefields, jungles, and mountains of Guam to split up and destroy enemy resistance after 21 days of grim fighting.

Carrier-air support was extensive before and after the landing phase at Guam. The first night ashore more than 100 planes were used in helping repel counterattacks on both flanks of the beachhead. Frequent Japanese night "Banzai" charges and night attacks forced the use of aerial illumination at the front lines and Marine Hellcat fighters of VMF (N) 532 flew combat air patrol from dusk to dawn over the battle areas. This unit, based at Saipan, began its initial operations over Guam two days prior to the landing and continued its night patrols during the campaign.

The major Marine air actions at Guam got under way when squadrons of Marine Air Group 21 flew off the carrier *Suwanee* to land at Orote field on August 4. Through the remaining days of infantry operation, Corsair squadrons 216, 217, and 225 and night fighter unit VMF (N) 534 supported the line troops.

As they had at Saipan, the Grasshopper planes flew continuous missions for both the infantry and artillery. VMO 1 landed its green-hued planes on Orote field the day of its capture. [*During the Cape Gloucester campaign on New Britain, beginning December 24, 1943, a Marine observation squadron, using borrowed Army Piper Cubs, was employed by the First Marine Division. Its pilots were a pick-up group of officers and men who had prewar flying experience or were Marine aviators on detached duty with the Division.*]

One day after Marines had cleared a portion of Agana field, the OY-1's moved up, though the Japanese still held the far end of the strip 3,000 yards away. Unable to use the field, the squadron flew off a near-by road which had been ground out by tanks and amphtracks. Deviled by raids, mud and mortar fire, the unarmed and unarmored "Madame Butterflies," which had a top speed of 130 mph, flew spotter missions for 27 artillery batteries. During the first ten days off Agana, every pilot in the squadron, commanded by Major Gordon Heritage, averaged more than 30 day and night missions. Two of its pilots were awarded the prized infantry medal, the Silver Star.

Lieutenant George Lovelace flew 12 miles behind the lines to locate his target. Discovering a large enemy concentration, Lovelace dropped down to 75 feet through intense machine-gun fire, calling directions to the artillery which wiped out 60 trucks, 2 tanks, numerous positions, and 400 Japanese.

Lieutenant Gerald Skogmo earned his award for "conspicuous gallantry and intrepidity in action" on a mission in which his plane hovered 50 feet over an enemy position. Bullets smashed into his cockpit, missing Skogmo, but badly damaging his plane. Nursing it back to the field, the Marine climbed out of the battered Grasshopper and into another and returned to finish his mission.

Six of the squadron's planes were hit by Jap fire, but none was lost and it had no pilot casualties. Staff observers of the Third Amphibious Corps estimated that 3,000 enemy troops, 100 trucks, 10 tanks, and numerous storage dumps, warehouses, and bivouac areas were destroyed by artillery fire directed by observation from the Stinson Sentinels.

Brigadier General Pedro DeValle, senior Marine artillery officer on Guam, wrote of the air-support efforts of the squadron: "VMO 1 did an excellent job. These planes flew innumerable missions in all sorts of weather. Flying so close that, at times, they almost skimmed the trees, they smoked out enemy guns, trucks, bivouacs, and dumps with great skill and persistence."

Senior shore-based air command in the Marianas was the Marine Air Defense Detachment, Forward Area, which operated administratively under the Fourth Wing and was originally commanded by Colonel William L. McKittrick. It went ashore with the assault waves at Saipan to direct the Army squadrons handling local air defense. Its Marine units were grouped at Guam under Colonel Peter Schrider, who served as Air Defense commander of the island and commander of MAG 21. By November, 1944, when McKittrick was replaced by Brigadier General Thomas J. Cushman, 2,200 officers and men of Marine Aviation were on duty in the Marianas with 11 operating squadrons. Their main activity was a neutralization bombing campaign against islands in the upper Marianas. Daily for four months, the fighter squadrons hit Rota, 55 miles away, or ranged 280 miles north to bomb the enemy base at Pagan. This by-passed island operation was in effect until the end of the war.

Blood and Hell Jelly at Peleliu

After the Marianas campaigns, the Allied offensive swung south and west. It was directed against western islands of the Carolines, the Palau group, which command the approaches to the Philippines from the east and New Guinea from the north. One thousand miles west of Truk and only 530 miles from Davao in the Philippines, the Palaus are a chain 20 miles wide and 77 miles long. Principal invasion target in this enemy mandate possession was the small, roughly terrained and wooded island of Peleliu in the southern Palaus. Its capture would join the Allied spearheads which had been driving up from the South Pacific and west through the Central Pacific.

First Division Marines drove across coral reefs and onto the southern beaches of Peleliu under fierce Japanese fire on September 15. They repelled several heavy counterattacks during the afternoon of the first day and by night were generally pinned near the beaches. At dawn of the second day, the Marines began cleaning out enemy caves and pillboxes, using flamethrowers, bazookas, mortars, and tanks. Veteran Japanese troops continued to counterattack during the day, but the airfield was taken by dusk.

Ground echelons of the Second Marine Air Wing started ashore to build an air camp, but were pressed immediately into the beachhead operations. One hour after the assault waves went ashore, the air Marines were forming boat platoons for unloading, beaching, and evacuation of wounded among the infantry. One week later, aviation personnel were still serving as front-line stretcher bearers and ammunition handlers after fighting as riflemen and grenade throwers. Six were killed and 11 wounded during this period of unusual "air support." Grasshoppers of VMO 3 landed on a 550-foot field on D-plus-2 to initiate their artillery observation and scouting missions.

After taking the southern part of Peleliu on the third day, the

Marines drove northward through limestone ridges and valleys impregnated with enemy cave positions, and by the 21st had secured the eastern coast of the island. Little progress was made on the left flank on the west coast, which was dominated by a three-to-four mile mountain called Umurbrogol. This natural fortress was infested with rifle pits and pillboxes. The southern extremity, about 1,000 yards north of the airfield, was called "Bloody Nose Ridge" by the Marines who stormed its heights for six days under intensive bombardment, suffered heavy casualties, and failed to overrun it.

Peleliu's airbase opened for traffic on September 24. Marine Commando transports navigating for eight planes of VMF (N) 542 and carrying Major General James T. Moore were the first to land. Moore set up headquarters for the Second Wing with its one Air Group and as the Commander, Garrison Air Forces, Western Carolines. His area command was charged with three major tasks: 1) Air defense of all American ground troops and convoys in the Western Carolines; 2) furnishing air support for the ground forces on Peleliu, Ngesebus, and other islands in the vicinity; and 3) neutralization of the remaining enemy bases in the Western Carolines. By the end of September, one Corsair fighter squadron (VMF 114) and half a night fighter unit were operating and the ground crews of three other squadrons were standing by for the arrival of their planes and pilots.

A battalion of the Fifth Marines, supported by Sherman tanks, crossed the coral reef along the northern coast of Peleliu on September 28 and landed at Ngesebus Island under cover of VMF 114, which bombed and later strafed the beaches for 30 minutes, until the infantry units were within 200 yards of shore. The island's airbase was captured by noon, and by nightfall all enemy resistance except a small pocket was eliminated. The Marines also captured two small near-by islands.

With the exception of the menacing Bloody Nose Ridge area, all organized resistance on Peleliu ended September 29. [During the period until the assault phase ended October 12, Marines and Army infantry units succeeded in narrowing the mountain pocket by continued attacks on its caves and ridges. The bitter fighting during the campaign resulted in 5,031 Marine casualties, with 842 killed and

128 missing. More than 11,000 of the Japanese defenders were killed.]

Corsairs of the Death Dealers squadron made their first close air support mission against Bloody Nose Ridge on the morning of September 29 and continued these strikes regularly for two months with "extreme accuracy." They dumped their bombs on a small horseshoe curve in the "Death Valley" sector just 15 seconds after passing over the ready tent on the airfield where they had been briefed. Ankle-deep in mud, the rain-soaked ground crewmen of the squadron watched the first of what came to be known as one of the shortest bombing hops in the Pacific war.

Major Robert F. Stout, Gaudalcanal ace and squadron commander, led the planes which plastered the target area on the first raid. Bomb concussions on the ridge shook the airfield and rocked its control tower while one pilot slipped his bomb into the mouth of one of the large enemy caves, sealing it up permanently.

Until the defenders were wiped out on November 27, the Marine fighter-bomber squadrons, now including VMF 121 and 122, pounded away at the Peleliu pocket. Early in October, the F4U's began fire bomb raids. The Napalm "hell jelly," ironically, was mixed with captured Japanese gasoline stores.

Making their runs with wheels down at extremely low altitude and close to friendly troops, the Corsairs were able to sear off the brush concealing enemy emplacements and suffocate or burn to death many of the cave-entrenched Japanese. Their early efforts were so successful that the F4U's continued to make these "flying flamethrower" attacks during the remainder of the mopping-up campaign.

Living within concussion blast of mortar and heavy artillery positions and under the low roof of steel they belched up at the Ridge, the Second Wing units continued their backyard air support for the troops of the 81st Army Division which had taken over from the First Division in mid-October and had contributed a combat team during the early Peleliu phases. Corsairs also provided air cover for infantry units landing at Pulo Anna island, 200 miles southwest of Peleliu, November 4, and for a further infantry landing at Ngregong Island.

Long before the last Japanese died in his cave on Bloody Nose

Ridge, General Moore's squadrons were concentrating on what was by then an old Marine tradition, the milk runs. His GAF, Western Carolines, included 11 squadrons, both Army and Marine, and two Air Groups.

Beyond the enemy base at Yap were the islands of Ulithi Atoll, site of the second airbase of Moore's command. The Ulithi invasion, a phase of the Peleliu operation, was ordered because Ulithi's large lagoon was to be used as the major fleet anchorage for the impending invasion of the Philippines. Its main island of Faleolap was taken without opposition by Army infantry on September 23. The first elements of MAG 45 arrived there October 8 and its night fighter planes were patrolling the area by the end of the month.

The Air Group entered its phase of the by-passed islands campaign when planes of VMTB 232 made their first run over Yap November 2. During four months on Ulithi, the TBM Avenger bombers of this 20-year-old squadron carried out a relentless campaign against Western Caroline bases: Yap, Fais, Sorol, and Woleai. Secondarily, it conducted a ceaseless antisubmarine patrol over the Fleet anchorage in the Ulithi lagoon. Two of its planes were credited with sinking an enemy submarine during a hunter-killer mission on November 20 against a reported wolf-pack of enemy subs.

Back at Peleliu, planes of Moore's GAF struck in a new direction when Army B-24's based at near-by Angar Island bombed Japanese fields on Luzon in the Philippines. The Liberators flew daily strikes thereafter against Philippine installations, with alternate targets in the northern Palaus which were receiving the brunt of Marine raids. In early December, air operations against the enemy-held Palaus had reached the milk-run stage.

Garrison Air Force, Western Carolines, was disbanded then and its Army and Navy personnel returned to other duties. On December 15, the Second Wing, consisting only of a headquarters squadron, was returned to Pearl Harbor for the planning stages of the Okinawa invasion. Marine Air Groups 11 and 45, with their six squadrons, were transferred to the Fourth Air Wing.

Through the final weeks of 1944, until the end of the war, the Peleliu squadrons kept thousands of Japanese troops pinned down to their bases while carrying out a systematic campaign of destruction against them. The main targets were Babelthuap, largest island in the Palaus, and Yap. During five weeks of milk-run raids, the Corsair squadrons at Peleliu flew 1,100 sorties, dropping 186 tons of bombs on predetermined targets. The pin-point bomb drops in this period netted a variety of destruction—112 barges; 58 trucks; 35 assorted oil, supply, and ammunition dumps; 1 dam; 2 radio stations; 10 power boats; 4 boat houses; 2 whale boats; 1 locomotive; 12 warehouses; 20 small motor boats; one 80-foot ship; one 100-foot ship; 3 piers; 3 planes on the ground and one in the air—along with undetermined, but considerable, personnel damage.

Peleliu airfield was designated as a Marine Corps airbase in January and put under command of Colonel Karl Day, a World War I flier. During and after the operation, Marine airmen served as Island Commander, Peleliu, a position which was held successively by Brigadier Generals Harold D. Campbell, Christian Schilt, and Ford O. Rogers.

Aerial Lifeline to Everywhere

With the Western Carolines on its roster, Woods' Fourth Wing was operating over an ocean area of several million square miles from its seven major bases in the Marshalls, Marianas, Palaus, and Ulithi. Knitting this vast network of Marine activity into a compact and effective whole and linking it to other theaters of war was an aerial lifeline to everywhere—the twin-engined transport squadrons which hauled tactical air traffic over the Pacific reaches.

This Central Pacific counterpart of SCAT—the infantry's combat airline in the Solomons—made what is considered the most significant contribution of the Marine Air Arm to continued front-line infantry support during the mid-Pacific campaigning. Like SCAT, the several Central Pacific transport organizations were a remarkable example of interservice cooperation, with Army, Navy, and Marine personnel operating jointly in all the major units. As in the South Pacific, Marine transport squadrons were the core and bulk of these airlines with Army planes in strong support.

First of this series of Central Pacific transport units which telescoped one into another was the Samoan Combat Air Transport Service, which began operations at Tutuila in September, 1943. Commanded by Major Edmund Zonne, former civilian airline pilot, this service had one squadron—VMJ 353—flying Douglas R4D's and serving the garrison forces in the Samoan area.

CENCATS, the Central Pacific Combat Air Transport Service, was activated under General Merritt's Fourth Wing in mid-November of the same year to handle air traffic from its headquarters at Tutuila over the small island network of Upolo, Wallis, Funafuti, Nukufetau, and Nanomea.

As the invasion forces drove upward into the Gilberts, the air transports hovered in their wake. The first large plane to land at Tarawa was a CENCATS freighter, which brought in the island's first radio transmitter and personnel to operate it. Next day one of its transport planes flew in Admiral Nimitz and other high-ranking service personnel for an inspection tour of the atoll battlefield. Both flights and succeeding trips into Tarawa brought out planeloads of wounded.

CENCATS planes flew an exhausting round-the-clock shuttle during the month of December, when its command was taken over by Marine Lieutenant Colonel T. J. McQuade with an Army Major as its executive officer. Ground crews worked on a 24-hour schedule to keep the transports operational for the emergency flights to and from the captured bases in the Gilberts. [Opening new terminals on their first flights into Makin and Apamama, the planes of the Marine squadron and three Army transports carried 2,229 passengers, 535,000 pounds of priority freight, 206,000 pounds of regular mail, and 500 pounds of top priority messenger mail during the month.]

Bulldozers had barely leveled portions of the captured airbases after the Marshall invasions in February, when CENCATS flights pancaked on one after another of the fields after pioneering hops over hundreds of miles of open water, weaving in and out between enemy-held islands to find the tiny atoll strips. They opened makeshift air terminals and began scheduled operations from the new fields under conditions that would have caused shudders in commercial airlines. One Marine plane even squeezed in a landing on the half-finished field at Eniwetok to bring in heavy construction gear needed to surface the strip.

Aerial cargoes into the combat zones were made up of priority passengers, mail, medical supplies, and the odds and ends of war needed to maintain the garrison forces and expedite the aerial siege campaign. One emergency flight brought in 6,000 pounds of soap because the filthy clothing of the troops ashore was infecting their battle wounds. At Roi, the infantry was suffering from a dietary deficiency and 10,000 pounds of canned tomato juice winged its way in to relieve the condition. Planes returning to bases in the south or east to Pearl Harbor loaded out with regular cargoes of medical patients, mail, and passengers. During one urgent transfer of a Marine Air Group, 488 officers and men and 71,700 pounds of gear were hauled in eight days by six planes.

To meet new demands on its services, CENCATS was reorganized as the Transport Air Group (TAG) during March and two new squadrons were added. Marine Utility Squadron 252, flying the high-speed, whale-bellied R5C Curtiss Commando transports, joined on the first of March and the Army's 10th Troop Carrier unit one month later. The new Commandos gave additional impetus and range to the tactical airlines because of their advantages over the traditional Douglas R4D's in speed, capacity, and distance.

Prowling the sky highways of the Pacific under the ambitious title of the Victory Air Line, with large white shipping tags painted under the noses of its transports, TAG planes made 545 flights during April. By month's end, the freight squadrons had been in operation for half a year and their records showed not a single serious accident in hauling 15,200 passengers, 3,380,000 pounds of freight, and 2,386,000 pounds of mail on its atoll runs. The squadrons were then hauling an average of 2,500,000 pounds of cargo a month, and that total rose steadily.

TAG transports operating under the Fourth Wing entered their biggest phase of combat air support during the invasions of the Marianas. At Saipan, Guam, and Tinian, the twin-engined planes were the first large planes to land on the captured fields. During the battle for Saipan, the transports rushed 48,000 pounds of urgently needed supplies to the battlefront from Kwajalein, more than 1,200 miles away, and then returned with heavy loads of wounded infantry-men. In two weeks, at the height of the campaign, the TAG terminal at Saipan handled nearly 5,000 passengers and 1,500,000 pounds of airfreight. One of its R4D's was specially fitted out to spray DDT over island camps to combat a rising epidemic of dengue fever. Another pilot was cited for saving his load of medical patients in an emergency landing by using parachutes rigged to the plane to stop it before it crashed beyond the end of the runway. In four and one-half days of the Tinian battle, the aerial ambulances hauled out 1,400 battle casualties to rear-base hospitals and established a new Pacific evacuation record.

The Marine transport planes performed another spectacular air support mission in the early days of the Peleliu campaign when the combat troops were without food and their field hospitals, still under fire, were crowded far beyond capacity with scores of battle casualties. The transports at Saipan made their emergency run when foul weather and surf conditions made supply and evacuation by small boat impossible.

All available planes of VMR 952 were stripped of their original cargoes and jammed with rations. At dawn, 16 TAG Commandos headed for Peleliu in one of the largest emergency air operations of the Central Pacific war. Flying unarmed and unescorted over miles of enemy-held territory, the planes landed safely. After an overnight stop under sniper fire, the transports loaded dozens of emergency patients on hurriedly rigged stretchers and litters and made the stormy 900-mile return trip without incident.

October 9, TAG was moved forward from the Marshalls to the Marianas, where it set up headquarters of Agana Field, Guam. Two units, VMR 253 and 952, handled the forward traffic while the two other Marine squadrons, VMR 252 and 353, remained as the mainstays of ATG, the Air Transport Group, flying the local runs in the Gilberts and Marshalls. [When ATG disbanded in March, 1945, its Marine squadrons were moved up to operate with TAG. During the last year of the war, the forward-area Marine transports were assisted by TAU, a special transport line handling "hot cargo,"

which operated out of MCAS, Ewa, under the Third Marine Air
Wing. This squadron, VMR 953, operated over the entire Pacific
Theater and by July, 1945, had flown its 25 millionth passenger mile
without incident or accident.]

The land-based twin-engined transports of TAG and the other
Marine transport units continued to wing out day and night over
thousands of miles of ocean on their runs from atoll to island in
the Central and South Pacific, serving the Marine and Army divisions, the naval bases, and the Marine air units. Special hops took
them to Samoa, Australia, the Philippines, and the Admiralties as
they toted strange combinations of VIP's (Very Important Per-
sonages), Jap prisoners, USO performers, penicillin, Marine war dogs,
blood plasma, and war plans. Their performance over the ocean areas
without the loss of a single passenger or a serious accident in 23
months and 14,191,000 plane miles of air travel was tactically spectacular in its routine, undramatic fashion.

Next way-station of the TAG planes took them half way up to
Tokyo on a bearing north by west from Saipan.

"Eight Square Miles of Hell"

During the first days of 1945, the word was spread deliberately
through the bistros of Honolulu that the next American offensive
would be against Formosa, the Beautiful Island, called Taiwan by
the Japanese. Instead, in the dawn of February 19, the 800-ship invasion armada of the Fifth Fleet stood off an inconspicuous little
island of the Volcano group in the Kazan Retto.

It was Iwo Jima. Precisely at 0903, the first assault wave clawed its
way up the black volcanic sands of this "eight square miles of hell."
These were the first of Major General Harry Schmidt's 61,000
Marines of the V Amphibious Corps which was composed largely
of the Third, Fourth, and Fifth Marine Divisions which were committed to action against the 22,000 Japanese hidden in Iwo's earth
and rock defenses.

Prior to the landing, an unparalleled naval and air bombardment had turned the island into what was described as a "pork chop with a bump, frying and sizzling in the ocean."

Ashore, the Marines fought up the heights of Mount Suribachi, planted the flag, and then pressed their relentless assault on the central and northern parts of the island and the three airfields. At the end of 36 savage days, and at the price of 5,500 Marine dead, Iwo Jima was taken. Lieutenant General H. M. Smith, commander of the expeditionary troops, marked down Iwo as "the toughest we've run across in 168 years of Marine Corps history." Admiral Nimitz described it as a battle in which "uncommon valor was a common virtue."

The strategic value of Iwo Jima, some 600 miles from Tokyo, again highlighted the fact that the Pacific conflict was basically a war for airfields. As a forward fighter base screening the Marianas, Iwo made possible vital over-the-target fighter cover and heavier bomb loads for the B-29 Superfortresses hitting targets in Japan from bases in the Marianas. Its price in Marine lives was staggering, but the investment paid off twice a life for a life, as hundreds of crippled B-29's and their Army crews used Iwo as an emergency haven when they were unable to return to their home fields.

Marine air support of the Iwo operation began with the fighter-bomber missions during the landing phase by the Corsair squadrons aboard the fast carriers Essex and Bennington. First planes to land on the island at Motoyama Field No. 1, were two OY-1's of VMO 4 from the carrier Wake Island, on February 26. Their artillery-spotting missions began immediately, with more Grasshoppers of that unit and VMO 5 landing the following day. Two planes and one pilot of Lieutenant Frank Rozga's VMO 4 were lost when the carrier Bismarck Sea was sunk by a suicide plane. Other planes of Rozga's squadron were launched by special gear from a new type "baby carrier," the LST 776, fitted with a flight deck. As usual, the Sentinel observation planes were holed and torn by enemy ground fire during their 19 days of operation for the Marine artillery concentrations. Two planes hovered on station during the daylight hours over Iwo and the 6 planes of VMO 4 managed 194 combat flights with only one pilot wounded.

Up from Saipan on March 1 came the first air support plane of TAG. The Commando made five low passes over Motoyama, dropping 4,400 pounds of mail by parapack to the front-line troops. Two days later, another R5C nosed up to Iwo and landed on a portion of the field to unload 5,500 pounds of badly needed mortar ammunition. Again, on March 4, a TAG emergency mission, flown by planes of VMR 952, swept in over Iwo and para-dropped 51,000 pounds of mortar shells from their nine planes. Seventy-nine flights into Iwo were made by planes of VMR 952 during March on priority missions. Return flights evacuated 625 wounded infantrymen.

The third phase of Air Arm combat at Iwo was the operation of VMTB 242 which landed its first planes there March 8. Eighteen more of its type TBM-3 Avengers were ferried in from Tinian the next day to begin inshore antisubmarine patrols on a 24-hour basis. Eighteen pilots ranged out over the day sectors and 24 flew the night sea patrols on a rugged schedule in which the squadrons flew 3,300 combat hours in the first month at Iwo.

Night marauding PBJ bombers, commanded by Lieutenant Colonel Jack Cram, who won the Navy Cross at Guadalcanal, landed at Iwo on April 6 to put Marine land-based planes within range of the Japanese homeland for the first time. Cram, who had been experimenting with fast night-search radar bombers since the summer of 1943, stripped his Mitchells of all armament except tail guns to make weight and room for special radar gear, additional gas tanks, and eight 5-inch rockets slung on the wings.

Four days after arriving, a PBJ of VMB 612 made the first night run to Japan and severely damaged a cargo ship near the naval base at Kobe. Then, joining the neutralization campaign for the Okinawa operation, planes of the squadron on April 16 made rocket attacks on airfields in southern Kyushu, Japan, with Army P-51's as fighter escorts.

Throughout May and June, Cram led his squadron on a relentless series of long-range antishipping searches along the southern coast of Japan, with some of the missions more than 1,500 miles in length. In late May and June, the PBJ's experimented extensively with "Tiny Tims"—new 11.75-inch rockets which had the fire blast of an artillery broadside. Twenty-three attacks were made on enemy ships in June during the 74 low-altitude missions flown by the squadron along the coastal and inland waters of the Empire. Cram's pilots, despite weather and enemy night fighters, sank one ship and damaged 16 others during the period to bring the VMB 612 score to 5 Jap ships sunk and 53 damaged.

During the summer VMB 612 moved to Okinawa, and Iwo Jima settled back into the routine of rear-area existence as a dismal, unfriendly, well-blooded monument to valor, and another air terminal for TAG's transports droning northwest toward Japan.

ighter bombers of the Fourth Marine Air Wing swing out to the taxiway of
heir atoll air base on another mission to pound Jap strongholds in the Marshalls.

Aerial strangulation sorties against the by-passed islands in the Central and
Western Pacific gave the Marine airmen ample opportunity to test their
new technique of using the fast Corsair fighter as a pin-point divebomber.

Their target for the day to Marine SBD, F4U and
SB2C pilots who flew the milk run circuit in the
Marshalls was inevitably like this intelligence photo
of the remnants of Wotje.

A Jap's eye view of the shambles left by Marine bombers, this photo was
taken from a low-flying plane after one of the by-passed atolls had received its
daily battering.

A fire bomb sears a Japanese infantry position in a Peleliu gorge as Corsairs of the Second Air Wing aid Marine and Army troops in mopping up after weeks of bloody fighting.

A TAG transport receives a Peleliu battle casualty for air evacuation to a naval hospital as Major General William H. Rupertus (second from the right with cane), commanding the First Marine Division, watches the careful loading of the Curtiss Commando.

Workhorses of the Air Arm were the Avengers torpedo bombers shown here during a hazardous several thousand mile flight across the vast reaches of the mid-Pacific to a new battle area.

R.S.V.P. in Bombs requested "Welcome Yankee" message c eled in the airstrip on Babelth Island by its Japanese garrison the eyes of the Marine pilots were daily visitors.

A Jap shows the way to his own headquarters as Lieutenant Minoru Wada voluntarily directs a formation of Marine Mitchell bombers and Corsairs on a mission to wipe out his former division command post during the Philippines campaign.

A disaster in profile, the listing carrier *Franklin* shows her battle wounds, flames still pouring out of her aftersection following a Kamikaze attack off Japan.

Marine Corsairs are stacked in neat rows aboard the fast Navy carrier *Essex* as elements of a huge task force move into position for an attack in enemy home waters off Japan.

Informal briefing for the pilots of his two Marine fighter squadrons is handled on the carrier flight deck prior to a mission by Lieutenant Colonel William A. Millington.

His face tense as he roars past the carrier's island, a Marine pilot guns his fighter down the deck for a take-off.

Japan bound on an escort mission for Navy torpedo bombers, a Marine Corsair lifts off the carrier flight deck as two war correspondents watch it claw for speed and altitude barely above the waters of the Pacific.

☆ 8 ☆

RETURN TO THE PHILIPPINES

THE Marine dive-bomber pilots on Luzon are well qualified for the job they are doing and I have the greatest confidence in their ability. On our drive to Manila, I depended solely on the Marines to protect my left flank from the air against possible Japanese counterattack. The job they turned in speaks for itself. We are here.

"I can say without reservation that the Marine dive-bomber outfits are among the most flexible I have seen in this war. They will try anything, and from my experience with them, I have found that anything they try usually pans out. The dive-bombers of the First Marine Air Wing have kept the enemy on the run. They have kept him underground and enabled troops to move up with fewer casualties and with greater speed. I cannot say enough in praise of these dive-bomber pilots and their gunners for the job they have done in giving my men close ground support in this operation."—Major General Verne D. Mudge, Commanding, First Armored Cavalry Division.

"The excellent close support furnished by Marine dive-bombers in the advance of ground troops east of Manila in the Wawa–Antipolo sector between February 1 and March 15 was a major contribution to the success of operations in that area. The coordination and skill displayed by these pilots with the resultant effectiveness of their strikes was a continuation of the fine work accomplished on Bougainville. It has been my experience, gained from association with that operation and the present one, that Marine dive-bomber pilots can always be depended on to render outstanding support to the ground troops."—Major General O. W. Griswold, Commanding, XIV Army Corps.

"Please express to the officers and men of the Marine Air Wing, on the eve of their transfer to another assignment, my sincerest appreciation for their splendid support of the Sixth Army during the Luzon campaign. Their effective efforts were instrumental in keeping ground casualties to a minimum and contributing materially to the success of the operations."—General Walter Krueger, Commanding, Sixth Army.

"I have heard a great number of reports from Major General Franklin C. Sibert of the Tenth Corps and other unit commanders on results of Marine-type dive-bombing in the Philippine theater. The value of close support for ground troops as provided by these Marine fliers cannot be measured in words and there is not enough that can be said for their aerial barrages that have cut a path for the infantry. From all quarters, commanders down to the men with the bayonets, I have heard nothing but high tribute. Great going and keep blasting."—Lieutenant General Robert L. Eichelberger, Commanding, Eighth Army.

From these lavish tributes by its infantry commanders in the Luzon operation, it is safe to assume that in the Philippines campaign, the United States Army infantry "got the word" about Marine close air support.

The occupations of Peleliu in the Central Pacific and Morotai, north of Halmahera in the Southwest Pacific, kicked open the doors to the sprawling Philippine Archipelago which had been heavily under the Japanese thumb since the surrender of Corregidor on May 6, 1942. Its reconquest came sooner than had been expected.

Admiral Halsey's Third Fleet had been sortying against the Central Philippines in early September when he received word from a retrieved carrier pilot who had been downed there that Japanese strength in the area was considerably less than estimated.

Further investigation and reports on the widespread activities of the Filipino guerillas confirmed the pilot's story. Halsey recommended to his superiors that the proposed intermediate invasions of Yap and Mindanao, in the Southern Philippines, and two smaller islands be called off and that Leyte be invaded as soon as possible rather than in late December as had been planned.

General MacArthur agreed to invade on October 20, two months ahead of schedule.

Retaking of the Philippines would serve two vital purposes. It would help the white race to regain "face" in the Far East and would provide the large land base necessary for staging the half-million or more troops which would be needed in the "inevitable" invasion of the Japanese homeland.

Halsey's Third Fleet carried out the task of isolating the new battlefield by striking along an arc marked by the Philippines, Marcus Island, the Ryukyus, and Formosa. In late September, his carrier pilots destroyed 357 planes in the Manila area, then struck Leyte, Panay, and Cebu to the south. They shambled Manila again in mid-October. Those naval actions were implemented by the Seventh Fleet which intensified its savage submarine warfare against enemy shipping in the Philippines area. The Army's China-based Superfortresses ranged against Formosa, its 5th and 13th Air Forces against the southern Philippines, while Chennault's 14th Air Force worked over the China Coast.

Under heavy naval protection, General Krueger's Sixth Army went ashore on the northeast coast of Leyte on October 20. More than 600 amphibious vessels debarked its two elements, the X and XXIV Corps. Their separate landings were made against light resistance.

Three days later, as it fanned out against elected targets, the infantry was given orders to secure the beachhead areas and stand by.

Virtually the entire Japanese Navy had come out for a showdown. It was moving on Leyte in three separate forces in an attack aimed at wiping out the invasion shipping and smashing the landing attempt by a pincers coordinated with enemy land-based planes which had escaped the softening-up attacks.

Though under attack, and with the element of surprise lost, the three Jap task forces bored on, bullheadedly, toward Leyte and what became one of the greatest victories of American naval history—the Battle for Leyte Gulf.

After the naval battle, the Sixth Army moved ahead as the forces of the Tiger of Malaya, General Tomoyoki Yamashita, withdrew slowly into the difficult terrain of Leyte's rice paddies and mountains. In early November, the south coast of Samar island, to the near northeast, had been taken and another spearhead inched toward Ormoc, the principal enemy installation on Leyte. Bitter fighting, in progress at every point, was hampered by typhoons ushering in the islands' rainy season as the enemy brought in heavy reinforcements including its crack First Division of the famed Kwangtung Army.

Back at Tacloban field, the only major operating airbase on Leyte, the Fifth Army Air Force was ready to admit that the campaign "was a dud from the beginning" and that Leyte was "the closest we had come in a long time to losing a show." While mud delayed airfield operations and construction, Japanese planes raided Tacloban and the beach areas almost at will.

Without an overt attempt at dramatics, this was where the Marine Air Arm came in. In numbers, the flying Marines did not play the dominant part in the balance of Philippine campaigning, but their support role developed into one of the finest of its kind in the Pacific theater.

Major General Ralph Mitchell wangled permission from MacArthur's airmen to send First Air Wing elements into the Philippines show. On October 10, 1944, Mitchell issued orders for certain Wing units to prepare for a close support mission. With the issuance of those orders, Marine Aviation passed an important milestone. Close air support for infantry had been the prime mission of Marine Aviation for two decades. It had done a great deal of it from World War I to the caves of Peleliu, but this was the first time that its squadrons had been given a major air support assignment prior to an operation.

Somewhat disconcerting was the fact that this large-scale mission was not for Marine infantry, but for the Army ground forces, which did not officially believe in what the Marines knew as true "close" air support. Neither was their close support a doctrine of the Army Air Forces under which the air Marines would operate.

General William Mitchell, Chief of the Air Service, American Expeditionary Forces, in a report dated February, 1921, to the Commander-in-Chief AEF, wrote, "The attack by aircraft upon troops, using machine guns and small bombs, showed clearly that this had a most demoralizing effect. When properly employed, this aid from the sky in assisting during an attack by our own troops or in repelling an attack or counterattack by the enemy greatly raises the morale of our own forces and much hampers the enemy . . . this project should be thoroughly developed in the future." This, like other of Mitchell's recommendations, was not followed.

In "Attack Aviation," a document by the Army Air Corps Tactical School, Langley Field, Virginia, dated January, 1938, the following evaluation was carried, "In the event the situation is so critical that attack aviation is assigned to operate against hostile ground forces and their logistical systems, its striking power should be used against those targets which cannot be reached by the weapons of the ground arm . . . to use this force on the battlefield to supplement and increase the firepower of ground arms is decidedly an incorrect employment of this class of aviation, since it would neglect the most distant and vital objectives."

In the War Department's FM-100-20, Command and Employment of Air Power (Field Service Regulations, dated July, 1943), there is no mention of air support. It assigns third priority to aviation participation in gaining objectives on the immediate front of the ground forces. "However," it states, "in zones of contact, missions against hostile units are most difficult to control, most expensive, and are in general less effective than other forms of air effort, restricted by necessity for safety lines, and justifiable only at critical times . . ."

The First Wing order for the Philippines was transmitted to Colonel Lyle H. Meyer's MAG 24, which had spent most of the previous year on Bougainville. The group had four VMSB squadrons flying the Dauntless SBD's, which by this time were supposedly outmoded by several generations of new plane development. MAG 24's pilots accepted the new mission with relish and then asked, none too politely, "What the hell is close support?" They had all the usual training received by Marine Corps pilots, but they had no combat experience in air infantry support. What basic knowledge they had of Marine infantry tactics and procedures varied somewhat from those used by the Army.

Air support was too ticklish a task to play by ear, so MAG 24 began an extensive educational program based on data gathered from dozens of sources—Marine Air operations, a report on air support in Burma, a New Zealand summary of air support in New Guinea, and the operating procedures of various Army and Navy units along with the air support plan outlined in the Navy's Landing Force Manual.

Under Lieutenant Colonel Keith B. McCutcheon, Group Operations officer, a workable doctrine fitting the Philippines campaign was finally drawn up. It was based on the general Marine principal that "Close Air Support is an additional weapon to be employed at the discretion of the ground commander. He may employ it against targets that cannot be reached by other weapons or in conjunction with the ground weapons in a coordinated attack. It should be immediately available and should be carried out with deliberation and accuracy and in coordination with other assigned units."

This definition was followed in a detailed operating procedure and implemented by an intensive training program. The core of the SOP (Standard Operating Procedure) was emphasis on good communications and the Air Liaison Parties, called ALP's.

It was here that MAG 24's viewpoint disagreed with most existing and then practiced procedures. The Fifth Air Force, which commanded the operation, did not plan direct communication between the front lines at the point of support and the supporting planes. The AAF idea was that a Support Air Party (SAP) operating behind the front lines, usually at division headquarters, could supply all necessary data and direction for strikes. In this, the Navy too agreed.

MAG 24, on the contrary, proposed to have ALP's in radio jeeps right at the front lines. These Air Liaison Parties consisted of a radio man and a pilot or intelligence officer who could "talk" the support planes right on to the target by using radio, rocket signals, panels,

smoke, or any other workable means of target identification. The
thesis was simple and direct and most applicable to the terrain in
which the Marines would operate. Air support would be used like
a bayonet.

The Group worked out its tactics and learned those of the infantry
while on joint maneuvers with the Army's 37th Division, then
bivouacked on Bougainville.

Also at Bougainville and recently transferred from Pearl Harbor
were the SBD squadrons of MAG 32, commanded by Colonel Clayton C. Jerome, formerly Chief of Staff for ComAirNorSols. The
name Jerome was to become the byword for close support in the
coming operation. As the year drew to a close, the bomber groups
prepared to move into the combat area.

Action at Leyte and Samar

The first Marine air activity of the Leyte landing was credited to
General Mitchell himself. He went ashore on S-Day as an observer
on MacArthur's staff. [*Air units in the original landings were the
Air Section, Corps Artillery, Fifth Amphibious Corps, serving two
battalions of Marine 155-mm. artillery and an air liaison section of
the Marine Corps 2nd and 3rd Joint Assault Signal Companies.*]

When some 40-odd Navy planes were forced to land on bomb-
pocked Tacloban field after their escort carrier had been sunk during
the sea battle, Mitchell grabbed a pair of signal flags, ran to the
end of the strip, and acted as landing-signal officer, wagging in each
plane safely. Mitchell reported in the early assault phases that,
while he had spent a good deal of his Solomons duty in foxholes,
Leyte set a new record. He dived into a foxhole 26 times in a single
day as Jap planes raided the area.

Another sidelight on Leyte which Marines will long remember
was the task assigned to a Marine dive-bomber pilot serving as an
air support adviser on a carrier flagship. He flew the first official Marine
air mission of the invasion, dropping not bombs, but a cargo of
leaflets carrying the slogan "I Have Returned" to announce General
MacArthur's arrival to the Filipinos.

The first Marine squadron to land at Leyte was VMF (N) 541, a night fighter unit commanded by Lieutenant Colonel Peter D. Lambrecht. Originally attached to the Second Wing at Peleliu, this F6F unit was called in hurriedly because the Army P-61 night fighters lacked range, climb, and pilots with experience to cope with the Japanese night bombers. For several weeks after its landing on December 3, Lambrecht's squadron did not operate as a true radar night fighter unit. Local commanders didn't believe in using fighters throughout the night to hunt intruders by radar. Instead, they were confined generally to dusk and predawn operations.

During the month VMF (N) 541 operated at Leyte, it found the dusk and dawn hunting excellent, shooting down 22 planes, sinking 4 small surface vessels, and destroying 6 planes on the ground. Four of these air kills were credited to Technical Sergeant John W. Andre, one of the few Marine enlisted pilots then still flying in the Pacific.

Andre scored twice in one night by casually joining up on two Japanese "Jacks" returning to their base on Luzon after a raid near Tacloban Field. The Japanese pilots failed to notice Andre. Over their home field, they turned on their lights and went into their landing approach. Andre slid in behind one, fired, and it burst into flames. He gunned up behind the second plane, firing a long burst. That enemy plane smashed into the field, spewing fire in all directions as its gas tanks exploded. The Hellcat followed up with six strafing passes over the enemy field, burning at least three planes on the ground.

On December 3, four Marine squadrons added their Corsairs to the jam at Tacloban strip. For several weeks, this airfield was called the most crowded in the world.

Four days after arriving, these fighter-bomber units of MAG 12 (VMF 115, 211, 218 and 313) made their first major contact with Japanese shipping convoys. In this attack and in subsequent ones on December 11 and 12 in the Leyte–Ormoc–Mindoro areas, 14 enemy ships were sunk and 5 damaged.

Japanese air activity lessened considerably during December. Of the 26 planes which Marines shot down during that period, 11 were destroyed on December 11.

MAG 12 fighter-bombers covered the landing of the Army's 77th Division at Ormoc and joined VMF (N) 541 and carrier pilots in supporting landings by elements of the Sixth Army on Mindoro Island, several hundred miles northwest of Leyte. In early January the Corsairs made a long run north to join the air cover for the Army landings on Luzon Island.

The Marines flew routine fighter missions and operated regularly against land targets in the Central Philippines during January in attacks which netted numerous vehicles, buildings, bridges, freight cars, and assorted Japanese installations.

Infantry-support missions for the F4U's became common in early February during extensive operations with the Filipino guerillas in the Visayan Islands and on Mindoro. Although native leaders made enthusiastic reports from time to time on the air strikes, few results were reported because of a lack of good communications.

Support missions for the guerillas continued during February while MAG 12 prepared for another campaign. Meanwhile, another fighter-bomber group was in action near by.

Marine Air Group 14 and its four squadrons, VMF 212, 222, 223, and 251, began operating from Guiuan on Samar in early January, after staging in from the South Pacific. During their first weeks of action, MAG 14 planes flew a heavy schedule of air patrols, convoy cover, and tactical air missions, but had little contact with the Japanese air force which, by then, had judiciously vanished from the area.

In April, the tactical situation in the Philippines was such that the major fighter squadron assignment was supporting the 8th Army (which had relieved the 6th) and the guerillas in mopping-up and expansion campaigns. The majority of the Corsair missions were flown against targets on Cebu and Negros Islands. MAG 14 squadrons were commended regularly for "very effective close support" strikes which rapidly became routine and, as the weeks passed, of little note because of the lack of suitable enemy targets in the areas under attack.

During their months of operation in the Central Philippines, the Corsair groups had enjoyed little wholesale contact with the Japanese, but they had thoroughly established the effectiveness of the fast Corsair as a more-than-adequate infantry air support weapon.

The Diving Devildogs of Luzon

While the two First Wing fighter groups were holding forth on Leyte and Samar, the two dive-bomber groups were in action on a new front. On December 11, the ground echelons left the South Pacific by ship for the Philippines. About a week later, the flight echelons began their hazardous journey. With Marine Douglas transports navigating and carrying key personnel, the SBD's followed behind like broods of chicks in the wake of mother hens. They flew into action via Emirau, Owi, Biak, Peleliu, and Leyte. Their destination was the Lingayen beachhead.

On January 9, Krueger's Sixth Army, now composed of the First and Fourteenth Corps, went ashore at Lingayen Gulf and by nightfall had established a 15-mile beachhead against negligible opposition. Krueger left a strong force to seal off the enemy forces in the north and concentrated his offensive on a drive to the south and Manila. Yamashita made several attempst to bottle up the Army on the Luzon plain, but failed. His divisions either arrived too late or not at all. He took the only obvious course and retreated slowly into the foothills and the mountains. The troops of the XI Corps (Eighth Army) went ashore on the west coast on Luzon near Subic Bay on January 29 and moved eastward against light opposition to cut off Bataan Peninsula.

The Marine dive-bombers landed at Luzon on January 25 and began operations two days later as Marine Air Groups, Dagupan, under Colonel Jerome. To the infantry and the war correspondents, this combined enterprise was known as "The Diving Devildogs of Luzon."

The seven SBD squadrons operated under colorful nicknames: Flying Eggbeaters (VMSB 133), Wild Hares (VMSB 142), Sons of Satan (VMSB 241), Black Panthers (VMSB 235), Flying Goldbricks (VMSB 243), Bombing Banshees (VMSB 244), and the Torrid Turtles (VMSB 341). Their strip at Mangaldan airdrome in

Pangasinan Province was a temporary field out in the rice paddies. Low dikes separating the paddies had been bulldozed and scraped flat, but there were few other improvements. Any of the usual heavy Philippine rains left the 6,500-foot runway a morass.

On January 27 Major Ben Manchester led the first air strike of the dive-bombers, an 18-plane attack on San Fernando La Union. This and other early missions against targets in Southwest Tarlac, Neuva Ecija, Bulacan and Cayagan Provinces, and in the vicinity of Clark Field near Manila were a disappointment because they were not of the close-support variety. The only resemblance they bore to the intensive training on Bougainville was that the strikes had to clear through the SAP regardless of the closeness of enemy troops. Little by little, however, as Army confidence in Marine accuracy grew, the targets moved closer to our own front lines.

SBD missions in January destroyed two small towns, 90 huts, and storage buildings and two barracks areas. In return, one Japanese bomber raided Mangaldan Field but did no damage to the Marines.

At dawn on February 1, Jerome's bombers began their celebrated mission of supporting the 100-mile dash of Mudge's First Cavalry Division, down Highway Three to Manila. In a tactic with few if any major precedents in the history of air-ground warfare, the SBD's were responsible for covering and guarding Mudge's left flank from the air. A flight of nine SBD's was on constant patrol from dawn to dusk over the flank and searching for enemy strongpoints ahead.

By evening of the first day, the advance column forded the river opposite the town of Cabanatuan. Reconnaissance flights by the SBD's indicated the disposition of enemy troops south of the town and permitted the First Brigade to continue its rapid advance. VMSB 142 had nine bombers harassing advance targets principally at the town of Angat. Fording the Pampanga River at dawn of the second day, the Brigade moved south. The SBD's were in constant patrol on its left flank, clearing the area for 20 miles behind and 30 miles ahead.

At dusk on February 2, the infantry column reached Balinag on the Angat River, where it met with the 37th Division. The dive-bombers, meanwhile, hit targets at San Isidro and Neuva Ecija. Next day, the infantry advance continued across the river and swung east to the near-by foothills with dive-bomber support so precise that General Chase commented, "I have never seen such able, close, and accurate support as the Marine fliers are giving us."

While some units covered the First Cavalry, other Marine bombing and strafing missions were sent out against a wide variety of targets close to and behind the enemy front lines. During the period from February 8 to 14, the two Marine groups attacked some 34 name-targets in addition to those hit as targets of opportunity. The SBD's rained down their loads on Corregidor Island where the Fourth Marine infantry regiment had been the unpublicized bulwark of the island's defense during its last days in 1942; and on Fort McKinley, Nichols Field, Balete Pass, Mount Oro, Rosario, Fort Stotsenburg, Antipolo Wawa, and other points. Highlights of the period were the annihilation of two ammunition dumps and Japanese Military Police headquarters and barracks at Baguio on February 11, and close-support missions on the same date near the Labayug River in which all designated targets were destroyed. Two days later the Marines hit antiaircraft positions and personnel in the Malago River valley. This enemy strongpoint was hidden in a position 100 yards long and a few feet wide. After the bombing and strafing, the Army liaison party radioed the SBD's "area blasted, supplies demolished, and gun positions destroyed."

Throughout this "trial" period with the Army infantry in February, the Marine pilots flew an exhausting variety of missions to prove that their air-support weapon was a workable combination of flying artillery and sniping.

One incident among the many which helped sell Marine air support to the Army ground forces occurred when a patrol of the Sixth Division was stranded after falling down a cliff. The officer-in-charge was dying and three other men were seriously wounded. The remaining 12 men refused to abandon their position, although their food was exhausted and a Japanese position was only 300 yards away. Attempts were made to relieve the patrol, but failed because of fire from the enemy position.

A flight of Dauntlesses was assigned to wipe out the Japanese strongpoint, even though the Army Colonel in charge of the relief effort was afraid of possible injury to friendly troops. The Colonel requested the flight leader to make a dummy run. It was right on. He requested the leader to drop one of his wing bombs. It hit the target. Then the SBD flight was cleared for the the attack. Of the nine planes making runs, one dropped 80 yards from the target. The other bombs were within a 30-yard circle, all bull's-eyes. Next night, the Colonel evacuated his stranded patrol without interference.

Generally, the planes of MAG 24 and 32 operated under two types of tactical situations in handling these close-support missions. In the "ground alert" condition, the bombers were at their field, loaded and ready to take off the moment an order came from the Support Air Commander. The "air alert" provided for planes to be continuously on station in the air orbiting a stand-by point designated by the Air Coordinator.

A typical close-support situation shaped up in this fashion:

The infantry company or battalion commander bumps into an enemy strongpoint. With him on the front lines are his artillery observer and the Marine Air Liaison party. It is decided that the Jap position can't be handled by the artillery because of the time element involved or because the position is on the reverse side of a ridge and unreachable. The infantry request for planes is relayed back over the air network to the Support Air Commander, giving full details including the position of friendly troops, the enemy target, the number of planes and the type of bombs required.

If the condition is "ground alert," the SAC briefs the pilots thoroughly. They take off and arrive over the designated target at the prescribed time. If the condition is "air alert," this information is relayed to the Air Coordinator overhead. Usually, if the attack calls for precision, the planes are told to report to the Marine ALP on the front lines. In this case, the ALP radio jeep marks its own position by a panel or reports it in relation to a landmark easily visible from the air. Then the air-ground conversation starts, with "K-ration" as the radio jeep and "Red Dog" as the leader of the dive-bombers overhead:

"K-ration to Red Dog. Do you have my position spotted? Over."

"Red Dog to K-ration. Roger. Out."

"K-ration to Red Dog. We will mark our target with one burst of William Peter. Watch for it, 500 yards due north of us." (William Peter is phonetic for WP, meaning white phosphorous.)

"K-ration to Red Dog. William Peter on its way." (A mortar or howitzer had fired the phosphorous shell.)

"Red Dog to K-ration. I see William Peter. Over."

"K-ration to Red Dog. Roger. Make one dummy run on William Peter." (The infantry commander and the ALP watch critically as the little plane breaks out of formation at 9,000 feet and dives.)

"K-ration to Red Dog. Roger. You are right on. You may make your runs."

"Red Dog to K-ration. Roger and Wilco [Will comply]." (The bombers make their separate runs on the marked target. If one deviates slightly, the ALP radios an immediate correction to the next plane coming down. Finally all bombs are dropped and a strafing run follows.

"K-ration to Red Dog. Well hit. That smears them nicely. Thanks again."

"Red Dog to K-ration. Anytime, Mac. Over and out."

The code calls for the planes changed frequently, but all the Marine ALP radio jeeps were "K-ration," plus an identifying number to distinguish them from other ALP's operating near by. This code call was supposedly devised by Captain "Frisco" Godolphin, who pointed out that the three components of the packaged K-ration were supper, breakfast, and dinner, or "SBD." Since the jeeps were directing SBD's, their code call properly should be "K-ration."

The use of white phosphorous was general throughout the campaign except in areas unreachable by artillery or mortars or where strong wind might dissipate the marker smoke. Colored smoke was used, but it proved hard to see from the high altitudes where the dive-bombers began their runs.

Sometimes the Japs tried confusing the issue by dropping smoke shells of their own on Army lines to make the Marines bomb friendly troops. In one instance, the enemy dropped a shell close to an ALP jeep.

Over the radio, the Marine ALP queried, quite unperturbed, "K-ration to Blue Boar. Do you see that William Peter?"

"Roger, I see it."

"Hit just 1500 yards north of it. Got it?"

"Roger. Coming down."

Occasionally, as they had in the South Pacific, the Japs broke into our radio channels to give the SBD pilots misleading instructions. But the meticulous Japanese lacked a knowledge of American idiom and their efforts were usually without success, except in two recorded instances near Baguio, summer capital of the Philippines.

Nine SBD's requested permission to hit Baguio when they were unable to reach their target at Balete Pass because of weather. Permission was given and the bombing attack was successful except for AA which hit two planes. After the strafing run, the flight leader received a message purporting to come from his Support Air Party: "You are bombing and strafing friendly troops." The SBD's immediately returned to base to verify the charge, but found that there was no record of the message ever having been sent. Sometime later, another SBD strike was halted by a message to return to base with their bombs. Returning, they discovered no such message had been issued.

Without Jap planes to bother them, the dive-bomber pilots met their only opposition from enemy antiaircraft fire which ranged from intensive but inaccurate to light and ineffective. Air casualties during the month of February for more than 4,000 Marine combat sorties were only two pilots and one gunner. This was in spite of the fact that the SBD's were boring in low to get pin-point accuracy on bomb runs and then strafing in their slow planes at low altitudes. [Bomb loadings for the Dauntless varied with the targets assigned. The usual load per plane was one 500-pound bomb on the belly rack plus either two 250-pound or two 100-pound bombs on the wing racks. When a 1,000-pound bomb was carried, it usually constituted the entire load. The average SBD attack was made at an indicated airspeed of between 240 and 260 knots, at an angle approaching 70 *degrees. Release was made between 2,500 and 1,500 feet. The planes pulled out of their steep dives at between 2,000 and 1,000 feet.*]

Tactically, the biggest problem of the air support missions was target location. Maps were all too frequently incomplete and the aerial photos, at first, were outdated. Even when maps were finally complete and accurate, they were not of much use except for the general orientation of the pilots unless their target was some prominent landmark. The Air Liaison Party in the K-ration jeep proved to be the best possible method of target designation when working at the front, because the air liaison officer could see usually both the target and the planes.

Mission after mission of SBD's winged out from the Dagupan strip, ranging in size from the usual 9 planes to as high as 81 aircraft. Relations with the Army infantry and its commanders improved daily. Colonel Jerome received an increasing number of commendations from the infantry commanders either by personal letter or via official channels as commendations. The official reports regularly carried unsolicited written or oral comments by ground observers on the air support efforts of the dive-bombers. These were terse tributes to their effectiveness:

February 11: Enemy position on ridge near Labayug; SAP reported, "Target blasted."

February 12: Specified target in O'Donnel area; SAP reported, "Very satisfactory results."

February 13: AA east of Nichols Field; SAP reported, "Good coverage."

February 14: Enemy concentration; report, "Japs in disorder, you have killed a mess of them with your bombing and strafing."

February 16: Gun revetments and fuel dumps near Marakina; "Very good coverage of assigned area."

February 17: Troop concentration in a ravine; SAP reported, "All bombs in target area, good job."

February 20: Enemy troops and artillery positions; SAP reported, "Area well covered with bombs excellently dropped. Damage estimated as terrific." Barges on Taytay Esterpo River; "You have done more damage than you think."

February 21: Hilltop 4,000 yards south of Lumboy; SAP reported, "Bodies, guns, papers blown all over the place. Kisses from Commanding Officer of adjacent ground units."

February 23: Enemy entrenchments on hilltop; "Accuracy excellent."

These communications were of immense value to the airmen's morale, since for the pilot or rear-gunner, close support had many disadvantages. Though a precision task, it was one of the easiest they were called upon to do, particularly with ground fire at a minimum as it was in most of the Philippine campaigning. Close support offers no excitement or no special glory.

Major Ben Manchester, squadron leader, said: "It's dull as hell for a pilot. Remember, he hardly ever sees what he hits. To him, the target is either a hunk of ground or a hunk of brush, unless it happens to be a building of some kind. The pilot hits it and that's all there is to it. Unless the ground forces take the trouble to tell him the results, he never knows whether he has done any good for all his sweating."

But right down to the last private, the Marines agreed that operations in the Philippines were paradise compared to the aerial strangulation chore in the South Pacific. At least they saw towns and roads and other signs of civilization, even if they had to destroy them. The ragged but ecstatic Filipinos welcomed them noisily wherever they moved up. With these compensations and the incentive of offensive war, the "Diving Devildogs" kept hammering away at the Japanese. It was many weeks, however, before it was thought fitting to let the enemy and the American public know via the medium of the communiques that the Marine air groups were in action there. But that was an old story to the Air Arm, as it had been to the Fourth Regiment on Corregidor years before. Though it was hardly so intended, this lack of any recognition in the communiques exasperated the Marines to even greater effort.

As the campaign progressed, air-ground integration was intensified and more air personnel were assigned to serve with the front-line infantry units. Section-leader pilots worked with the ALP radio jeeps on a weekly rotation basis and came back to their squadrons very much aware of the infantry's problems and the need for even greater precision teamwork.

Notable among the ACI (Air Combat Intelligence) officers who did front-line duty with the infantry was 42-year-old Captain Francis R. B. "Frisco" Godolphin, a veteran of four major Pacific campaigns. [A professor of Greek and Latin at Princeton University, Godolphin volunteered for the Marine Corps at 40 because both he and the president of the university felt there would be a serious need on the postwar faculty for a professor with combat experience who could really understand the problems of servicemen returning to college.]

Godolphin was in the front lines for 38 days as a Support Air Party officer. Marine Combat Correspondent Staff Sergeant David Stephenson reported several of Godolphin's exploits:

"During the early part of February, the Seventh Regiment had captured the Balera water-filter plant northeast of Manila. The Japs, determined to destroy the plant and pollute Manila's water supply, had been directing mortar and machine-gun fire at the building from four positions. Finally they brought up rockets.

"The rocket attack began at midnight. Captain Godolphin went to the roof of the plant with a sextant to determine the azimuth of the rocket position. Six enemy rockets landed within 40 yards of his CP, but Captain "Frisco" got out alive with enough data to pinpoint the target for the SBD's the next morning.

"On another occasion, Godolphin and his party were studying a situation map when the enemy sneaked in close with a machine gun and wounded two of the men and destroyed the map.

"The largest Marine strike which the Captain helped direct on Luzon was an 81-plane attack east of the Marakina River. In preparation for it, the SAP sent a guerilla lieutenant—a civil engineer graduate of the University of the Philippines—into the area to be bombed. The officer, disguised as a native civilian, sketched and plotted the Jap positions by night. After sufficient information had been obtained, Godolphin called in the dive-bombers. He radioed his data to Major Manchester, the air coordinator, who was circling the target, picking out each point of attack as it was described to him. Then Manchester sent his planes down for the kill.

"In the last strike which Godolphin directed, two waves of nine planes each were to drop 1,000-pounders 250 to 300 yards in advance of the First Cavalry troops. The first wave came in and dropped its load. All nine bombs were duds. The Captain recalled 'You should have seen the looks of discouragement on the faces of the infantrymen!' Then the second wave came over and all nine bombs exploded right on the target."

Among the unusual close-support missions performed by the dive-bombers while holding the Cavalry's left flank was one which occurred northeast of Manila. The advance had rolled to a stop before a cave-infested hillside where intensive Japanese fire pinned the infantry to the ground. The mission of blasting out the caves was assigned to the "Torrid Turtles" squadron.

Nine of its planes on station listened to instructions from the ALP radio. They were told to be particularly careful because the enemy position was less than 200 yards from friendly troops. The strike leader, Captain Jack Canaan, peeled off and came down. His 1,000 pounds of assorted bombs scored a direct hit.

The Air Liaison Party grunted satisfaction, then radioed: "Don't bomb another foot north. The concussion is bouncing our troops around. Confine your hits within 30 yards to the south." The remaining planes did just that and the soldiers moved forward again.

It was about this time that Lieutenant Ewing Crutchfield, a dive-bomber pilot, got his radio jeep assignment to another Army division, on the right flank of the First Cavalry.

He reported in and was told by the commanding general: "We don't believe in close air support. As a matter of fact, the closest air support we want is 1,000 yards from our troops." Somewhat discouraged, Crutchfield went to work flying a tiny Stinson observation plane as a spotter for the artillery. He helped remove a postoffice and several big gun emplacements by directing gunfire and air strikes. But because of the local opinion of air support, he left shortly after to join Captain Godolphin's unit.

At that time, the First Cavalrymen had occupied high land west of the Pasig River and had taken the Balera water plant. They were opposing Jap forces on a ridge in front of the Marakina River. The enemy positions on the ridge were causing considerable trouble with their heavy machine-gun and mortar fire. The Japs had also launched several abortive "Banzai" attacks, making the infantry's situation generally uncomfortable.

When Crutchfield arrived, Godolphin was working in the water tower at which the enemy fired frequently, but without much accuracy. Godolphin had run wire from the tower to his radio jeep and was doing his broadcasting only 150 yards from the Japanese ridge. General Mudge called a strike regardless of the close quarters.

When the air strike arrived, Godolphin had some prominent spectators in the tower, both General Mudge and the doubting commander of the right flank division. Manchester, the strike leader, was instructed to hit the ridge on its further slope because an explosion on the near side would have sent bomb fragments whistling into the Army infantry. While a lively firefight went on below, Manchester made his run with only a patch of scrub brush to hit.

His bomb bounced just off the crest of the ridge, on the Japanese side. His wingman followed in, cloaking the ridge in smoke and flying debris. The cavalrymen cheered the performance as though it were a touchdown in a football game. One of the Army patrols moved up at once, walking over the ridge with no opposition. They found 8 machine-gun positions and 15 mortar emplacements. There were dead Japanese about, but no live ones. The enemy survivors were bandy-legging it in retreat to a point more than half a mile away across the Marakina River.

The doubting General, now convinced, asked Godolphin how soon his own division could have the same kind of air support. General Mudge reminded his infantry cohort that the planes would have to bomb a lot closer than 1,000 yards, to which the once-doubting General replied:

"I don't give a damn how close they hit!"

Some of the Marine K-ration jeeps remained with the handful of Army troops keeping Mudge's left flank secure over an 18-mile line from Laguna de Bay to Montalban. Here, the air support situation ran into difficulty because of the length and nature of the chain-of-command. If air support was needed, the request had to go from company to battalion, from battalion to regiment to division, from division to corps and from corps to the Sixth Army. There proper authorities took it up with the 308th Army Bombardment Wing under which the Marines were operating. The Wing then ordered the mission, and sent an O.K. grinding back down the same channels. This procedure often took as long as two days.

Captain Godolphin was beset by this red-tape menace in trying to knock out a portable rocket-launcher with which the Japanese were making local conditions extremely unpleasant. The launcher would be spotted or bracketed at night. Then a strike ordered. By the time the planes arrived, two days later, the launcher had moved to an unidentified position.

The Marine captain sang his tale of woe to General Mudge. He was told promptly, "When planes report on station, you tell them what you want hit. Never mind what they have been briefed for. I'll accept full responsibility."

Next morning, when the SBD's came over, expecting to hit elsewhere, Godolphin directed them to a clump of brush at one end of the Jap-held Marakina airstrip where the rocket-launcher had taken its latest stand. Shortly, a pilot reported seeing the twisted wreckage of the rocket rack after his bomb had hit. Its remains were later found by the infantry.

This incident was of great value to the success of the air support operation, because the practice from then on was to use the planes on targets as needed, and usually without prior briefing, unless the situation was fairly static. In such cases, detailed briefing produced uniformly excellent results, as in the case against a target west of Antipolo.

Beyond the town was a double bend in the road, forming a winding M where the Japanese had bored industriously into the near-by hills, emplacing artillery positions and antitank guns. These enemy defenses stalled the infantry advance for several days, causing heavy casualties and knocking out two American tanks.

Enlarged photographs of the M were used to brief the pilots of 54 SBD's assigned to the mission. So complete were their instructions

that they merely reported on station and went to work, singly, starting at one end of the road and working up. Reports from the infantry
said later that the dust clouds raised by the Marine bomb blasts
went along like the dust track of one fast moving truck. The caves
were sealed and the gun positions eliminated. The greatest bomb
miss was only 50 yards from the aiming point and most bombs were
directly on. This was a startling demonstration of accuracy, even for
experienced SBD pilots. The troops passed through the strongpoint
without casualties.

In connection with dive-bomber accuracy, some comments were
made by captured Japanese AA gunners. Their antiaircraft was fairly
intense in some areas and planes were lost by Army fighter outfits and
medium and heavy bomber squadrons. The Marines, however, were
not shot at quite so often because the Japanese had no intention of
divulging their position to "the little planes that dive." The Jap
gunners were frankly afraid that a few shots might anger the dive-
bomber pilots into retaliation. They had heard what could happen to
AA positions when the SBD's came down.

Advance infantry elements from Lingayen entered Manila on
February 4, meeting little early opposition and liberating war prisoners
along the way. It looked as though the city would fall easily and
cheaply, particularly since it had been supposedly declared an "open
city" by General Yamashita. But the sullen Japs fell back slowly
across the Pasig River, which winds through Manila proper, blowing up bridges and city landmarks one after another. For three savage
weeks, the Japs defended Manila as American infantry cleaned them
out of one big structure after another, fighting from floor to floor and
often engaging in point-blank artillery duels down the corridors of
buildings. When the enemy was routed finally, after heavy casualties
among Filipino civilians and the infantry, the city of Manila, once
regarded as the showplace of the Orient, was a desolate shambles.

Some Japanese moved from their crime at Manila to strongpoints
beyond the city, but generally they retreated to the mountains in the
north. A fast series of amphibious and airborne landings then bottled
up the enemy positions or eliminated them. Four thousand Japanese

died trying to hold Corregidor against a combined sea-air invasion
which had been preceded by a mighty naval and air bombardment,
participated in by Marine squadrons.

Marine planes covered infantry and guerilla landings at Burias
Island, Masbete, Capul, Biri, and Nasugou. On March 10, the Cor-
sairs joined in the air support for the landing of the 41st Division at
San Mateo on Mindanao, second largest island in the Philippines.
The Marines were in support during the Basilian landing in the Sulu
Archipelago. The performance was repeated in the landing on Panay
on March 18. Five fighter squadrons covered the landing on Cebu.
This action was followed by constant close-air support missions
throughout the Cebu and the Negros island operations.

VMB 611, a medium-bomber unit up from the Solomons, joined
Marine and other air units in covering landings in April at Sanga
Sanga, Bongao, and Jolo in the Sulu group. Marine fighters and
bombers also provided air cover for invasion operations at Malabang,
Parang, Cotabato, and Dumaguete in the Philippines.

Meanwhile the divisions of the Sixth Army met fanatical enemy
resistance in the mountain ranges between Baguio and Balete Pass.

At Balete Pass, the Japanese were fighting a rear-guard action in a
mountain fortress. The heavy crossfire from their cave positions disputed any entrance into the Pass, though artillery batteries had
blanketed the area for days.

General Mitchell's pilots, already staging for another campaign,
were called in. For five days of constant bombing, the SBD's pin-
pointed the enemy positions. Then the infantry moved in against
feeble resistance. Japanese dead, hundreds of them, littered the
target area, and many more bodies were found where the dive-
bombers had caught a Jap reinforcement column moving up to the
Pass from Baguio.

The raids against the mountain targets wound up the assignments
on Luzon for the SBD groups, which had moved from field to field
behind the advancing infantry they were supporting. Before the

Marines left, General Krueger of the Sixth Army sent his farewell message to them. It concluded:

"The war record of the First Marine Aircraft Wing is emblazoned with one success after another, from the bitter days at Guadalcanal, where they won the Presidential Unit Citation, to Luzon, where their record speaks for itself and from praises uttered by men of the Sixth Army who have done the land fighting."

"Magszambo" and the Final Phases

Though the Philippines campaigns were exclusively an Army ground force—guerilla operation, aviation Marines made one beachhead. It was at Zamboanga on the island of Mindanao on March 10. The landing force comprised the staffs and ground crewmen of the Marine Air Groups. Their mission was to set up an airbase from which the Corsairs of MAG 12 and the SBD's of MAG 32 could operate. Commanded by Colonel Clayton Jerome, the combined unit was called "MAGSZAMBO."

The Marines coming ashore from the landing craft were greeted on the beach by a single cobra, hood flared and poised to strike. The reptile's exact fate is unknown, but on the third night ashore, the Japanese launched a counterattack against the airfield and the Marines, many of whom had not fired a rifle in combat, set up defense lines and spent the night in foxholes, guarding the perimeter.

The attack was repulsed by troops of the 41st Division, but the enemy retreated only as far as the hills near the airfield. To eradicate them, the fighter planes were staged in from their base at Leyte. This provided a prime opportunity for the infantry to witness close air support from take-off to landing. The Japanese were so close their mortar shells were landing on the strip. As in the fight for Bloody Nose Ridge at Peleliu, the Corsairs took off, circled, and dropped their bombs in plain sight of their own field.

Later, the Corsairs used another facet of the support technique. Artillery observers, pinned down by enemy fire, could not move in close enough to spot for their own artillery. The Marines dropped Napalm bombs between the observers and the Japanese, throwing up a fire screen behind which the observers crawled up to better positions in perfect safety.

Five days after the landing, MAGSZAMBO were in regular operation off Moret Field [named in honor of Colonel Paul Moret, a First Wing Staff officer killed earlier in the war in a New Caledonia air crash]. After the transfer of MAG 14 to Okinawa, the arrival of MAG 24 at Malabang with Groups 12 and 32 at Zamboanga placed the entire Philippine complement of the Air Arm on one island.

On April 9, when troops of the 41st Army Division made a shore-to-shore landing from Zamboanga to Jolo Island in the Sulu Archipelago, the K-ration Air Liaison jeeps went along. By this time, the sight of the jeeps with their Marine insignia was a matter of course to the infantrymen. Close air support was no longer novel or a matter of unusual interest to the soldiers. It was always there. It always worked. It was now just a part of the first team.

During the drive against Davao on Mindanao during April and early May, air support again became of prime importance to the infantry. There, however, the pilots found the ground troops had been a little too well indoctrinated. The infantry was apt to call for planes to hit a pin-point target that any hard-driving rifle squad could have taken. However, such enthusiasm was much preferred to indifference. General Eichelberger, of the Eighth Army, later commended the Marine squadrons highly for the blows that they dealt enemy supply lines, troop concentrations, and artillery networks along the jungle trails of Mindanao.

Marine activity fanned out into a new theater of operations from Philippine bases when its squadrons provided day cover on April 30 for the convoys carrying Australian troops invading Borneo in the Sadau–Tarakan Island area. This landing and close support for Australian forces was repeated in July when Mitchell bombers of the First Wing hit invasion targets in the Brunei Bay area on the west coast of Borneo.

The Douglas Dauntlesses continued to ignore their "obsolete" status as military aircraft throughout the balance of the Philippines campaign. They performed as ably at Mindanao as they had back along the trail to the Battle of Midway. Though they were as beloved by the Marines and the infantry as the family Model-T, one squadron of SBD's was finally replaced, after an appropriate ceremony, by the bigger, faster, and longer-ranged Curtiss SB2C Helldivers.

Eight of the SB2C's were given as one of their first routine targets a large, white building at Korondal, northwest of Davao. But, it was an off-day. All eight planes missed the target completely. The last SB2C pilot came back a little disgruntled. He reported, "I pulled out so low I could see in the windows. Don't see why you want us to bomb it. There isn't anything inside the building."

That mission was typical of many of the later strikes—not the misses, but the lack of targets. Additional missions were carried out in the Sarangani Bay area on July 12, in support of a landing by troops of the 24th Division; but the big Philippine show was over.

In retrospect, the Marines felt that it had been a rather good performance. It had sold the Sixth and Eighth Armies on close air infantry support, Marine style.

Typical of the infantry attitude was that of Major General Jens A. Doe, USA, commanding the Sunset (41st) Division. During a combined air and ground ceremony, he presented to Colonel Jerome a plaque commemorating the close cooperation between the Army and Marines. Six feet high and four feet wide, the plaque was trimmed with Japanese naval signal flags. On it was mounted an enemy light machine gun and a Jap silk battle flag. It bore the legend: "IN APPRECIATION—41ST INFANTRY DIVISION." At the bottom were listed their combined campaigns: Jolo, Sanga Sanga, Basilan, and Mindanao.

During the ceremony, General Doe read this message:

"It is the desire of the commanding general, 41st Division, to present this plaque to the officers and men of Marine Air Groups, Zamboanga, in appreciation of their outstanding performance in support of operations on Mindanao, Philippine Islands. The readiness of the Marine Air Groups to engage in any mission requested of them, their skill and courage as airmen, and their splendid spirit of cooperation in aiding ground troops has given the division the most effective air support yet received in any of its operations.

"The effectiveness and accuracy of the support given by these groups proved a great factor in reducing casualties within the division. The work and cooperation of these groups has given the officers and men of the 41st Infantry the highest regard and respect for their courage and ability."

In hearing it, the airmen well knew that such tribute from the men with the bayonets was hard to come by, anywhere. Mitchell's Marines of the First Air Wing felt it was adequate testimony for their efforts from the beginnings on Leyte to the end in the hills of Mindanao.

$$\star \quad 9 \quad \star$$

WITH THE FAST-CARRIER TASK FORCES

O N NEW YEAR'S DAY, 1945, as Admiral "Bull" Halsey's great
Third Fleet steamed westward toward Formosa, two squadrons
of Corsairs, flown by Marines, were bedded down aboard the *U.S.S.
Essex*, one of the newest and largest carriers of the Fleet.

First-line carrier duty had been a long time coming for the Marines.
Prewar, it had been one of their regular missions. Expediency in the
early years of Pacific fighting, however, had made the Air Arm a land-
based force. Meanwhile, the Navy had been building up its carrier
might until just the sight of their horizon-to-horizon task forces gave
Japanese pilots gulping heart tremors. These carrier forces prowled
at will through the Western Pacific, taking on the enemy wherever
they could find him. For many months, the Marines longingly eyed
carrier combat activity from their by-passed bases.

Then the opportunity came. It was due to an urgent shortage of
available fighter replacements in the Fleet and the need for a higher
ratio of fighters to bombers aboard the carriers.

Though there was some question whether their prancing Corsairs
could take the pounding of flat-top operations, ten Marine fighter
squadrons were given the call for carrier duty. [*The only Marine
carrier action earlier in the war occurred when six pilots of VMO 155
joined Navy planes in supporting the Army's landing at Attu Island
in the Aleutians, in May, 1943. Flying Grumman Wildcats, they
operated from the escort carrier Nassau. One pilot was lost during
the operation.*]

Two long-time rivals of the South Pacific air war, VMF 124
(Checkerboards) and VMF 213 (Hellhawks), were the first units

assigned to the carriers. After a minimum of practice landings, or "bounce-drill," and with no opportunity for a shakedown cruise to familiarize themselves with the many quirks of carrier flying, the Marines joined the *Essex* at Ulithi, Western Carolines, on December 25, 1944. [A fast, 27,000-ton ship, the *Essex*, known by Navy designation as CV 9, was launched in December, 1942, as the first of a series of large carriers of that class. Its four-squadron Air Group, composed of 80-odd planes, operated from a 500-foot flight deck. Marine two-squadron fighter units later operated aboard four other carriers of the *Essex*-class: The Wasp (CV 18), Bennington (CV 20), Bunker Hill (CV 17), and the Franklin (CV 13). These units operated with approximately 36 planes and some 50 pilots.]

They were commanded by stocky, balding Lieutenant Colonel William A. Millington, who had led VMF 124 in the Solomons. Seven South Pacific veterans bolstered the ranks of the *Essex* Marines: Major Earl Crowe, and Captains Finn, Hartsock, Bedford, Clark, Agan (who had been a TBF pilot), and the triple ace, Gus Thomas, with 16½ planes to his credit. The remainder of the squadrons had no speaking acquaintance with the Japanese air force.

As the invasion force of the Sixth Army closed on Luzon in the Philippines, Halsey's carriers, under Vice Admiral John S. McCain, plowed through the Philippine Sea for a neutralization raid on the Formosan airfields. On the morning of January 3, as dawn failed to penetrate a solid 8,000-foot overcast, the *Essex* launched her Marine Corsairs on their first mission: to escort the bombers of Navy's Torpedo Four to Formosa.

Beyond the West Formosan mountains, the strike leader called the target. The torpedo planes, black AA bursts breaking around them, pushed over for Kagi airfield below. Right with them went the Corsairs. Bombs made their marks on hangars, shops, and runways. Corsair machine guns spat destructive rhythms at barracks and gun positions. Then the flight climbed back up to rendezvous.

En route home, the formation found two Nick fighters waiting high above the western peaks. Colonel Millington turned into them, wrapping up his Corsair sharply. His fire converged on the leading enemy plane and there was a neon-like spatter as the tracers went home. The Jap fighter staggered crazily and spun out, down into the reaching mountain peaks. The other Nick pilot took heed and ducked into the nearest cloud bank. The strike returned with one Corsair missing. A Navy pilot, back from an Okinawa sweep, reported that he had tried to give the Marine a bearing, but the latter had failed to get it. Last reported 90 miles north of the force and heading out to sea, the Marine never came back.

That loss to the weather was the first of a disheartening series. Four times the Daily Change Sheet (current action report) carried the curt notation: "Missing in action . . . he was last seen at ——— when he became separated from his division in the heavy overcast and failed to return." Expediency had not permitted the Marines to get sufficient instrument training for bad-weather flying in their schooling or in the period before boarding the *Essex*.

On the carrier they had to fly missions which experts said were "under weather conditions considered difficult even by experienced instrument pilots." In spite of these losses, Millington's pilots, after several weeks, were navigating through the murky Western Pacific weather with a facility approaching that of veteran carrier pilots.

Halsey's carriers swung south through unbelievably foul weather and launched their planes to support the landings of the Sixth Army at Luzon. Though they formed only a small part of the thousand-odd planes of the task force, the Marines doled out their share of damage. In return, their losses were not to the enemy, but to storm fronts that had no top or bottom.

The strain of weather flying, their losses, and the lack of enemy air opposition were a drag on pilot morale until the word was passed that the force was heading for the South China Sea. Never before had the U. S. Fleet invaded the closed waters between the Asiatic mainland and the Philippines. It looked like a gravy run for the carriers.

On January 12, Halsey launched the first carrier air strike in history against the coast of Asia. The main targets were three: Saigon, chief city of French Indo-China; Cap St. Jacque, at the mouth of the Saigon River; and Camrahn Bay, to the north. The Marines were assigned to raid airbases at targets with strange, exotic names: Trang Bang, Bein Hoa, Long Trans, and Than Son Nhut.

Planes returning from the morning raids reported the area fat with Japanese shipping, but very short on air opposition. Of the afternoon raids, Lieutenant Hal Goodwin, a Marine correspondent who saw the action from a torpedo bomber, wrote:

"After our Avengers had gutted shipping and shore installations, the Marines roared in. Captain Gus Thomas took his division down and made merry with a neat line of Tojos, stubby single-engine fighters.

"Irish got it as he went in low to get another plane on the ground. Automatic fire pounded his engine and he was suddenly out of altitude and grating along the ground of Saigon in a wheels-up landing. The other Marines came low to cover and saw him climb from his cockpit and raise his hand in salute. They dipped their wings and left him there, a lone, straight figure in an alien land.

"Millington arrived with the second Corsair sweep, each plane lugging a 500-pound bomb. The formation split, some going to Trang Bang, others to the Saigon River. Major Fay Domke let his load fly at a medium cargo ship and thereafter counted it among the Japanese chickens he had explosively hatched. Big Ben Bennewitz, who has the blond, innocent countenance of a cherub and the build of a Brahma steer, found a Jap hangar and spread it across the landscape in so many broken boards. Others, in Domke's flight, fired a second cargo ship and ripped huge chunks from a third."

The task groups counted up their eruptions and found that there had never been such a day of damage to the enemy with so little opposition. Four dozen Japanese ships had been sunk or damaged in addition to the havoc the carrier planes left behind on the ground. The only plane shot down by the Marines was a snooping bomber found over the Fleet.

Only Marine combat loss of the day had been the "Irish" of Goodwin's story. He was Lieutenant Joseph O. Lynch, who appeared months later after an amazing escape. While the Corsairs had strafed near-by Japanese gun batteries, Lynch left his crashed plane and was picked up by French native policemen. He was interned for several months in an underground prison by the local pro-Vichy French faction. When Lynch was finally freed, he and several Navy airmen sneaked through Japanese territory and eventually arrived at Kunming, China.

Halsey's rapier raids in strategic support of the Luzon landings took his armada north from Saigon toward three potential sources of Japanese air opposition: Hainan, Formosa, and Okinawa. After refueling in the crashing seas, the Fleet shivered its way up to Formosa. Off its coast, the planes were launched against targets on the southern end of the island, with the Marines joining in raids against Takao Harbor. For the first time, the Corsairs came back with well-ventilated wings and fuselages. They had found the strange, colored bursts of AA over Takao murderous as they bombed a factory and strafed a gunboat and a destroyer.

One day later, on January 16, the force turned slightly south and launched its aircraft against the enemy seaplane anchorages and airfields on Hainan Island, off the southeastern tip of China. The Admiral on the Marines' carrier passed the word:

"Be quick as a rattlesnake, sharp as a razor, and kill the bastards scientifically!"

The planes wallowed through the soupy weather to find little air opposition as they hit the shipping in Hainan harbor. The Corsairs sank one ship, burned two, and damaged several in bombing and strafing raids at Yulingan Bay and Saifa Point. One pilot, Lieutenant George Strimbeck, was lost when his belly tank exploded after being hit by a Zeke fighter. He parachuted, but was never heard from again.

As the carriers led the way out of the South China Sea through a dangerously narrow passage between Formosa and northern Luzon, combat air patrols on January 20 intercepted an enemy raid on the Fleet. The attack was broken up, with the Marines getting 8 of the 12 planes shot down.

Strikes were launched on the two succeeding days against Formosa and Okinawa. At Formosa, the Marines fired two large factories, one near Saimei and the other at Bhakko. Over Okinawa, they bombed the airstrip on tiny Ie Shima and strafed Naha town, the largest city on the big island.

Then, for a period, the squadrons flew routine combat air patrols, twiddled their thumbs, dealt endless games of acey-ducey in the coffee mess, swapped sea stories with the sailors, and battled boredom in air-conditioned comfort. Life was like that on the carriers, one week an inferno of action, the next an icebox of inactivity. The Marines who had known the perpetual motion of combat, heat rash, malaria, bad food, and the foxhole mosquitos of the South Pacific air war, didn't know quite what to make of the plush, but confined, existence aboard the floating city and citadel that was the Essex. They found the slide-rule luxury a bit nerve-wracking after a while.

"There Below Was Tokyo!"

While the carriers were taking their ease in Ulithi Lagoon after returning from the South China Sea, the Third Fleet became the Fifth Fleet as part of the Navy's SOPFEC (Standard Operating Procedure For Enemy Confusion).

Halsey and McCain were replaced by Admiral Raymond Spruance and Vice Admiral Marc Mitscher. Aboard sister carriers of the Essex —the Bennington, Wasp and Bunker Hill—were six more Marine fighter squadrons. The final Marine complement for the fast carriers was rounded out in March, when two Corsair units joined the task force aboard the Franklin. [VMF 112 and VMF 123, the Wolf Pack and the Eight-ball squadrons, commanded by Majors Herman Hansen and Everett Alward, reported aboard the Bennington on December 31 and began combat action with Carrier Air Group 82 in the Tokyo raids of mid-February. The Wild Hare and Bulldog units, VMF 216 and VMF 217, under Majors George S. Buck and George Dooley, joined the Wasp on February 3. Fighter Squadrons 221 and 451 (Fighting Falcons and the Blue Devils), commanded by Majors Edwin H. Roberts and Henry A. Ellis, went aboard the Bunker Hill in January.]

On February 10, the Fifth Fleet pulled up the hook and put out to sea. Then the word was passed that Iwo Jima was to be invaded by the Marines, and the carriers would support the landing. That put both of Millington's squadrons in good fettle. They had trained extensively with the Fourth and Fifth Marine Divisions in the Hawaiian area and were anxious to operate with the "Mud Marines" again.

But ahead of Iwo Jima on the action schedule was another mission, the long-awaited raid on Japan and Tokyo itself. The men of the Fleet froze even in their long underwear and foul-weather gear as the ships drove through winter seas and slid in almost undetected to pay the first call on the Empire of Nippon and Tokyo Rose.

In bitter cold and sleeting rain, the carriers launched planes on February 16 against targets along the eastern coast of Honshu, largest island of the enemy mainland. Corsairs of the eight Marine squadrons were sent out.

With the thermometer reading 55 degrees below zero at 25,000 feet, Colonel Millington led the first Marines ever to see Tokyo from the air in wartime. His divisions struck Vayzu airfield. Major David Marshall's planes roared over the Imperial City itself. Surprisingly, the Marines found the air opposition relatively light. Only four Corsair pilots shot down planes on the early strikes. Captain Thomas retained his multiple shooting eye by destroying two Zeke fighters in the air, raising his score to 18 planes. Lieutenants Hugh McQuillan and Clark Merchant ran a two-plane search until they found a convoy off Honshu. They mauled it to the tune of one cargo ship sunk, one left burning, and a destroyer dead in the water with smoke gushing from its ruptured boilers.

Major David Andre led the first Bennington Marines over Tokyo. The sweep downed one plane. Major Hansen took the second mission. It downed one more plane, and was barely fired upon by the surprised Japanese as it raided three airbases and destroyed 19 planes on the ground. Major Elward brought his flight back with two planes missing.

Andre's Corsairs went back again to the Tokyo fields. This time they shot down a Tojo fighter, burned ten bombers on the strips, and fired three hangars. Alward's second strike rocketed more planes from 15 feet off the frozen earth and the flight leader set a destroyer afire en route back to the carrier.

Weather on the second day was progressively worse around the task force. But over Tokyo, the sun shone. Some of the missing enemy air force appeared briefly as Major Alward's early sweep came in over Tokyo Bay. In a flurry of combat, both he and his wingman shot down planes. Alward came back with mud on his windshield from a freight locomotive the Corsairs had disemboweled with rockets. Then Major Hansen downed one more plane to end the *Bennington* scoring for the day. Storm-lost, Major Mobley made a lone rocket attack on a warship while his flight went on to damage a light cruiser.

The Avenger bombers of Torpedo Four went out that day to gut the mile-long Nakajima-Tama aircraft factory and came back smiling, for their Marine cover stuck so close that it was in the middle of the bomber formation most of the time. Two Oscar fighters were destroyed while they were attacking the Avengers.

During the two days, pilots of the Marine squadrons from the *Wasp* worked in sweeps and strikes over the Tokyo area. They shot down four planes while raiding shipping and the Yokosuka and Hamamatusu fields.

As the task force steamed away from Japan into warmer waters, the bewildered Marines pondered the meek performance of the enemy air force and the puny quality of the ground defense. They could find no adequate answer to the lack of violent Japanese opposition over the sacred homeland.

Corsairs Over Iwo Jima

Marine Aviation history was made on the morning of February 19, when Marine pilots aboard the *Essex* were launched at dawn to support the Marine divisions making their tortuous beachhead on the black sands of Iwo Jima. For the first time in history, the Air Arm gave carrier-based cover to its own infantry in a landing operation.

Colonel Millington led the combined Corsair and Hellcat fighter-bomber mission which concentrated on two strongpoints flanking the southeastern landing beaches of Iwo. The planes made run after run to dump their fire bombs on Mount Suribachi, which was bee-hived with gun emplacements, and on heavy gun positions at the opposite end of the beach. They went down through an inferno spawned by the guns and planes of the Fleet. Picking their targets through the smoke, the Corsairs strafed positions around the two airfields. H-Hour came and the tiny landing craft passed the line of departure like a host of water bugs, bearing their cargoes of Marines to the beaches. The Corsairs continued their strafing runs until the landing craft actually ran ashore. The final air attack came as the fighter pilots laid down a pattern of steel only a few hundred yards in front of the infantry footholds on the beachline.

After their one day of close-support missions, the *Essex* Corsairs were confined to CAP duty over the task force protecting the landing operation. *Bennington* units took over the Marine share of the air support work on the second day. This, too, was their first opportunity for carrier cover of the infantry Marines, and observers aboard the ship reported that the Corsair pilots literally begged to fly on every mission. Despite poor flying weather, the two squadrons bombed, burned, and machine-gunned enemy strongpoints on Iwo Jima for three days.

Then Task Force 58 turned north again. The Marine pilots were disappointed on one count with their first taste of carrier infantry support. It had made small history, but it had been all too brief to suit them.

Approaching from the southeast, the carrier task force moved in to deliver another cargo of steel orchids to Tokyo Rose on February 25. This raid failed to live up to expectations on several counts. The surprise element was lost when it was detected by an enemy picket boat the night before the strike. The weather was miserable in the extreme and the air opposition was negligible. The pilots again struggled with their major nemesis—guns frozen to inoperative condition in the sub-zero air over the Empire.

The Marine squadrons were sent out on missions around Tokyo. They met with few enemy planes and some tragedy. Millington made one kill while leading 16 *Essex* Corsairs. His divisions downed 4 other Jap planes, destroyed 11 more on the ground at Kamagaya, and 4 at Matsuyama Field. En route back to the Fleet, they shot up 8 Japanese cargo ships near Cape Inubo.

The *Bennington* Marines had even less to show for their efforts, plus a serious loss. While leading his fourth run on an 8,000-ton freighter-transport escaping from Tokyo Bay, Major Alward was killed when his flight was surprised during its low-level attack by 15 enemy fighter planes. The Marines fought their way out of the bad position, downing one enemy plane and losing another of their own pilots.

Mitscher's carriers left by night for the Nagoya area, hoping to find a more favorable weather situation there. However, the heavy weather persisted, the strike was cancelled, and the force moved south.

The three February raids on Japan had not been as productive as the Navy had hoped, although they had been profitable in every category: 359 planes shot down, 298 more destroyed on the ground, 17 ships sunk, and shore-based damage had been extensive. The Marine share of the scores, in proportion to their numbers in the force, was excellent but not spectacular. Their reactions were summed up by the wry words of one pilot, "There was Tokyo. I spent three hours over the place. What have I got to show for it? Frostbite!"

Okinawa received its second treatment from the carrier Marines on March 1 in a heavy routine raid that concentrated on the airbases. The Corsairs cleared the way for the bombers with rocket, bomb, and strafing runs and repeated the performance after the bombers had done their work. There was no air opposition, but the AA was so intense over Naha that the Marines came back talking to themselves. Several of their planes were badly hit; one pilot bailed out over the ocean and was promptly picked up by the Navy's efficient rescue service. [*This mission concluded carrier duty for Millington's squadrons on the Essex. During their three months with the Fleet, the two units were credited with shooting down 23 planes and destroying 64 on the ground, sinking one cargo ship and two picket boats. Twenty-nine other ships, from destroyers to patrol boats, had received assorted damage from their bombs and guns. Damage to land targets on their raids from Formosa to Tokyo and Okinawa was listed as "extensive." In flying more than 1,000 combat sorties, they lost 9 pilots and 24 planes, with only one pilot lost in actual combat.*]

The carriers of Task Force 58 wheeled and sortied about the Western Pacific with the adroitness of polo ponies during a fast chukker. They were off Japan again on March 18 for an attack on Kyushu, the southernmost of the main islands of the Empire. Targets for the Marines were three of the major airfields.

Major "Hap" Hansen led 16 Corsairs of VMF 112 toward Kanoya East Field. At 19,000 feet, his formation was intercepted by 20 Zeke fighters. The Corsairs came about in a violent turn, right on the rear of the Japanese formation. In six seconds, 5 of the enemy planes were in flames and the sky polka-dotted with parachutes as the Japanese abandoned their planes. The remaining Zekes pressed the attack until 4 more of their number were shot down and 6 severely damaged. When the action broke off, the Corsairs resumed course and attacked the airbase in low, sweeping runs that did considerable damage. Back aboard the *Bennington*, the 16 Marines probed their planes and found them sans bullet holes in spite of the dual action.

Next, Mitscher took his force northeast to hit Honshu and the island of Shikoku, which is between the former and Kyushu. There, for a change, the Marines found considerable air opposition.

At dawn on the 19th, Major Mobley (now in command of VMF 123) led a flight toward Hiroshima and Kure, the giant enemy naval base on the Inland Sea. Their mission was a fighter-sweep and strafing run to level opposition for a second strike which was to hit the remnants of the Japanese Fleet near Kure Harbor. Near the target, the Marines received a call for help from another carrier formation. As Mobley swung his group in the direction of the call, the Corsairs were hit from behind and above by some 30 Jap planes.

There was a variety of enemy fighter types in the formation, Zekes, Tojos, Jacks, and two new unidentified planes. The Japanese pilots flew as though they were the pride of the Imperial Air Force. Their tactics were American-style; passes were made in two- and four-plane groups; they used the scissors-weave to advantage, striking at opposite sides of the Corsair formation; all runs were well coordinated, hitting when the American planes were vulnerable on the outside of turns; when the enemy pilots opened fire, their 7.7 machine-gun tracers were right on target instead of the usual wandering all over the sky; with the 7.7's hitting, they closed in and opened fire with vicious 20mm cannon fire. The Japanese pilots picked on cripples and stragglers and used a variety of tricks to lure the Corsairs and Hellcats

into individual combat or over their AA barrages. As usual, the Corsairs had trouble fighting with the Zekes, Tojos, and Jacks since the
F4U's were not maneuverable enough to turn into them. With the
newer enemy plane types, which were as large as the Corsair, the
Marine pilots had no problem.

Two Marines were shot down in the initial attack. Eight minutes
later, however, 9 of the Japanese planes had been destroyed or damaged. Captain William Cantrel shot down 2 planes in two minutes.
Then, though badly wounded in the foot and with a damaged plane,
Cantrel shepherded the return flight, which developed into a running
battle, back to the carrier. He damaged and drove off 2 more enemy
planes. Nine of the Corsairs were so badly shot up they could barely
fly and several had to be pushed over the side of the carrier.

Sixteen rocket-bearing Corsairs of the *Bunker Hill's* Blue Devil
squadron swept in over Kure Harbor, where they sighted a nest of
enemy ships which looked big enough to be the remnants of the
Japanese Fleet. Leading the bombers, the F4U's picked out a battleship and poured a series of rocket hits into it in a low-level attack.
The antiaircraft fire they stirred up from the ships and shore batteries
was unbelievably intense. It was implemented by flights of Zeke
fighters which disrupted the attack effectively. Only the battleship
received major damage.

The final *Essex*-class carrier to bring the Marine squadrons into
the Pacific lasted two days in actual combat. It was the *U.S.S.
Franklin* with the Black Sheep and Sky Raider units aboard. [*These
two squadrons were aboard the Franklin when it sailed from Pearl
Harbor for the Western Pacific in late February. The only member
of Boyington's original Black Sheep squadron with the new unit was
Major Stanley Bailey, the squadron commander. He had been Executive Officer with the Black Sheep on their first tour of duty in the
Solomons. VMF 452 was commanded by Major Charles Weiland.*]

For two days, Corsairs from the *Franklin* roamed over the Japanese
home islands, looking for a dogfight behind every cloud. A fighter
sweep over Kagoshima Field on March 18 was their first assignment.
Japanese planes, however, remained in their revetments and were

well strafed. Next was an escort mission for Hellcat photo planes. No opposition was encountered until the flight was returning over Kago-shima Bay where a call was received from a near-by Navy fighter plane having trouble with 3 Zeke fighters. The Black Sheep broke off and went down to find not 3, but 15 Zekes. They broke up the melee in several minutes, getting 4 planes while the F6F photo-fighters downed 3. Other missions followed at Kobe and Shikoku, destroying planes on the ground.

Then in the sunrise of March 19, a lone Japanese suicide plane turned the *Franklin* into an inferno. Lieutenant Jim Hardin, a Marine radio correspondent aboard the *Franklin*, wrote an eye-witness account of the disaster:

"The bomber came out of a heavy black cloud that was near the *Franklin*. He put his plane into a shallow dive and made a run from bow to stern, very, very low. The bomb was released amidships. There was a tremendous explosion. Instantly, a great ball of flame shot along the hangar and flight decks. Great clouds of smoke poured out, as the carrier turned out of the wind. Then there were heavy explosions on the flight deck. In a few minutes, the entire ship was engulfed in smoke, broken only by the glare of explosions. Debris was landing in the water 500 yards from the carrier.

"Flashes of flame and thick smoke were blanketing the flight deck. I heard a voice from the bridge yelling. 'Keep the flames aft, if you can!' Everyone was choking but we groped around for the fire lines . . . and played them on the center of the flames. We had to give ground or suffocate. At the edge of the deck, I found two Marine pilots helping each other; one had a broken ankle. A large section of the flight deck exploded a few feet away. We seemed unhurt. The pitch between the flight deck planks at my feet was bubbling . . . the hangar deck below was a mass of flames. On the flight deck, a terrific explosion lashed out when the planes still on deck disappeared as their bombs exploded . . . their rockets fired and flashed by in great orange streaks a few feet over our heads . . . the carrier shuddered as though in an earthquake.

"Panic was in men's eyes . . . but they didn't give in to it. The fire-fighting team was amazing. Trapped men on the deck went over the side . . . one pilot near me had badly burned hands . . . he slid over the side and grabbed a rope . . . his life jacket fouled in the line . . . someone cut him loose. He worked his way to the water and disappeared. The word was passed to go to the forecastle deck just below . . . where we breathed fresh air for the first time in an hour. The deck was packed with several hundred men awaiting the inevitable. It seemed impossible that the carrier could remain afloat. The wounded began to arrive. Marine Warrant Officer Carl Omasta eased the pain of a fatally wounded sailor who kept telling his buddy to make sure his wife got word of what had happened.

"Navy Lieutenant Graham had taken time out from his fire-fighting duties and was sitting on a charred bomb, gravely unscrewing its live fuse. By noon, the *Franklin* had developed a pronounced list . . . its lower decks were flooded to prevent more explosions in the ammunition lockers. The fire was coming under control. Marine and Navy pilots manned the undamaged antiaircraft guns. Then the explosions ceased." [*Marine and Navy survivors of the Air Group went aboard the Santa Fe while the cruiser fought the rough seas to remain close to the carrier's side. In a heartening display of courage and seamanship, Captain L. E. Gehres, USN, and his crew of the Franklin sailed the charred hulk of their carrier back across the Pacific to New York Harbor for repairs. Seven hundred and seventy-two officers and men were listed as dead or missing in the disaster. Of the dead, 15 officers and 62 enlisted men were Marines.*]

Task Force 58 moved south again from Kyushu to continue the pre-invasion softening up of the Okinawa battlefield area. Beginning on March 23, the carriers sent out their planes in a continuous series of fighter sweeps and bomber and fighter-bomber raids against the "ships and strips" of the Nansei Shoto islands, which extend like a net for some 570 miles across the eastern approaches to the East China Sea. From the Sakashima group off Formosa, up north through the Okinawa Gunto, the Amami Gunto and the Osumi Gunto near Kyushu, the Nansei Shoto contained a series of feeder airbases, harbors, and ground installations which endangered the upcoming invasion of Okinawa.

Through March until the end of June, Marine carrier squadrons operated extensively in tactical, strategic, and close support of the Tenth Army forces engaged in the battle for Okinawa. When Marine and Army divisions went ashore at Okinawa on April 1, the Marine Corsair fighters from the *Bennington*, *Bunker Hill*, and *Wasp* joined the Navy squadrons in a continuing series of strikes and combat air patrols in tactical and direct support of the invasion operations.

After their early missions in support of the infantry ashore, the fast carriers withdrew to serve as the outer screen protecting the invasion area and to sortie against strategic targets in all directions from the battlefield.

During a fighter sweep over Amami Gunto on April 3, VMF 451 planes splashed 11 Zeke fighters. Lieutenant William Peek knocked down 3 while other Corsairs were raiding the airfields and shore emplacements at Saki Shima. Two days later, the Corsairs were battering the Tokina Shima field with fire bombs, rockets, and strafing.

Initial enemy air opposition at Okinawa was minor until April 6, when the Japanese lashed out against the ground and supporting naval forces. That day's air battles were the first major introduction of the carrier pilots to the wholesale suicide attacks which dominated the enemy's air efforts during the spring and summer of 1945. Carrier planes shot down 248 attackers in the day's spree and lost but 2. VMF 221 paced the scoring for the Marine squadrons. Eight of the Fighting Falcon pilots disposed of 13 planes, with Lieutenant George Royal Johns splashing 3.

The task force nosed into the north again, this time to "seek out and destroy" strong Japanese Fleet units which had been sighted off Kyushu. During the early search for the battleship *Yamoto*, pride of the Imperial Navy, Major Edwin Roberts, commander, VMF 221, searched Kagoshima Bay. Though they failed to find the battleship, Roberts and his two wingmen caught 6 Rex-type float planes over their base and shot them down.

Carrier striking units finally located the *Yamoto* and its escort screen off Kyushu. Despite heavy cloud cover, torpedo planes gutted and sank the battleship and the cruiser *Yahagi* after the fighters and dive-bombers ripped open the protecting screen, sinking 4 destroyers and burning 2 others.

On April 11, when Japanese suicide pilots resumed their attacks on Task Force 58, 17 were destroyed. The following day, the weight of the Kamikaze strikes was directed against the ships anchored off the Okinawa beachhead. In the battle to protect the shipping, the carrier Marines ran up their highest day's score during their tour with the Fleet.

Intercepting a series of raids that came in from all directions, the Marines literally fought until they were out of ammunition and gas. Paced by Major Archie Donohue, the two *Bunker Hill* squadrons downed 25 planes. Donohue, a Solomon's ace, brought his three-year total to 14 planes by splashing 3 Val dive-bombers and 2 Zeke fighters.

During a respite from the Kamikazes, the carriers turned their attention to the northern islands of the Nansei Shoto and to southern Kyushu. For two days, raids were sent against airbases at Kakai and Taenga Shima and Minami Daito in the Empire.

Major Hansen, a South Pacific veteran, celebrated his 25th birthday by shooting down 3 planes over Amami O Shima on April 12. With 11 other planes of his squadron, VMF 112, Hansen was on intercept patrol over the island when a Japanese formation was sighted coming in high above them. A full-power climb from 9,000 feet brought the F4U's in contact with 30 suicide planes, Jack and Tony fighters protecting Kate-type dive-bombers.

Hansen's division hit the dive-bombers on the first pass and got 4 or five. The other Corsairs tangled with the fighter escort and the battle broke up into what one pilot described as a "rat race from deck to ceiling." Flamer after flamer went down as the Marines splashed 20 of the 30 planes without loss to themselves.

Facets of the weird legend of the Kamikaze pilots grew out of incidents such as happened to a flight of Marines on April 14. The F4U pilots intercepted 9 suicide planes over Iheya Shima. In the process of shooting down all 9, the Marines noticed that 5 of the Japanese pilots were dressed in flowing robes of the Arab variety, topped by white hoods. Several Japs were seen in the garb when they were shot out of their cockpits. To substantiate the story, Lieutenant Gene Dennis, who blew up 3 planes, returned to the carrier with a section of white robe cord, from an exploding plane, lodged in his wing-root.

Suicide planes reappeared April 28. They damaged 2 destroyers before the planes and guns of the task force tolled off 25. VMF 221 shot down 14 of the enemy raiders. Two kills each were credited to Captain Donald Balch and Lieutenants William Bailey and Earl Langston. Lieutenant Dean Caswell, who had flamed 3 planes on March 18, repeated the performance by downing 3 enemy fighters and a possible fourth.

Lieutenant John McManus purportedly flew with one leg over the side of his cockpit because of perennial engine trouble. He developed supercharger difficulties in his Corsair on the 28th, when his CAP was vectored up to intercept a Japanese raid coming in at 25,000 feet. Long after his wingmates reached the enemy formation, Mc-Manus got into the dogfight as it worked itself down to his level.

A Zeke split-essed out of the scramble overhead and McManus chased the Jap downstairs and blew him up. Climbing back, he found a Tony on the tail of Lieutenant Caswell's plane. One snap burst from McManus' guns and the enemy fighter exploded. Joining up on Caswell, McManus was returning to the carrier when they discovered 8 more Zeke fighters streaking for home, low over the water. The Marines picked out 4 apiece and peeled off after them. One Zeke kept eluding McManus so often that the Marine had to close in to 50 feet to disintegrate it. Caswell, in the interim, had dumped 2 into the ocean, and went after a third with only one of his machine guns firing. Finally, Caswell dropped back and McManus shot down the Zeke in flames for his fourth kill of the day.

In a large-scale raid timed to support a counteroffensive by their troops ashore, the Kamikazes came down in force on May 4 after shore targets and shipping. Carrier pilots joined with Corsairs of the Second Wing and batted down 98 of them with a loss of 5 planes.

One week later, on May 11, another major air battle was fought over Okinawa and the ships of the task force. Carrier planes downed 69 of the Japanese attackers, 3 more went down before the guns of the Fleet, and two Kamikaze pilots died while crashing the *Bunker Hill*. The carrier was badly damaged by the suicide attack, though not as seriously as the *Franklin* had been. Of the carrier's personnel, 373 were killed and 19 listed as missing in action. One officer and 21 enlisted men of VMF 451 and 10 men of VMF 221 were killed.

Marine pilots returning to the *Bunker Hill* after an interception in another area saw the bombs explode aboard the ship and were forced to land on a near-by carrier. [*Among them was Captain James Swett, Medal of Honor winner who had just destroyed a Jill bomber, to raise his score to 16½ planes.*]

Following the withdrawal of the squadrons on the *Bunker Hill*, Marine activity on the fast carriers was centered on the squadrons remaining aboard the *Wasp* and the *Bennington*, with the pilots of the latter carrying the major portion of the load.

The task force went back to Japan in mid-May on its usual mission to blot out the sources of the suicide raids at their initiating points on Kyushu. The Marines destroyed 8 planes in combat on the 13th and 14th over the Kyushu fields and the Kumamoto aircraft factory. Lieutenant Robert H. Cook, of VMF 112, added his own footnote to Marine air history by shooting down a barrage balloon near Kanoya East Field, the only Pacific kill of its kind for the Air Arm.

Clean-up sweeps against the Kyushu fields and a few last sorties against targets in the Nansei Shoto at the end of May and the first days of June completed the carrier duty of the last four Marine squadrons.

During their six-month period of operation with Task Forces 38 and 58, the ten fast-carrier Marine squadrons flew more than 5,000 combat sorties or in excess of 20,000 combat hours. They shot down over 200 enemy planes in combat and destroyed 202 on the ground, while losing some 20 of their own pilots in air combat or to anti-aircraft fire. The *Bunker Hill* Marine units led the carrier scoring with more than 100 planes destroyed in the air.

The carrier Marines added up their plane scores and the extensive shipping and shore-based damage for which they were credited. It added substantially to the battle story of the Air Arm in the Pacific. Beyond that, they proved the value of the Marine-Corsair team on the flat-tops and were acknowledged as an integral and necessary part of what had been the Navy's private carrier warfare.

The Marine commendations from naval airmen were many and gratifying, particularly the one from the Admiral aboard the *Bennington*: "Your squadrons have done a wonderful job . . . I wouldn't trade them for any I have seen in action."

☆ 10 ☆

THE BATTLE FOR OKINAWA

THE mighty amphibious operation against Okinawa in the Ryukyu Retto was, in a sense, a dress rehearsal which turned out to be the last act of the protracted Pacific war.

To close the gap between Iwo Jima and Japan, the Joint Chiefs of Staff directed that one or more islands in the Nansei Shoto (Ryukyus) be taken to provide adequate bases to intensify air operations against the Empire itself, and to cut the already harassed supply lines between Japan and the China Coast and the outlying remnants of the Greater East Asia Co-Prosperity Sphere.

The island of Okinawa was selected as the prize target. Only 350 miles from Kyushu, its topography and land mass of almost 500 square miles would provide excellent airbase facilities, several of which the enemy, with his usual providence, had constructed there.

Planning for the capture of Okinawa envisioned it as the largest operation of the Pacific war because of the magnitude of forces, problems, and distances involved. More than 1,200 ships of the Pacific Fleet and its supporting echelons were committed along with 450,000 troops and 10,000 aircraft. It was so planned that, in addition to the tactical value of its capture and defense, the Okinawa campaign was to serve as a giant testing laboratory for all the techniques and material thus far developed in the Pacific theater. The war machine, thus perfected, would be hurled against Japan itself.

The mission of its capture, development, and defense was assigned to the Joint Expeditionary Force under Admiral Raymond Spruance. Lieutenant General Simon Bolivar Buckner, USA, directed the amphibious forces ashore, which were composed of the XXIV Army

219

Corps, the III Amphibious Corps, and the Tactical Air Force (TAF).
Commanding the troops of the Third Corps was the most versatile
triphibious veteran in the Pacific, Major General Roy Geiger, the
Marine aviator.

Marine Major General Francis P. Mulcahy was named commanding general of the Tactical Air Force, Tenth Army, after relinquish-
ing his post at Aircraft, FMF, Pacific, to Major General James T.
Moore. Mulcahy was also put in command of the Second Marine Air
Wing which was the TAF for the first six weeks of the Okinawa
campaign.

Marine Aviation was picked to carry on the initial tactical air work
ashore at Okinawa because its air groups were geared to move fast
and operate flexibly and it had extensive experience with similar campaigns in the Pacific. Its squadrons had been trained to a fine edge,
in recent months, by the job of pounding the by-passed islands.

The Second Marine Air Wing was selected because it had recently finished the Peleliu operation and its organization, as an
experienced staff nucleus, was available in Hawaii.

When planning for Okinawa got under way in December, 1944,
General Mitchell's First Wing was committed to large-scale operations in support of Army forces in the Philippines, with continuing
action in the New Britain area. The widely scattered Fourth Wing
under General Woods was polishing off its aerial strangulation work
in the Central Pacific and the Third Marine Air Wing at Ewa, Oahu,
was serving as a training and replacement unit.

The TAF was activated at Schofield Army Barracks, Oahu, T.H.,
in December, 1944, and occupied staff quarters there in the com-
pound of the Tenth Army Headquarters. Staff operations of the
Second Marine Air Wing continued at near-by Ewa Air Station.

To meet the complex demands of the role which the TAF would
play in the combined operation, General Mulcahy peopled both the
staff of TAF and the Second Wing with long-time veterans of tactical
air warfare in the Pacific. Brigadier General William A. Wallace, veteran of the Solomons, took over the Air Defense Command. Army
Colonel Bernard A. Bridget who had served ably on the joint air
staff at Peleliu became Chief of Staff, TAF. The legendary Colonel

Hayne D. Boyden was named second in command of the Air Wing. Hardiest Navy veteran was the chief medical officer, Lieutenant Commander Tom Flaherty, MC, USN, who had pioneered air evacuation at Guadalcanal and who was to die in a plane crash soon after the Okinawa landing.

Air units participating were assigned early in the planning stages by Marine AirFMFPac, Navy's COMAIRPAC, and AAF, Pacific Ocean Areas.

The majority of Marine air elements involved were released from other operating Wings in the Pacific. Units of MAG 31, 33, and later 22 were detached from the Fourth Wing. MAG 14 joined from the First Wing in the Philippines.

Most of the squadrons slated for the target had seen combat of sorts which consisted, in the main, of milk-run bombing or combat air patrol during which the enemy air force was seldom encountered. Many of the pilots were replacements with a maximum of training and a minimum of combat. The personnel rosters showed a bare handful of the pilots who had made headlines in the early phases of the Pacific war. Men like "Mad Jack" Cram and the fighter ace Ken Walsh arrived too late in the Okinawa campaign to add much to their past records.

The TAF planned nothing radically new for Okinawa, although there were many modifications and minor innovations in strategy and weapons. The most notable of these improvements were: better integration of air and ground offensive units, more efficient radar gear, better-trained night-fighter pilots, and a wider latitude of emphasis and responsibility for the air-warning squadrons.

As conceived in the planning stages, the TAF missions at Okinawa were, primarily:

1) To establish headquarters and tactical units ashore as soon as practicable after L-Day.

2) To execute the air support mission assigned by the Commander, Joint Expeditionary Force, as long as he functioned as such in the area.

3) Thereafter, to provide for air defense and air support for the ground and supporting surface forces in the Okinawa area by applica-

tion of available air power as dictated by the over-all situation and as directed by higher authority.

Initial mounting stages for TAF began February 22, 1945, when 46 officers and 102 enlisted men sailed from Pearl Harbor for San Pedro Bay, Leyte, P.I., where their ship arrived in convoy March 16 to join the gathering might of the XXIV Army Corps or Southern Attack Force.

Ground personnel of Colonel J. C. Munn's MAG 31 units went aboard AKA's and LST's at Roi-Namur with the ground crews of VMF 224, 311, and 411. Two escort carriers loaded the squadrons' pilots and planes along with the flight personnel of VMF (N) 542.

Colonel Ward E. Dickey's MAG 33 embarked on an APA and LST's at Espiritu Santo, New Hebrides. His flight echelons flew their Corsairs to Manus Island where two CVE's embarked the planes and flight personnel of VMF 312, 322, and 323, and VMF (N) 543 which had previously loaded. The two flight echelon convoys arrived at Ulithi for the final staging March 30. Ground echelons were routed to the target via Saipan.

L-Day for Okinawa was set for Easter Sunday morning, April 1, 1945.

For months prior to the invasion date, elements of the Third and Fifth Fleets, including the Marine fighter squadrons, had been hammering at installations, harbors, and air fields in the Ryukyus, Formosa, Kyushu, China, and the satellite islands in the target area in a mounting softening-up effort. The Navy had been well assisted in its strategic bombing and raiding by units of the British Pacific Fleet and the Army Air Force bomber commands.

The bulk of the preliminary Allied effort was concentrated on neutralizing enemy air installations within striking range of Okinawa. As L-Day approached, the entire weight of Allied air strength in the Western Pacific was directed against enemy airfields which lay roughly within the quadrilateral of Kyushu, China, Formosa, and the Ryukyus. The mounting toll of damage to enemy planes, ground installations, and normal existence was heavy, but not sufficient for wholesale destruction or even continued neutralization. The enemy, from this network of airbases, was able to maintain a considerable number of attack planes over Okinawa during the invasion phases and all too consistently thereafter.

As the assault armada converged on the target in the final hours of March, the invasion forces were convinced that the landing in the Ryukyus would be the traditional "This is it" with a vengeance. They expected the bitterest of resistance from all quarters. And they got it, but with variations on the theme as they had known it.

In a startling silence after the preliminary bombardment, the assault waves went ashore standing up, on that sunlit, almost pastoral Easter Sunday morning. They moved inland quickly over Okinawa's southeastern central beaches through that same ominous, unbelievable silence. Two major objectives—Yontan airfield to the north and Kadena field about one mile south of it—were easily secured on L-Day.

The first American planes to land on Okinawa were the observation planes of VMO 3. On April 2, two yellow Grasshoppers landed at Yontan from escort carriers offshore. The remainder of VMO 3, augmented by three pilots of VMO 2, landed soon after. The unit's full-scale operations began on April 4. Captain W. J. Slappey's squadron, organized as spotters for four artillery battalions, by April 11 was serving 11 Army and Marine artillery units.

Landing casualties were nominal for all units of TAF, and General Mulcahy and his staff went ashore April 2 to establish TAF and Second Wing Headquarters at a site less than a mile southeast of Yontan field.

When the first-phase traffic bottleneck broke, heavy equipment and supplies poured ashore. By April 7, the engineers and Seabees had punched through the debris and leveled off enough of Yontan's runway to permit fighter operations.

Hovering offshore 100 miles east of Okinawa were the carrier-borne-Corsairs of MAG 31. Led by the veteran Munn, the gull-winged F4U-ID's were catapulted off during a Kamikaze attack on the carriers. A lone Jap bomber had wiggled through the defensive screen of carrier-based fighters. He came in low over the water on the CVE group, then busy launching its fighters.

Eight planes of VMF 311 on combat air patrol splashed the bomber a few hundred feet off one of the CVE's. This single kill on the way to battle was a significant introduction to the enemy suicide tactics which played a dominant role in the air battle of Okinawa.

Kamikaze pilots, whose title translated as "The Divine Wind," were dedicated to "body-crashing" tactics. Sporadic suicide attacks of an unorganized variety had been one of the feature attractions of the enemy war effort as far back as 1932 in China where three Jap infantrymen saddled themselves with a bangalore torpedo to obliterate a barbed wire entanglement in Shanghai, and, incidentally, themselves. Tokyo's propagandists recognized a good thing. Ignoring the evil rumor that it might have been an accident, they deified the splattered dead. Tokyo's incessant harping on the glory of suicide for the Emperor, the Oriental's usual disregard for human life, and the guarantee of a berth in a slant-eyed Valhalla, all helped produce the weird Banzai charge and its airborne equivalent, the Kamikaze attack.

The Kamikaze Corps was an instrument of desperation and not a secret weapon in the atom bomb sense. But, until weapons and tactics were adapted to cope with him, the Kamikaze served his purpose.

These Jap suicide missions concentrated on three objectives: elimination of the radar picket craft serving as the outlying screen; destruction of the combat naval forces covering the operation; and destruction of the troop transports, cargo ships, and other elements of the supporting amphibious forces supplying the impetus to the campaign.

Elements of the enemy air force in the Okinawa battle were not all members of the Kamikaze Corps, but the latter were sufficient in number and successful enough to do major damage to the naval forces. Thirty ships of the supporting forces were sunk and 223 damaged. The corresponding loss of life was equally startling, but on both sides. Except for overwhelming American air superiority and the accuracy of the gunners in the Fleet, the final effect of the Kamikaze effort might well have been appalling, even to the point of defeating the Okinawa venture.

After splashing the bomber near the carriers, planes of VMF 311 (Hell's Belles), VMF 441 (Black Jacks), VMF 224 (Fighting Wildcats) and VMF (N) 542 landed at Yontan on April 7. Two days later, elements of MAG 33 pancaked at Kadena Field. Colonel Dickey's command on the first day of operation included VMF 312 (Day's Knights), VMF 322 (Fighting Cocks), VMF 323 (Death Rattlers), and VMF (N) 543 (Night Hawks).

The two air groups mounted patrols their first day ashore even though the enemy and the elements seemed to have conspired to make operations impossible for the TAF.

The usual hard work required in this critical period was hamstrung by a combination of incessant Jap bombing and strafing, enemy artillery fire, a cascade of our own AA shell fragments, heavy rains and foul weather, all of which slowed construction work on the fields and made air operations hazardous.

The combat-hungry Marine pilots took their first good bite out of the Japanese air force on April 12. After an all-night Jap bombing, Kadena planes scrambled to meet an incoming morning raid and downed two Tony's and a Judy. In the early afternoon, VMF 312 pilots Johnson, Revnes, Webb, and Holden took on 20 Zeros and 4 single-engine bombers at 18,000 feet over the Motobu Peninsula.

The enemy formation broke up on contact and the ensuing dogfight ranged over a 40-mile area from 18,000 feet to sea level. Forty-five minutes later, the score was 8-0. Though it was their first time in combat, Johnson got three, Revnes two, and Webb and Holden one each. Landing while the field was under a heavy artillery barrage, they reported that the Zero's evasive tactics were poor and that four Jap pilots had bailed out during the battle. One hour later, another larger Marine formation shot down three Zeke fighters and a Betty bomber for the day's total of 15.

Beginning on April 13, the Corsair squadrons which were doubling in brass as fighter and fighter-bomber units, flew their first of the long series of air support missions in the campaign. Thirty-six Corsairs, each loaded with two 500-pound bombs and eight 5-inch rockets, worked over enemy artillery positions four miles behind Japanese lines. The results were highly satisfactory, according to ground observers. Pilots reported hits on 18 gun emplacements concealed in caves.

It was a good beginning. Weather permitting, and many times when it didn't, the Corsairs flew strike after strike in direct support of both Marine and Army infantry throughout the long campaign, but the major fighter activity during the first weeks at Okinawa was a continual aerial turkey shoot.

Another killing came April 16, when, after enduring a hectic night of bombing and shelling, the F4U pilots bagged 36 planes. The dawn CAP and early morning patrols downed 18½ planes. Shortly before noon, the climax of the day's action came when four divisions from VMF 441 attacked a mixed flight of 25 Japanese planes, destroying 15½.

During the early morning battle another indication of the enemy suicide trend of mind made its appearance. This one-way ticket looked like a large torpedo with a canopy and stubby wings. Carried by a "mother" plane, the piloted bomb was directed at its target and then released. The pilot, well sealed inside, had a bare minimum of control to guide his flying warhead. Models captured earlier on Okinawa had been promptly labeled the Baka (fool) bomb by invasion troops. Young Dewey Durnford, a lieutenant in the Death Rattlers, was raking the flanks of a Betty bomber when it loosed the Baka. Startled, Durnford radioed "Look, you guys, it was carrying a papoose!"

A bizarre and profitable period for the TAF began in the early evening of April 22 when a 7-plane patrol of the Death Rattler squadron ran amok over the East China Sea. Intercepting 39 enemy planes about 40 miles north of Aguni Shima, the Marines downed 25 of them in as many minutes. In the action, three pilots who had never scored previously emerged as aces.

Twenty-one-year-old Lieutenant Jerry O'Keefe, destined to be a top Okinawa-made ace, squinted in on 5 bombers and dropped them all. Only one gave him a bad time. The Jap plane burst into flames and, instead of going down, turned head-on into O'Keefe. He pushed the gun pipper down and sweated. When they were less than 50 feet apart, the Jap Val shuddered, rolled off, and exploded on the ocean.

By all scoreboard counts, the belle of that evening battle was Major Jefferson David Dorroh, the squadron's executive officer. He ran his score from zero to 6 in 20 minutes of squirrel-cage fighting. Dorroh burned 5 and exploded his sixth.

It was a rare day for Major George C. Axtell, Jr. who had shot down 5 Japs in fifteen minutes. The intense, "Big Axe," at the tender age of 24 years, was probably the youngest regular Marine fighter skipper of the war. If that honor was not his, certainly the record of his squadron was. His "deadly passel of kids," as one elderly veteran of 28 tagged them, played havoc with the Japanese air force and percentages. In less than two months of operation, the Death Rattlers topped all existing Marine air records by shooting down 124½ enemy planes without a single loss of their own in aerial combat.

Axtell readily admitted that, by critical comparison, their lopsided score was easier to come by than those records earned earlier in the war against the cream of the enemy's fighter pilots. As Sol Mayer, the unit's mess officer, purportedly pointed out over his pork chops, "They had it good in the Solomons, but they didn't have Kamikazes!"

Combat analysts who studied the Okinawa air campaign in contrast with its predecessors agreed, by inference, that there was considerable sagacity in Sol Mayer's statement.

Japan's startlingly high proportion of losses in aerial combat did not properly mirror the expertness of the enemy's air tactics or the considerable success of his mission at Okinawa. In spite of overwhelming American air superiority and the number of Japanese planes shot down, many of the Kamikaze Corps died, doing damage all out of proportion to their individual losses. Thousands of American seamen died aboard destroyers, destroyer escorts, picket boats, transports, LST's and LCT's, and the larger ships of the Fleet from these suicide attacks. Thousands more were wounded and the materiel damage was major.

The primary mission of the enemy fighter planes was not to dogfight for supremacy of the air. The queer variety of protecting Jap fighters tried only to herd the suicide bombers through the fighter craft of TAF as best they could. These motley Jap plane assortments often looked to Marine pilots as though the Smithsonian Institute had suddenly taken to wing.

The losses to American shipping would certainly have been appallingly higher, according to those at sea, had it not been for the marksmanship, tenacity, and courage of the fighter pilots. Message after message from the harassed Navy congratulating TAF pilots and squadrons bumped their way down the chain of command to General Mulcahy's sandbagged headquarters in acknowledgment of the Marine efforts on behalf of the Fleet.

TAF pilots found another "gold mine in the sky" on April 28, when 35½ more Japanese planes were shot down. Then the fitful air war lapsed into another breathing spell, marked by foul weather, Jap night raids, and the shelling of Pistol Pete.

Indicative of the lull was the May 2 news summary of TAF activity sent to all war correspondents:

> It rained all day,
> The fields were goo,
> Nothing happened
> No news for you.

With the infantry, it was a different story. In an attempt to break the stalemate along the southern front, Tenth Army troops launched a strong attack May 2 against the heavily fortified Japanese positions. Weather denied air support to the offensive, and only small gains were made.

During the period from May 3 to 5, the enemy launched a strong counteroffensive supported by sea and air forces. Several heavy attacks were hurled against Buckner's main positions on the southern front and Japanese raiding parties landed small units behind Tenth Army lines on both coasts. The main Japanese attacks and infiltrations were broken up with the enemy infantry losing an estimated 4,000 men.

The enemy air counterattack reached its peak the morning of

May 4. Rather than saturation of TAF's air defense by single mass attacks, the Japanese used infiltration by small groups attacking from all over the compass.

The Japanese turned their hangars inside out for the occasion. Marines reported shooting down at least 12 known types of enemy bombers and fighters during the day. In return, Marines provided their own brand of variety. Thirty-three pilots were credited with victories on May 4 for a total of 60 kills.

Again the Death Rattlers took scoring honors with 24¾ planes for a squadron total of 80½ planes. The unit's ace roster rose to seven as three more pilots—Lieutenants Rusham, Wade, and Dillard—shot down 4 apiece.

VMF 311, second ranking squadron of the TAF, added 17 more Jap planes to the day's total. On a dusk patrol intercept west of Naha, 4 of its planes scratched 11 Jap Tonys and Dinahs. Before the last of the enemy planes were disposed of, Lieutenant William Brown, who had gotten 4 of them, reported that the Corsairs were firing at silhouettes in the evening sky.

Not one TAF plane was lost during the day's fighting which raised the Second Wing's score to 205 planes shot down in less than a month of action.

But the month of May was not without its rigors. The suicide rat races at masthead level had hardened the fighter pilots to riding the Kamikazes down through the clawing blanket of ship-based flak regardless of the danger. A lieutenant named R. O. Hansen, on May 7, splashed a Tony on a suicide run 50 feet off the port bow of a destroyer. To make this kill, he was forced to fly through a barrage of AA fire spewed up by the guns of 5 friendly LCI's and 2 destroyers.

There occurred that day one of those weird happenings which seem to be an inalienable part of battle, particularly of high-speed air warfare. Two Corsairs patrolling at high altitude peeled off to investigate what appeared to be enemy planes at 3,000 feet. The section leader held fire in his dive. After closing in, he radioed his wingman that they were friendly planes. The wingman continued to close and fired when in range. His target, a Corsair, fell off and crashed in the ocean. The wingman announced his "victory," but was told it was a friendly plane. En route back to Okinawa, the wingman's plane developed engine trouble and he was killed while crash-landing in the water. His "victim" survived the earlier crash and was picked up by a surface craft.

Four days later occurred what was called by General Wallace "one of the most remarkable achievements of the Pacific air war."

Sandy-haired Lieutenant Robert R. Klingman, one-time enlisted man in both the Marine Corps and Navy, was on CAP May 10, with three other planes of VMF 312. Cruising at 10,000 feet, his wingman, Captain Kenneth R. Reusser, spotted suspicious vapor trails high above them over the tiny island of Ie Shima.

As they climbed to investigate, the Jap, a Nick-type fighter on a photo mission, banked and headed back home. As the Corsair division climbed beyond 32,000 feet, two pilots found their planes unmanageable and turned back. Klingman and Reusser continued the chase.

At 35,000 feet, the F4U's leveled off. Their extra gas load was jettisoned to lighten the sluggish planes now high above the absolute operating ceiling for the Corsair. Klingman and Reusser kept their heaterless guns operative by firing short bursts.

Above 38,000 feet, Reusser was able to close in on the enemy's tail. With his last burst, he damaged the Nick's wing and left engine. Then Klingman slid into position as the three fighters maneuvered about the thin air as if in slow-motion ballet.

Klingman's guns froze when he was barely 50 feet behind the Jap. He felt he had not enough gas to get back to Okinawa and decided to buzz-saw the Jap plane.

Klingman made his first ramming pass.

"I overshot by a few inches," he said, "and my propeller nicked the top of his rudder, sliced off a foot of fabric, and chewed into the rear cockpit where a very scared rear-gunner had been pumping and pounding his guns to get them to fire."

The Nick remained in almost level flight but lost altitude. Klingman made a second run while fighting the wobbling effect produced by the enemy's slipstream. This time the Marine succeeded in cutting the Nick's rudder completely off and damaging the right stabilizer. Still the Jap pilot maintained control.

Convinced that he "had to knock down the Jap or crash in the attempt," Klingman settled his plane on top of the Nick for his third attempt. This time the propeller performed the coup de grâce by severing the Nick's stabilizer.

The Jap plane went into a spin. Klingman and Reusser watched it pull off both wings at 15,000 feet and go down like a plummet. Klingman herded his staggering plane toward Okinawa and ran out of gas in sight of the field, but he landed safely.

Not to be outdone by Klingman, a bomber pilot of VMTB 232, in the dark morning hours of May 17, turned in his own bizarre incident.

At 0235 while on a night heckler mission behind enemy lines, Lieutenant Fred Folino spotted an enemy plane in the darkness. After checking with his ground controller and verifying that it was Japanese, Folino hauled his loaded bomber up for an altitude advantage. In his first pass, the Marine fired all the ammunition in his two wing guns without apparent damage to the ghost plane. Folino maneuvered his very unfighter-like Avenger into position again and fired a wing rocket without effect. However, his second and third rockets tore a wing off the Jap plane, which crashed in flames.

Veterans of antisubmarine patrols and milk-run raids at Ulithi, the pilots of VMTB 232 arrived at Okinawa in late April. Flying TBM-3's, the General Motors version of the Avenger, the squadron established itself as the workhorse of the TAF. Its pilots did everything but deliver milk and the morning paper.

During May, VMTB 232 flew 50 strikes in support of the ground troops, 50 night harassing sorties, 151 combat observation missions, 125 antisubmarine patrols, 74 air-drop missions, and a candy-counter assortment of flights which included spraying DDT, aerial photography, message and propaganda leaflet drops, and hunting enemy radar stations. It encountered enemy AA on 240 of these low-level missions.

One air support mission in which VMTB 232 participated was described in the *Gunto Graphic*, the newspaper of the XXIV Army Corps:

"There have been countless U. S. air strikes on Okinawa since L-Day, but no other quite like this one. The Marine pilots who undertook the mission struck the enemy from the south, behind the Jap lines, and zoomed out of their dive-bomb attacks northward over American lines. And that is playing the game of air support mighty close.

"The planes made a dummy run and word was received from the air-liaison party that they were right on target. Then Captain J. E. Nauss of VMTB 232 led the squadron on the wet run. He came in at a terrific speed. It appeared as though he would never come out of his dive. Observers behind the U. S. lines lost sight of his plane below the 200-foot crest of the hill. Then suddenly the plane came out of nowhere with a roar, climbing almost straight up. A moment later a terrific explosion was heard. Then the rest of the squadron dived on the hill, each loosing a bomb. None of them, however, surpassed the daring dive of the squadron leader, who later admitted his plane had been within a few feet of the ground.

"A second bomb run was made. Then the torpedo bombers made a rocket strike while the Corsairs strafed. During the bomb runs, mud, trees, and Jap bodies were tossed a hundred feet in the air.

"Not one plane overshot its mark. That would have been disastrous to the waiting Doughboys who, once the runs were over, advanced and seized the hill."

Supply drops by VMTB 232 and VMTB 131, which arrived later in the campaign, were a major contribution to air infantry support at Okinawa. During a 12-day period, Feldmaier's unit racked off 327 supply sorties for troops of the Third Corps. All types of infantry ammunition, water, rations, batteries, 28 miles of wire, and a telephone switchboard were included in nearly 200,000 pounds dropped by the TBM's. In June the two squadrons made 485 extremely accurate drops to Army and Marine front-line units when Okinawa's weather quagmired the infantry's normal supply routes.

During its entire supply-drop operation, the Second Air Wing parachuted more than 600,000 pounds of food, ammunition, and medical supplies to the infantry on 760 sorties. Ninety-eight percent of the supplies were actually recovered by the ground troops.

Middleman between the infantry and the airmen on these air supply missions was the Air Delivery Section of the III Corps. This small unit, commanded by Lieutenant Richard Sinclair, a former Para-Marine, had served on nine previous combat operations in the Solomons, New Britain, and the Marianas.

The TAF, showing serious signs of wear and strain after five intensive weeks of operation, was bolstered May 14 by three P-47 squadrons of the AAF's 318th Fighter Group. Two days earlier, the first elements of MAG 22, under Colonel Daniel Torrey, had arrived at Ie Shima after a 2,500-mile flight from the Central Pacific. [*Ninety-three planes of squadrons VMF 113, 422, and 314, and VMF (N) 533 flew the hazardous overwater trip from their bases in the Marshalls, shepherded by TAG's R5C Commandos.*]

Shaped like a fat peanut, Ie Shima, five miles long and half that in width, was the American-held island airbase closest to the mainland of Japan. It was three and one-half miles off the tip of Motobu Peninsula, 25 miles northwest of Yontan field. Under constant fire from Jap bombers and enemy raiding parties, Ie Shima was an outpost in the shadow-war waged by the Marine air warning and night fighter squadrons.

Night fighter operations were integrated with TAF's Air Defense Control Center. Its radar spotter stations served as the outer warning screen for Okinawa. The radar network which plotted incoming enemy planes day and night began initial operations aboard ship. The first AWS station went ashore at Zamami Shima in the Ryukyus March 29 and the station at Nagannu Shima was in operation two days later. This network expanded rapidly until it numbered 28 stations in two months. These, including six Ground Intercept stations for night fighter control, were strategically located on Okinawa and five outlying islands.

Night kills in the first five weeks showed a thin total of ten, although enemy bombers were over Okinawa night after night. Perfected operations between the expanding AWS net and squadrons VMF (N) 542 and 543 were badly hampered by constant trouble with the delicate electronic gear, lack of adequate sites for the radar screens, poor field operating conditions with bulldozers and enemy bombs defying the planes to take off or land intact, costly interference from the understandably trigger-happy AA gunners of the Fleet, and the mine-run troubles of early-phase campaigning.

Then up from Eniwetok in the Marshalls on May 13 came the 15 Hellcat planes of Lieutenant Colonel Marion "Black Mac" Magruder's VMF (N) 533.

Five days later the balky night fighter operation at Okinawa had jelled and the "Crystal Gazers" and their "Night Chicks" began their own series of eerie turkey shoots. ["Crystal Gazers" and "Night Chicks" were terms in the strange language that was part of night air combat. The "Gazer" was the fight director, who guided the airborne "Chick" or pilot into a close-up position for the kill.]

Under a bright three-quarter moon the night of May 18, two pilots of Magruder's squadron made five radar night kills between them in less than two hours.

Lieutenant Harold H. Martin, a Marine correspondent, recounted in the lingo of the night fighters how Lieutenant Robert Wellwood shot down the first three Japanese raiders.

"At the station called 'Poison,' Lieutenant Hugh Gallarneau, the old Stanford football star, began scanning the glowing dials which cast a sheen of bluish light over the radar panel at the end of the dark control van. His chick, Wellwood, was already in the air.

"Miles away at the station called 'Raccoon,' Lieutenant Jack Wilson heard his chick, Lieutenant Edward LeFaivre, report airborne.

"For a while nothing happened. On the softly glowing dials at Poison and Raccoon, only two tiny sparks of light showed where the two chicks circled, each in his orbit, in the dark above. Then, far to the northeast, toward Japan, another faint spark glowed on Gallarneau's scope. He studied it, marking its course and altitude. Bogey —unidentified aircraft. Off to the left of the board a new light glowed, querying the stranger. No answering signal came back. He was an enemy now, beyond a doubt, a target instead of a bogey. Hugh clicked on his microphone.

"Hello, Muscles One Seven, I have a customer for you, starboard three-five-zero."

"One Seven to Poison. Three-five-zero. Roger and out."

"Hello One Seven. Target range 25 at 11 o'clock and 17,000 feet indicating 160 mph. Firewall! Poison, Out!"

"She had altitude on me and was closing fast," Wellwood said. "When Hugh told me to firewall, I jammed the throttle forward and started to climb. We were closing fast . . . 10 miles . . . 7 miles . . . I charged my guns again, just to make sure.

"Hello One Seven," called Gallarneau, "Target range 3 at 10 o'clock starboard two-two-zero. Target crossing . . . Punch! [Get him!]"

Wellwood said, "When I went into my turn, I knew this was it. If Hugh had judged his vectors right and if I'd followed him as I should, I'd be coming right in on her tail. If either of us had doped off, there wouldn't be anything out there but empty sky. As I came out of my turn, I flipped my finder and peered at the little orange colored gauge on my panel. There wasn't a blip [a tiny light on the radar screen] on it. Then I got her signal. It came swimming down from up in the left-hand corner of the screen and I yelled 'Contact' so loud Hugh could have heard me even without his radio.

"I watched the blip getting bigger and bigger and coming nearer and nearer. When I thought I was close enough, I started squinting through the windscreen out into the dark. Then I saw her . . . dead ahead and 300 feet above me . . . a vague black shape in the light of the moon. I nosed up to climb a little and swung to port to get on the dark side of the moon from her, and started closing in. The twin-engine Betty didn't know I was in the sky. At 300 feet I gave the trigger a short quick squeeze. At the wing-root, between the Jap's left engine and the fuselage, I saw the white sparks flickering where the armor-piercing incendiaries were going in . . . little glints of light . . . dancing along the wing . . . like the sparklers the kids play with on the Fourth of July.

"I gave the Betty another squirt . . . the port gas-tank blew up in a red glare . . . and her right wing was gone. She went down in a tight spin. I followed a bit. She hit the water and her bombs blew up."

Five minutes later Wellwood was after a second bomber, chasing her in a graveyard spin to the left, firing as he went. The Jap kept right on going down and so did Wellwood. He reported:

"The first thing I knew, I felt my stick loose and wobbly between my knees. I was in a spin too. That scared me to death. I broke out in a cold sweat because spinning in the daytime is bad enough, but at night it's murder. I was weak as a kitten and shaking. I didn't know then what happened to the Betty and I didn't much care.

"I was fighting to get back some altitude and to get my head clear. I had vertigo so bad every time I looked out of my cockpit, the moon was whirling all over the sky. I ducked back and went on the gauges, climbing and trimming the ship. I had a little bottle of brandy the Doc issues in my pocket. A nip of that helped a lot."

Minutes later Gallerneau had another customer for him. This contact was even rougher. The bomber led him down through flak from our ships. AA punched a hole in Wellwood's wing and knocked out one of his guns. Another jammed. His radio went out.

"The Betty saw me the same time I saw her. That same blue blowtorch flame broke out from her top turret as her gunner opened fire. I bored in and sat there pouring them into her. I must have gotten the pilot because the Betty went into a tight spin to the right. I didn't follow her. She hit—a gush of flame came up—and that was all."

Radio Tokyo, which had once preened about "control of the air over Okinawa," was now muttering dire threats of a new suicide wrinkle, the Giretsu.

Past 2230 the night of May 24, that new Special Attack Corps of airborne suicide troops arrived. A Sally bomber laden with these human bombs crash-landed on Yontan, in what was termed "the most audacious and destructive attack on aviation installations in the campaign."

With the turning of the enemy Shuri line by the infantry, the land campaign had gone into its last phases. Artists at delaying the inevitable, the Japs withdrew to a final defense line on the southern tip of Okinawa, asking their air force for diversionary attacks. These came in sustained fury over a five-day period, touched off by the spectacular Giretsu raid on May 24.

That night there was a break in the bad weather which had turned the battlefields into red rivers of mud. The Japanese took quick advantage of the moonlight and clear skies In a spider web of search-

Flaming tracers light the night sky at Okinawa as ground batteries pump up a webbed pattern of flak to beat off a heavy Japanese bombing raid on Marine squadrons based at Yontan Field.

The ruins of Naha, capital of Okinawa, show starkly beneath the wings of a Marine Grasshopper plane out on an artillery spotting mission.

A rocket broadside blasts towards an enemy position on Okinawa in this unusual photograph made by Marine Lieutenant David D. Duncan in a belly tank slung beneath the wing of a P-38 which followed the Corsair in on its target run.

Marine escort carrier air groups had their own night fighter protection as evidenced by these Corsairs warming up on the flight deck of a Marine CVE.

USS Vella Gulf was one of the Marine escort carriers which entered combat in the final months of the Pacific war.

Wake Island is retaken at war's end by a surrender party headed by Brigadier General Lawson H. M. Sanderson, commanding the Fourth Marine Air Wing. The American flag is raised again after four years while in the foreground the Japanese garrison salutes.

High over Fujiyama and the rugged terrain of the Japanese "Alps," this echelon of Marine Corsairs flies a vigilance patrol as part of its duties during the occupation of the enemy homeland.

Consolidated PB4Y Liberator

Curtiss SB2C Helldiver

Grumman F7F Tigercat

Women Marines served ably with the Marine Air Arm throughout the United States and in Hawaii in a variety of duties from mechanics to aerial photographers.

Production lines in dozens of aircraft plants across the nation fed thousands of planes and vital components into the rapidly expanding Air Arm during its crucial battles in the Pacific war.

lights, two bombers plastered the area around Yontan and moved on. The red alert continued. Sergeant Leroy Halle on duty in the Yontan field tower reported:

"At 2225, as ack-ack broke out to the northeast, we ducked behind the sandbags. Tracers were cutting right over our heads. This bomber was coming in at treetop level. It burst into flames 500 yards away. Ack-ack caught it again and it exploded 30 feet off the ground. I didn't know the bomber was carrying a suicide squad until daylight when I saw a roasted Jap and pieces of several others in the wreckage.

"A few minutes later, I saw the next Jap turn in the lights and come down the runway. I looked for him to start flaming, but he went past the tower. The engines were cut and he came in noiselessly for a perfect belly landing about 100 yards away."

While he watched, Halle saw two, then five or six more figures crouch by the side of the Jap plane. He shouted a warning and men in near-by dugouts and foxholes grabbed rifles and took up positions along the runway. The Japs fanned out toward planes parked near-by, their progress garishly lighted by moonlight and flames. Giretsu incendiary bombs burned three Commando transports as a full-scale fire-fight broke out around the crashed Sally. Then the Giretsu wriggled away from their plane, firing as they went.

Two other Jap planes loaded with raiders swung in over the runway, but were shot down in flames before they could land. The Giretsu on the field died one by one.

At daylight, Sergeant Halle saw six or eight men peering at a dead Jap when the last of the Giretsu leapt from the ruins of a transport and threw a grenade into the crowd. With rifle bullets thudding into him, the Jap held a grenade to his belly and blew himself five feet in the air.

The suicide raid had been of some value to the enemy. With a loss of 4 transports and 69 men in the actual attack, the Jap suicide party had wrecked 29 planes and destroyed 70,000 barrels of gasoline. Two Marines were killed and 18 wounded. The raid also had a temporary morale effect on the American forces, which was lost when the Japanese failed to follow with similar attacks.

Night fighters had taken some of the sting out of the night attack.

Lieutenants Trammel and Smurr (of 533) were directed to simultaneous kills by Gallarneau that night. A pilot named Davis of 543 shot down two Bettys. A. F. Dellamano, a lieutenant of Magruder's squadron, made three radar kills during the melee at Yontan. His last victim was a Sally bomber, believed loaded with more Giretsu, which exploded when it crashed.

Magruder's pilots continued to swing their scythes at the moon and in seven weeks they downed 35 Jap planes to lead all Marine night fighter squadrons. In spite of the hazards of night flying, only one of their pilots was lost in combat.

The three Hellcat-flying Marine night squadrons piled up a total of 68 kills in the Okinawa campaign with VMF (N) 542 adding 18 and VMF (N) 543, 15 enemy planes to those of Magruder's unit. A less spectacular but effective phase of their operations were the night heckling raids. Throughout their stay on Okinawa, the night fighter squadrons raked targets behind enemy lines on Okinawa with bomb, rocket, and machine-gun fire, and haunted northern Ryukyus installations with clocklike precision.

After the Giretsu episode, the day squadrons rode hard through bad weather and leaden skies on May 25 to turn in their best day of the Okinawa campaign. With the help of two AAF squadrons, TAF Corsairs shot down 75 planes. The Army P-47's, which had made their first kill of the campaign over Kyushu the day previously, were credited with 34 victories.

The Japanese air effort on the 25th was the high point of their attempt to divert attention from their troop withdrawals on southern Okinawa. Heavy attacks on shipping were made by what amounted to the cream of the Japanese air force. Some of the newer and faster planes which appeared were not the Kamikaze type. But the Corsair and Thunderbolt pilots made no distinction and Tojos, Tonys, Hamps, Zekes, Oscars, Irvings, Jills, Nates, Bettys, and Vals all flamed or crashed with equal facility as did one unidentified survivor of the Nazi *Luftwaffe*, which had black swastikas painted on its wings.

Pilots of the Death Rattler squadron made 8 kills on the 25th, raising their unit total to 105½ planes in six weeks. This broke the previous record for a similar period set by VMF 215 over Rabaul.

Okinawa weather, by now as infamous in curse and song as that of the Solomons, interfered with TAF action for two days, but the Japanese came down on May 28 and lost 37 planes.

As the infantry campaign on Okinawa moved into its final weeks, the air war slumped. Except for two good scoring days on June 3 and 22, the well-mauled Japanese air force offered little further opposition. Its heavy losses to the TAF and the effects of fighter sweeps and bombing raids on enemy homeland airbases by the TAF, the Fifth Fleet, and the B-29's finally cracked its offensive power. Except for sporadic raids, the remaining Japanese planes were carefully saved for the anticipated invasion of their Empire.

Command of TAF changed June 11 when Major General Louis E. Woods of the Fourth Wing replaced General Mulcahy as head of the Tenth Army's Tactical Air Force.

June 22, the last big day in the air battle for Okinawa was, oddly enough, the day after organized enemy resistance on Okinawa was declared at an end by General Geiger, then commanding the Tenth Army. [Geiger succeeded Lieutenant General Simon Buckner who was killed on June 18 by enemy artillery fire. Geiger was appointed a lieutenant general on June 9 to become the highest ranking Marine aviator in the history of the Corps.]

The aerial fracas of June 22 was marked by several headline incidents. Captain Robert Baird, VMF (N) 533, downed a Francis and a Betty, to become the first night fighter ace of the campaign. Captain Ken Walsh, Medal of Honor winner for his 20 kills in the Solomons, finally found another victim. He pushed his fast new F4U-4 in on a Zeke and splashed it for his 21st victim of the war. [The new Chance-Vought F4U-4 was first flown by Marines at Okinawa in early June. It was noted for its giant four-bladed propeller and its 2300 horsepower Pratt and Whitney radial engine. Prior to its arrival, TAF Corsair squadrons had been flying Chance-Vought F4U-1D's and Goodyear FG-1's.]

The Japanese pattern of combat on June 22 was unusual. The appearance of a large number of skillful, aggressive Jap pilots flying fast fighter types made the action comparable to those over Kahili and

Rabaul. Though 4 TAF pilots and 5 planes were lost, 44 enemy planes went down, with Second Wing pilots getting 32 of them.

Weirdest action of the day was that by First Lieutenant John Leaper, VMF 314, who, with his wingman, Lieutenant W. L. Milne, shot down 4 planes while on early morning CAP.

Leaper had just finished his final pass at a bomber which he shot down. In the pull-out, the Marine spotted a Zeke fighter making a head-on run at him. Leaper nosed around and fired 10 rounds when his ammunition gave out. The Marine pulled up and over the Zeke in a split-S and closed on the Jap from behind and below. Leaper pulled up trying to buzz-saw the Zeke's tail surfaces with his propeller. Shattered glass and oil on the windshield spoiled his accuracy.

Failing to connect the first time, the Marine jockeyed into position and came down on top of the Jap as his propeller sawed into the enemy fighter in front of its cockpit. Simultaneously, the right pylon tank on the Corsair exploded and the Zeke disintegrated. Then the entire right wing of the F4U ripped off.

The Corsair spun violently to the right. Leaper tried to bail out, but the centrifugal force of the spin held him back. He finally risked bailing out on the wrong side. As he pulled the rip cord, his parachute split from top to bottom. The impact of the chute's opening blacked Leaper out momentarily, broke two shroud lines, and tore the dye marker off his Mae West.

While floating down in this precarious state, the Marine saw another Zeke fighter diving directly at him with 6 Corsairs on its tail. Leaper avoided becoming a statistic by jerking hard on his shroud lines. This collapsed the parachute and dropped him like a brick before the Jap got close. After 4,000 feet in a free fall, he reopened the ripped parachute. It absorbed the second shock without further damage and landed Leaper safely in the water where he was picked up by a destroyer.

The defensive phase of the air battle for Okinawa was set at an end June 30. Mainly as the result of night fighter action in the last week, the TAF score reached 600½ kills on that date. During the three-month period (lacking one week) squadrons of the Second

Marine Air Wing had accounted for 484½ planes or 81 percent of the TAF kills at Okinawa. Twenty-one new Marine aces came out of the campaign.

The air battle for Okinawa was the second most profitable of the war for Marine aviation in the actual number of kills. At least 32 different types of identified Japanese planes were shot down by Marine pilots, who maintained the startling odds of better than 120-1. Only four Marine pilots were known to have been killed in combat with planes of the Japanese Air Force.

While air combat was the spectacular contribution, there was another major phase of TAF action which was most gratifying to the air-ground team at Okinawa. It was the precision close air support of the infantry.

Second Wing planes were responsible for a major portion of air-infantry support actions during the furious and bloody campaign to take the 485 square miles of land that was Okinawa Shima. Carrier-based planes of the Fleet carried out close-support work during the first phases, and Navy CVE squadrons ran a steady flow of infantry support strikes during the latter part of the campaign.

After April 10, the entire load of heavy tactical support traffic was handled by three Marine Landing Force Air Support Control Units. LFASCU One, under Colonel K. H. Weir, controlled aircraft in support of ground units of the III Corps, first on the northern and then on the southern front. LFASCU Two, commanded by Lieutenant Colonel Kenneth Kerby, handled all planes supporting the XXIV Army Corps on the southern front after April 8.

These LFASCU units handled the complex maze of details and finesse necessary for large-scale coordination between Marine and Army troops and their supporting aircraft. The types of air strikes and missions they controlled fell mainly into the following categories: a) Rocket, bombing, strafing, and Napalm attacks on enemy targets of immediate concern to the ground forces; b) similar attacks on enemy targets which were of secondary importance to the infantry, such as Japanese landing craft, supply dumps, troop bivouacs, and other rear-area installations; c) observation missions; d) air supply drops to front-line troops. [Second Wing planes flew another type of mission for the ground troops in June, when the OY-1 observation squadrons began evacuating wounded from behind the front lines. Operating off a narrow road below Naha, which was often under artillery fire, planes of VMO-7 made 271 evacuation flights between June 11 and 22, taking out wounded patients for treatment at rear-area hospitals.]

Second Wing planes flew big missions and small missions in support of the infantry. On occasion only four Corsairs went down to answer the call for help. Often there were 130 planes directed against a single target. At one time during the day of May 19, LFASCU Two was controlling 376 planes in the air at once, using them to batter seven different Okinawa targets simultaneously.

As action increased on the southern front, the radio channels were filled with urgent requests for direct air support from companies, battalions, regiments, and divisions, to knock out enemy positions which were holding up an advance or needed softening up prior to an attack.

Repeatedly, TAF planes laid their loads on targets close to friendly troops, often within 100 yards. Out of more than 7,000 sorties in direct infantry support, there were only three recorded occasions in which bombs were dropped behind friendly lines. In these instances, casualties were minor.

In the bloody seesaw battle to take Sugar Loaf Hill in the south, the Marine air-liaison parties regularly directed bombings within 125 yards of the front lines without injury to the infantry, but with great damage to the enemy.

Against heavily fortified positions like those at Shuri Castle, planes used 1,000- and 2,000-pound bombs effectively and without injury to friendly troops.

The usual routine in these direct support missions employing fighter bombers, torpedo or dive-bombers, was a bombing run, then a rocket run, often followed by a strafing attack to rake up and riddle the debris left by the heavier explosives.

The use of rockets, usually the 5-inch type, made Second Wing planes more than ever the galloping gun platforms and flying artillery that had always been envisioned by Marine air-support experts. While trained pilots were able to drop bombs with a high degree of accuracy inside a 16-foot circle in dive or glide runs, it was the use of rockets that made even deadlier aerial snipers out of them. Records revealed that the Marine air groups were getting better than 80 percent of their bombs in the small target areas. Rocket accuracy, however, often came close to 100 per cent hits on target.

One of the aerial cannoneer units that played havoc with enemy infantry on Okinawa were the pilots of VMF 322. On one of its missions, the enemy, rodent-wise, was intrenched in a series of deep caves which infantry weapons were unable to knock out.

The squadron commander led four Corsairs attacking seven separate caves. The planes came in singly on fast, low runs, firing rockets directly into the cave openings. They returned a second time and funneled in fire bombs. As flames seared the area, the Japanese defenders fled in shrieking terror. An observer only 50 yards away called to the planes,

"They're running all over. Come on down and strafe."

The Marines came back for another run, this time spewing machine-gun bullets over the terrain. Next day, the infantry walked in and took over the Jap position.

That afternoon, a group of tired, bedraggled men walked into the VMF 322 camp.

"We're looking for the guys who worked over that ridge yesterday. We've got something for them."

They unloaded a pile of gifts—Jap rifles, flags, medals, and wrist watches, the kind of souvenirs most pilots never had a chance to obtain.

After their few words of thanks, the infantrymen quietly went back to the front lines.

As on June 14 when 64 Corsairs seared a cave-pocked ridge and ravine containing a heavy enemy concentration, front-line air parties regularly used heavy Napalm attacks to denude a suspected area of all burnable matter in order to expose enemy positions.

During the whole of the campaign, Marine troops received direct air support on 562 missions, which ranged in size from one to 75 planes. Planes on these support missions dropped 1,800 tons of bombs, fired 15,800 rockets, and dumped 680 tanks of Napalm.

The XXIV Army Corps received 817 support missions, during the first 70 days of the Okinawa battle. Forty-three separate attacks were executed in a single day to aid the Army troops, with one of the missions numbering 139 planes.

According to observers, not all of these Air Arm support missions were letter-perfect. Generally, however, they were of exceptional value to the infantry because they were credited with expediting the ground campaign and saving hundreds if not thousands of infantry casualties.

In his comments on air support at Okinawa, the Commander of the Army's 7th Division said:

"In the main, both attack and reconnaissance missions were very successful. Ground forces attacking with close air support were materially aided in taking enemy strongpoints and suffered no casualties from front-line air."

The Army's 96th Division Commander reported:

"The close air support during this operation was superior throughout."

These commendations for Second Wing air support activity at Okinawa were strongly supported by those of the Marine infantry and the Navy commands.

The Okinawa campaign had provided the first large-scale opportunity for the highly-trained Marine personnel to demonstrate their conception of tactical aviation and ground support. The Air Arm answered the opportunity with a record of expert effectiveness, testified to equally by the Army and Marine ground teams. It was a fitting climax for two decades of intensive operations devoted to attaining this degree of excellence in tactical aviation.

OPERATION VICTORY

THE latest weapon of the Air Arm—escort carriers of its own—made headlines on June 30, 1945, when planes from two Marine CVE's were launched against enemy targets at Balikpapan, Borneo. For three days, Corsairs, Avengers, and Hellcats from the *Block Island* and the *Gilbert Islands* supported amphibious operations by Australian troops against this oil center of the Netherlands East Indies. Joining Army, Navy, British, and Australian planes, the Marines, on more than 300 sorties, covered the landing phase and then concentrated on cutting up armored reinforcement convoys in the hills and destroying troop concentrations, supply depots, and oil storage facilities.

Some six weeks prior to the Balikpapan landing, a long-time goal of Marine airmen was realized when planes from the CVE *Block Island* made the first combat sorties from a "Marine carrier." On this initial mission, May 10, F4U's and TBM's hit ground targets on Okinawa and airfields in the near-by Sakashima Group.

Long prior to the war, and particularly when milk-run assignments left their squadrons far in its backwash, Marine air generals campaigned for a small, all-Marine escort carrier force to support their own infantry in amphibious operations.

They based the repeated requests on the practical premise of sound tactical integration: that in any amphibious campaign, the Marine air-ground team was inadequate and incomplete unless "Marines were over Marines" from start to finish. Numerous landings were planned throughout the war for the Marine divisions on the island steppingstones to Tokyo. Marine airmen pointed out that their own

bayonet-type of infantry support would be even more vital to the
Marine infantry during the crucial assault phases of landings than
in the latter stages when they covered as land-based planes.

After a campaign as zealous as Lieutenant Cunningham had waged
in 1912, it was announced October 10, 1944, that Marine-carrier air
groups were in training. As initially planned, the Marine CVE program called for the activation of four Marine Air Support Groups
(MASG), with each group including the air complement aboard
four CVE's. The air complement of a single CVE was labeled a
Marine Carrier Group (MCVG) and comprised a fighter squadron
and a torpedo bomber squadron. A Marine ground crew or carrier
air service detachment (MarCASD) was to handle both squadrons
aboard a CVE. Early plans allotted 18 fighter planes (F4U's and
F6F's) and 12 torpedo bombers (TBM's). However, with the addition of night fighter planes and others for photographic work, the
number and types of aircraft varied slightly with each carrier, but
provided a well-rounded striking force.

Colonel Albert Cooley, a veteran of the Solomons, was named
commanding officer of the initial carrier unit, Marine Air Support
Group 48 (MASG 48), and its higher echelon, Marine Carrier
Groups, AirFMFPac. Based at MCAS, Santa Barbara, MASG 48
began a rigid and extensive training program based on the Navy's
carrier training system for all its personnel, many of whom were
veterans of the South and Central Pacific fighting.

The Navy assigned four CVE's of the Commencement Bay type
(105-class) to MASG 48—the Block Island, Gilbert Islands, Cape
Gloucester and Vella Gulf. These were delivered at intervals to the
Marines, complete with naval crews, for use in training and shakedown cruises before leaving for the combat areas.

The first all-Marine carrier air group, commanded by Lieutenant
Colonel John F. Dobbin, eight-plane Guadalcanal ace, arrived at
Ulithi in April, 1945, aboard the Block Island. The first air strike
for its squadrons, VMF 511 and VMTB 233, was the infantry-support mission May 10 which plowed up Japanese mortar concentrations near the front lines at Okinawa. For 43 consecutive days,
the Block Island squadrons operated deep in Japanese home waters

as a part of Rear Admiral C. T. Durgin's Escort Carrier Force. The rocket-firing Marine fighter bombers and TBM's divided their missions between air support strikes at Okinawa and round-the-clock neutralization raids against enemy airfields in the Sakashima Gunto. The latter were potential staging points for enemy air forces moving on Okinawa from Formosa and China. Sustained operations by the Marine planes were carried out against four major Japanese airbases in the chain at Miyako Jima and Ishigaki Jima. Though they had no contact with the Kamikazes, the Marine squadrons suffered considerable damage from AA fire on their low-level raids. When the *Block Island* returned to Leyte for supplies June 17, it had lost 4 fighter pilots, 2 TBM pilots, and 4 aircrewmen to Japanese flak during the 550 target sorties of its total of 1,100 combat flights.

June 1, the *Gilbert Islands*, with MCVG 2 aboard, joined the *Block Island* and the Navy escort carriers in their continuing operations in the Okinawa area. Commanded by Lieutenant Colonel William Campbell, the squadrons of Air Group Two—VMF 512 and VMTB 143—flew direct infantry-support strikes at Okinawa and bombed, rocketed, and strafed airfields and installations at Ishigaki, Miyako, Erabu, Ikema, and Irimote in the Sakashimas. On June 16, the carrier joined the CVE raid on Amami O Gunto and returned to Leyte. [*In the period, Gilbert Islands squadrons flew nearly 750 missions and downed one Jap bomber.*]

While the *Block Island* and the *Gilbert Islands* were in action off Borneo, the third Marine CVE put out from Leyte on July 1 for the China Coast. Aboard the carrier, the *Cape Gloucester*, was MCVG4, commanded by Lieutenant Colonel Donald K. Yost, another South Pacific veteran. Its squadrons, VMF 351 and VMTB 132, provided air cover for a task force on a mine-sweeping operation in the southern sector of the East China Sea and participated in shipping strikes against the Saddle and Parker Island groups at the mouth of Hangchow Bay. Three enemy planes encountered by the Marines on their operations were shot down. At the end of July, the *Cape Gloucester* dropped anchor at Buckner Bay, Okinawa, from which it later operated against Nansei Shoto targets.

The fourth and final member of the First Marine Carrier Division, the *Vella Gulf*, arrived at Saipan in mid-July to add its brief contribution to the CVE story. On July 24 and 26, its squadrons, VMF 513 and VMTB 234, made a series of milk-run raids on the by-passed islands of Pagan and Rota in the Marianas.

These brief but diversified combat baptisms for the first Marine carriers were eminently successful and well praised by naval airmen and the infantry. The initial missions were intended as a prelude to joint action by one and possibly two divisions of the Marine CVE's in Operation Olympic in the fall of 1945. During this projected invasion of southern Kyushu, the Marine CVE's were tentatively slated to support the Marine infantry divisions in the operation. [*En route to the Pacific in the final weeks of war were two CVE's of MASG 51, the Salerno Bay and the Puget Sound. The remaining ten Marine CVE's, their Air Groups 42 and 46, and squadrons, were still in the States in various stages of preparation when the war ended.*]

Though the combat actions of the Marine escort carriers in the final weeks of war were not of spectacular note, they were adequate evidence that the Marine Corps now possessed the most versatile and complete triphibious striking force of its kind in American military history.

Target Japan

With the reduction of Okinawa by the end of June, 1945, the Allied Pacific campaign concentrated on the Japanese home islands with accelerated B-29 raids from the Marianas, air attacks and raids by the Third Fleet, and intensified sorties by Okinawa-based planes.

Land-based Marine Corsairs of the TAF made their first fighter sweep over Japan June 10 in a 24-plane raid led by Major George Axtell. The F4U pilots roamed over nine air bases on southern Kyushu hoping to draw up enemy interceptors. In spite of several low-altitude strafing missions, Japanese opposition did not materialize in quantity and only one plane was shot down. Radio Tokyo reported that the Marines destroyed 17 planes on the ground during the mission.

The Corsairs continued to add their firepower to the now routine

Kyushu missions made by Army P-51's and B-24's of Major General Louis E. Woods' Okinawa air force during the balance of June and July. Most of the southern Japan sorties, however, were flown by the longer-ranged Army Mustang fighters, while the Marine Corsairs and Avengers concentrated on targets in the Nansei Shoto.

When TAF, Tenth Army, became TAF, Ryukyus, on July 1, General Woods commanded the largest combat air force in the history of Marine Aviation. It consisted of four fighter-bomber groups of the Second Wing, three fighter-bomber groups of the 301st AAF fighter wing, and four medium and heavy bombardment groups of the AAF's Seventh Bomber Command. Woods' tenure over this sizeable force was short-lived. TAF, Ryukyus, was disbanded July 14. Its Marine groups reverted to control of the Second Wing and the Army units were absorbed by the Far Eastern Air Force. [*On July 15, in the South Pacific, ComAirNorSols was disbanded and replaced by a Royal New Zealand Air Force command known as the New Zealand Air Task Force. MAG 61 and its squadrons remained as part of the new organization.*]

With the Second Wing then responsible for the air defense of the Okinawa area, its routine operations were broadened to include large-scale fighter-bomber raids and Dumbo and photo-escort missions against Kyushu targets; milk-run strikes against numerous Nansei Shoto land installations; China Coast patrols and routine elimination of Japanese shipping and barge traffic wherever it could be found. This extensive and successful whittling-down process against enemy remnants continued unabated except for foul weather.

During the closing weeks of July and into early August, the Second Wing air groups, now based at Yontan, Chimu, Awase, and Kadena, met little or no Japanese air opposition during the daylight hours. Only at night were the Marines able to contact and destroy a meager number of lone raiders or suicide planes.

As the Ryukyus area passed into the strangulation phase, the Second Wing announced its contributions to the lopsided air battle for Okinawa. In the first 100 days of the campaign, its pilots shot down 500 enemy planes and probably destroyed 22 more. Seven enemy ships were sunk or destroyed and 28 others damaged. Thirty-six small craft were destroyed and 54 damaged. A total of 37,126 sorties were flown. Nearly 1,600 tons of bombs and 11,480 five-inch rockets had been expended along with more than 4,500,000 rounds of machine-gun ammunition.

These records had been achieved with a loss of only 11 planes in air combat—4 to enemy pilots and 7 to AA fire. One hundred and forty-eight other aircraft were lost in combat flight. Thirty-two pilots were killed by enemy action, with 39 listed as missing in action.

Meanwhile, strategic bombing attacks and task force raids were stepped up against vital Japanese homeland targets to maintain pressure during the period of Allied preparation for the invasion of Kyushu in November. The startling lack of enemy air opposition during this literal mauling of their home islands was due to a policy of extreme conservation by the enemy. The entire remaining Japanese air strength, some 5,400 planes of all types, was ordered saved for an all-out suicide defense against the expected Allied invasion forces. All planes were elaborately dispersed away from airfields and in underground revetments which were well camouflaged.

In the midst of elaborate invasion preparations, the long-tottering Japanese Empire and its war machine were rocked by the atomic bomb drops at Hiroshima and Nagasaki and the last-minute entry of Russia into the Pacific war. Then the end came abruptly. On August 14, after several days of wild rumors, the Japanese accepted the Allied surrender terms. Stunned and unbelieving, the Marine Air Arm joined its fellow services in celebrating and praying that the long and bitter fight was over and done.

White Flags and the Aftermath

Immediately after the formal Japanese surrender aboard the battleship *Missouri* in Tokyo Bay September 2, the Marine Air Arm completed its cycle of destiny in World War II. Brigadier General Lawson H. M. Sanderson, commanding the Fourth Air Wing, accepted the surrender of the enemy garrison at Wake Island on September 4. Joining in the flag-raising ceremonies following the surrender was Colonel Walter L. J. Bayler, USMC, who had been the last man off Wake when it was still in American hands. Appropriately, Bayler was given the honor of being the first man ashore from the American surrender party.

With the formal surrender of the Japanese government, Marine Aviation coped with two major problems: occupation and demobilization. The Air Arm joined the Allied forces which moved into all centers of former enemy-held territory to disarm the Japanese troops, search out and repatriate surviving Allied prisoners of war, and establish garrison control of the conquered possessions.

Squadrons of the Second Wing supported the V Amphibious Corps in carrying out its occupation mission in Japan proper. By September 7, VMF 441 was operating from the airfield at Yokosuka naval base below Tokyo. The Second Wing retained its headquarters at Okinawa and two groups, and sent MAG 31 to Yokosuka and other units to Omura on Kyushu and to Nagasaki.

The largest occupation mission of the Air Arm was that of the First Wing in China in support of the troops of the III Amphibious Corps. Wing headquarters was established at Tientsin and taken over in late October by Major General Woods, who had turned over the Second Wing to Brigadier General Schilt. The First Wing's MAG 12 and 24 were based at Peking and MAG 25 and 32 at Tsingtao. [The Fourth Air Wing moved its headquarters from the Marshalls to Guam for a brief period of duty and was then deactivated as had been the Third Wing at Ewa, Oahu.]

On December 7, 1941, there had been only 4 Marine squadrons overseas. At the war's end, the command of Aircraft, Fleet Marine Force, Pacific was composed of 4 air wings; 21 air groups, including 2 air support units; 59 tactical squadrons, of which 12 were aboard carriers; a total of 19 transport, photographic, observation, and utility squadrons; 9 air-warning units; and other miscellaneous groups for an aggregate of 42,000 officers and men in the Pacific. [Ninety-three percent of Marine Aviation's total personnel saw duty overseas at least once during the war.]

Due to extremely rapid demobilization caused by the hue and cry at home, the Pacific personnel figure was reduced by one-half in a matter of several months. Throughout 1946, the Air Arm continued to reduce the number of units and personnel to meet regular peace-time quotas. In the meantime, the Air Arm was building an aggressive air reserve program for future needs, whatever they might be, in the Marine tradition.

As the vanguard Air Arm of a U. S. Marine Corps, ready for another era of nominal peace, it predicated its future on its past. As for the future security of the country it was ready to guard, Marine Aviation could only hope that America would never forget the most urgent lesson of the global war—the advent of air power as the greatest striking force the world has ever known.

GLOSSARY

The following letters indicate the combat functions of the principal Marine Aircraft as designated under the Navy system. Preceded by the letters "V" (Heavier-than-Air) and "M" (Marine), the letters alone or in combination indicate the type squadrons using the planes:

B—Bomber   O—Observation
F—Fighter   R—Transport
D—Photographic   T—Torpedo
J—Utility   S—Scout

Principal combat types of planes used by the Marines in World War II as mentioned in the narrative are:

Navy Designation	Name	Manufacturer
F2A	Buffalo	Brewster
F4F	Wildcat	Grumman
F6F	Hellcat	Grumman
F7F	Tigercat	Grumman
F4U, FG-1	Corsair	Chance-Vought, Goodyear, Brewster
OY-1	Sentinel	Stinson
PBJ	Mitchell	North American
PBY	Catalina	Consolidated, Boeing, Naval Aircraft Factory
PB4Y	Liberator	Consolidated
PV-1	Ventura	Vega
R4D	Skytrain	Douglas
R5C	Commando	Curtiss-Wright
SBD	Dauntless	Douglas
SB2C, SBW, SBF	Helldiver	Curtis-Wright, Canadian Car & Foundry, Fairchild

| SB2U | Vindicator | Chance-Vought |
| TBF, TBM | Avenger | Grumman, Eastern Aircraft, General Motors |

MARINE CORPS ACES IN WORLD WAR II

No.	Name	Number of Planes Shot Down
1.	BOYINGTON, Gregory, Lieutenant Colonel Medal of Honor	28
2.	FOSS, Joseph Jacob, Major Medal of Honor	26
3.	HANSON, Robert Murray, First Lieutenant (Deceased) Medal of Honor	25
4.	WALSH, Kenneth A., Captain Medal of Honor	21
5.	ALDRICH, Donald N., Captain	20
6.	SMITH, John L., Lieutenant Colonel Medal of Honor	19
7.	CARL, Marion Eugene, Major	18½
8.	THOMAS, Wilbur, Captain	18
9.	SWETT, James E., Major Medal of Honor	16½
10.	SPEARS, Harold Leman, Captain (Deceased)	15
11.	DONAHUE, Archie Glenn, Major	14
12.	CUPP, James N., Major	13
13.	GALER, Robert E., Lieutenant Colonel Medal of Honor	13
14.	MARONTATE, William P., First Lieutenant (Deceased)	13
15.	SHAW, Edward O., Captain (Deceased)	13
16.	FRAZIER, Kenneth D., Captain	12½
17.	EVERTON, Loren D., Major	12
18.	SEGAL, Harold E., Captain	12
19.	TROWBRIDGE, Eugene A., Major	12
20.	SNIDER, William N., Captain	11½
21.	DELONG, Philip Cuniffe, Captain	11⅙
22.	BAUER, Harold W., Lieutenant Colonel (Deceased) Medal of Honor	11
23.	BALDWIN, Frank B., Captain	10

No.	Name	Number of Planes Shot Down
24.	Conger, Jack E., Captain	10
25.	Mann, Thomas H., Jr., Captain	10
26.	Sapp, Donald H., Major	10
27.	De Blanc, Jefferson J., Captain Medal of Honor	9
28.	Long, Herbert H., Major	9
29.	Magee, Christopher Lyman, Captain	9
30.	Thomas, Franklin C., Jr., Captain	9
31.	Morgan, John L., Jr., Captain (Deceased)	$8\frac{1}{2}$
32.	Case, William Northrup, Captain	8
33.	Dobbin, John Francis, Lieutenant Colonel	8
34.	Gutt, Fred E., Captain	8
35.	Herman, Edwin James, Jr., Captain	8
36.	Hollowell, George L., Captain	8
37.	Kunz, Charles Murphy, Major	8
38.	Post, Nathan T., Lieutenant Colonel	8
39.	Overend, Edmund F., Major	8
40.	Warner, Arthur T., Major	8
41.	Yost, Donald K., Lieutenant Colonel	8
42.	Payne, Frederick R., Jr., Lieutenant Colonel	$7\frac{1}{2}$
43.	Brown, William P., First Lieutenant	7
44.	Caswell, Dean, Second Lieutenant	7
45.	Crowe, William E., Captain	7
46.	Haberman, Robert A., Captain	7
47.	Hamilton, Henry B., Warrant Officer (Deceased)	7
48.	Jensen, Alvin J., First Lieutenant	7
49.	Loesch, Gregory K., Captain (Deceased)	7
50.	McClurg, Robert W., Captain	7
51.	Narr, Joseph L., Second Lieutenant	7
52.	O'Keefe, Jeremiah J., First Lieutenant	7
53.	Owens, Robert G., Jr., Major	7
54.	Pittman, Jack, Jr., First Lieutenant	7
55.	Reinburg, J. Hunter, Major	7
56.	Rusham, John W., First Lieutenant	7
57.	Wade, Robert, First Lieutenant	7
58.	Williams, Gerard M. H., First Lieutenant	7
59.	Mullen, Paul A., Captain	$6\frac{1}{2}$

No.	Name	Number of Planes Shot Down
60.	DILLARD, Joseph V., First Lieutenant	$6\frac{1}{3}$
61.	DURNFORD, Dewey F., Second Lieutenant	$6\frac{1}{3}$
62.	TERRILL, Francis A., First Lieutenant	$6\frac{1}{2}$
63.	AXTELL, George C., Major	6
64.	BAIRD, Robert, Captain (First VF (N) Ace)	6
65.	BAKER, Robert M., Major	6
66.	BOLT, John F., Jr., Captain	6
67.	CHANDLER, Creighton, First Lieutenant	6
68.	CONANT, Robert W., Captain	6
69.	DILLOW, Eugene, Captain (Deceased)	6
70.	DORROH, Jefferson D., Major	6
71.	DRURY, Frank C., Major	6
72.	FISHER, Don Holms, Captain	6
73.	FRASER, Robert Buchan, Major (Deceased)	6
74.	HALL, Sheldon O., Captain	6
75.	HUNDLEY, John C., Captain	6
76.	JONES, Charles David, First Lieutenant	6
77.	McMANUS, John, First Lieutenant	6
78.	PERCY, Gilbert, Captain	6
79.	PIERCE, Francis E., Jr., Major	6
80.	POND, Kenneth A., Second Lieutenant (Deceased)	6
81.	PRESLEY, Frank H., Captain	6
82.	SHUMAN, Perry L., Major	6
83.	STOUT, Robert F., Major (Deceased)	6
84.	VALENTINE, Herbert J., Captain	6
85.	VEDDER, Milton N., First Lieutenant (Deceased)	6
86.	HANSEN, Herman A., Major	$5\frac{1}{2}$
87.	HOOD, William L., First Lieutenant	$5\frac{1}{2}$
88.	KIRKPATRICK, Floyd C., Lieutenant	$5\frac{1}{2}$
89.	SIGLER, Wallace E., Captain	$5\frac{1}{3}$
90.	ALLEY, Stuart C., Jr., First Lieutenant	5
91.	BRAUN, Richard Lane, Captain	5
92.	CARLTON, William A., Major	5
93.	DAVIS, Leonard K., Lieutenant Colonel	5
94.	DAWKINS, George E., Jr., Captain	5
95.	DOYLE, Cecil J., Second Lieutenant (Deceased)	5
96.	DRAKE, Charles W., Second Lieutenant	5

No.	Name	Number of Planes Shot Down
97.	ELWOOD, Hugh McJ., Lieutenant Colonel	5
98.	FARRELL, William, First Lieutenant	5
99.	FINN, Howard J., Captain	5
100.	FONTANA, Paul John, Lieutenant Colonel	5
101.	FORD, Kenneth M., Captain	5
102.	FREEMAN, W. B., Lieutenant	5
103.	HACKING, Albert C., Captain	5
104.	KENDRICK, Charles, First Lieutenant	5
105.	IRELAND, Julius W., Major	5
106.	LAIRD, Wayne W., First Lieutenant	5
107.	McCARTNEY, H. Allen, Jr., Captain	5
108.	McGINTY, Selva E., First Lieutenant	5
109.	OLANDER, Edwin L., Captain	5
110.	PHILLIPS, Hyde, Major	5
111.	POSKE, George H., Major	5
112.	POWELL, Ernest A., Captain (Deceased)	5
113.	RAMLO, Orvin H., Captain	5
114.	SCARBOROUGH, Hartwell V., Jr., Captain	5
115.	SCHERER, Raymond F., Captain	5
116.	SEE, Robert Byron, Captain	5
117.	SYNAR, Stanley, Captain	5
118.	WEISSENBERGER, Gregory J., Lieutenant Colonel	5
119.	WELLS, Albert P., First Lieutenant	5
120.	YUNCK, Michael R., Major	5

INDEX

☆ ☆ ☆